Rereading Victorian Fiction

Rereading Victorian Fiction

Edited by

Alice Jenkins
University of Glasgow

and

Juliet John
University of Salford

Foreword by John Sutherland

palgrave
macmillan

Selection, editorial matter and Introduction © Alice Jenkins and
Juliet John 2000, 2002
Foreword © John Sutherland 2000
Chapter 3 © Daniel Karlin 2000
Chapters 2, 4–14 © Palgrave 2000

Published by
PALGRAVE
Houndmills, Basingstoke, Hampshire RG21 6XS and
175 Fifth Avenue, New York, N.Y. 10010
Companies and representatives throughout the world

PALGRAVE is the new global academic imprint of
St. Martin's Press LLC Scholarly and Reference Division and
Palgrave Publishers Ltd (formerly Macmillan Press Ltd).

First edition 2000
Paperback edition with corrections 2002

ISBN 0-333-71445-8 hardback (*outside North America*)
ISBN 0-312-22643-8 (*in North America*)
ISBN 0-333-97385-2 paperback (*worldwide*)
ISBN 13 978-0-333-97385-1 paperback (*worldwide*)

This book is printed on paper suitable for recycling and made from fully
managed and sustained forest sources. Logging, pulping and manufacturing
processes are expected to conform to the environmental regulations of the
country of origin.

A catalogue record for this book is available
from the British Library.

The Library of Congress has cataloged the hardcover edition as follows:
Rereading Victorian fiction/edited by Alice Jenkins and Juliet John:
foreword by John Sutherland.
      p.   cm.
Includes bibliographical references and index.
ISBN 0-312-22643-8
1. English fiction – 19th century – History and criticism.
I. Jenkins, Alice, 1970–   . II. John, Juliet, 1967–   .
PR873.R47   1999
823'.809–dc21
                                                    99–15615
                                                        CIP

Printed and bound in Great Britain by
CPI Antony Rowe, Chippenham and Eastbourne

For Geoff Jenkins and Rebecca John

Contents

vii

List of Illustrations

Foreword

John Sutherland

This volume and its through-the-looking-glass companion, *Rethinking Victorian Culture*, are the written residue of a conference held at the University of Liverpool in 1996. It was a productive occasion bringing together, as it did, different generations of Victorian scholars and strikingly variant practices of British and American Victorian scholarship. As the programme unfolded, echoes could be heard of any number of established, influential voices: F. R. Leavis, Christopher Ricks, Harold Bloom, Gillian Beer, Louis James, Edward Said, Elaine Showalter – even Humphry House; together with the newer accents of D. A. Miller, Peter Brook, Gayatri Spivak and the pervasive Foucauldism of the younger school. Yet the general tone of the occasion was, if not harmonious, quarrelsome in a creative way.

The 'Re-' prefix has been much used in contemporary critical discourse. If one wanted to be cross-grained, the point might be made that more 'reading' of Victorian fiction is desirable. Forget rereading. The needful thing is to know more, to have read more of the primary matter, than scholarship currently does, has or prescribes its students to undertake. How many authors are extensively dealt with in this volume? A dozen? And many of those are the usual suspects: George Eliot, Bram Stoker, Lewis Carroll, George Gissing, Olive Schreiner, Hardy, Dickens and Dickens and Dickens. Thackeray, and the lesser Thackeray – Trollope – are in temporary eclipse, as are the Sensationalists (the absence of Collins is particularly striking, given his revival in the classic reprint libraries). Permanent obscurity shrouds the minor hosts of the silver-fork novelists, the evangelical novelists, the social problem novelists. (Trefor Thomas's chapter on G. W. M. Reynolds stakes a claim for a minor, if influential and incredibly fluent talent; but one wonders how many attendees at the conference could have averred, honestly, that they were in any condition to 'reread' *The Mysteries of London*?)

Griping apart, the nucleus of Victorian writers discussed in this volume are (in Frank Kermode's term) 'patient'. Their texts reward rereading and revisiting. And, on the edge of the conference, a strikingly new topic of critical discussion was formulated: those 'rereadings' of Victorian fiction that result in contemporary rewriting by, for example, John Fowles and Michèle Roberts. Victorian novels, as Robin Gilmour argued, can be written in the 1990s. As Juliet John and Alice

Jenkins (organizers of the conference) remind us in their judicious introduction, we must relax our definitions.

Where will it end? Do we actually, after a conference and the digestion of its papers in the form of books, 'know' more about Victorian fiction? Has that mythical 'store of human knowledge' been enlarged? I like to think of the problem as a conundrum: if you had a time machine capable of forward or reverse travel, and wanted – by some absurd whim – to use it to find out about Victorian fiction, which way would you go? Back to Victorian England or forward to the last conference on the subject, millennia hence? I accept we see the literature more clearly as time passes, but the clarity is that of the wrong end of the telescope. Textures and the feel of the original are lost. At some point, it will be lost altogether. The texts will be buried under the annotation necessary to understand them.

We have to accept we are where we are and Victorian fiction is where it is, and that the gulf between us and it is widening. We shall never, however hard we try, understand the Victorians as well as they understood themselves (and their books). But we read, and reread and, as G. M. Young once put it, if we do it well enough we can, again, 'hear' the Victorians.

This collection can be read for its many local illuminations but also – symptomatically – as an exemplary demonstration of where criticism of nineteenth-century fiction is, as the twentieth century comes to an end. There is, on the evidence of the essays collected here, a palpable drift away from materialist, biographical and historical explanation. Explication of text is the predominant flavour, but explication which anchors itself to particular (and in some cases minute) *topoi*: sentimentality in *Cranford*, hands in *Middlemarch* (a *tour de force* performance by Danny Karlin), clothes in *Great Expectations*, textuality in *Dracula*, Godhead in *The Water Babies*, the epistemology of the dream in the *Alice* books. If there is a predominant tone in the essays, it is a kind of oblique brilliance. Context seems to have dropped away, leaving a brilliant, if introverted, clarity.

Different generations of critics ask different questions about their canonical literature and look for meaning in different places. It is reasonable to predict that at some point before 2099 the pendulum will swing and broad, sweeping, materialist exegesis will enjoy a revival. *Rereading Victorian Fiction*, however, is a good sampling of where we are and what we do best in the 1990s.

Acknowledgements

The editors are very grateful to Kelvin Everest, Miriam Allott and the Department of English at the University of Liverpool, particularly to Philip Davis, Val Gough, David Mills, Jill Rudd and Karl Simms, as well as to Cathy Rhys, Barbara Smith, Jagori Bandyopadhyay, Mary Clinton, Lucy Crispin, Liz Hedgecock and Jo Knowles for their help with the conference which initiated this volume. We would like to thank Blackwell's Bookshops for their generous financial support of the conference. We are grateful to Helen Hackett and Dominic Rainsford for their assistance in the early stages of the preparation of this book. We would also like to express our gratitude to Susan Rowland, to Des O'Brien for invaluable technical assistance and to Hazel Clarke for administrative support. We are very grateful to Charmian Hearne for her help and guidance.

Notes on the Contributors

Bernard Beatty is Senior Lecturer in the Department of English Language and Literature at Liverpool University. He edits the *Byron Journal*, has edited three collections of essays on Byron including *Essays on Byron's Dramas* and written two books on him, *Byron's Don Juan* (1985) and *Byron's Don Juan and Other Poems* (1987). He has written articles on the Scriptures, Dryden, the Romantics, Oscar Wilde and historicism.

Philip Davis is Reader in the English Department at the University of Liverpool. His publications include *Memory and Writing, In Mind of Johnson, The Experience of Reading, Malamud's People,* and *Sudden Shakespeare*; and he has edited *Real Voices: On Reading,* a selection of Ruskin's writings, and *All the Days of My Life,* an anthology of religious and meditative verse. He has just completed the *Victorians* volume of the Oxford History of English Literature.

Gary Day is a Principal Lecturer in English and Cultural Studies at De Montfort University, Bedford. He is a general editor of the Insights series and of the Literature and Culture in Modern Britain series. He has edited a number of books including *Varieties of Victorianism: The Uses of A Past* (Macmillan, 1998) and is the author of *Re-Reading Leavis: 'Culture' and Literary Criticism* (Macmillan, 1996) and *Class* (Routledge, 2001).

Angus Easson is a Research Professor in English at the University of Salford. His publications include *Elizabeth Gaskell; Elizabeth Gaskell: The Critical Heritage*; and editions of Dicken's *The Old Curiosity Shop* and Elizabeth Gaskell's *Mary Barton, North and South, The Life of Charlotte Bronte,* and *Wives and Daughters.* He is currently working on a book on Dickens.

Robin Gilmour was Reader in English at the University of Aberdeen, where he taught mainly in the field of nineteenth-century literature. His chief publications were *The Idea of the Gentleman in the Victorian Novel* (1981) and *The Victorian Age: The Intellectual and Cultural Context of English Literature 1830–1890* (1993). He also wrote a history of the Victorian novel, *The Novel in the Victorian Age* (1986), and a short study of *Vanity Fair.* He edited *The Warden, Barchester Towers* and *Great Expectations,* among others.

Michael Irwin is Professor of English Literature at the University of Kent. His chief academic interest is novelistic technique: most of his published work concerns eighteenth- and nineteenth-century fiction. He has also published novels and translated numerous opera libretti and cabaret songs.

Alice Jenkins is a Lecturer in English Literature at the University of Glasgow. She is the co-editor (with Juliet John) of *Rethinking Victorian Culture* (2000). She has published articles on literature and the history of science and is completing a study of spatial discourse in nineteenth-century literature and science.

Juliet John is a Senior Lecturer in English at the University of Salford. She is the author of *Dickens's Villains: Melodrama, Character, Popular Culture* (2001) editor of *Cult Criminals: the Newgate Novels* (1998) and the co-editor (with Alice Jenkins) of *Rethinking Victorian Culture* (1999).

Daniel Karlin is Professor of English at University College London. He is the author of *The Courtship of Robert Browning and Elizabeth Barrett* (1985) and *Browning's Hatreds* (1993), and co-editor with John Woolford of the annotated English Poets edition of Browning's poems (vols 1 and 2, 1991). His *New Penguin Book of Victorian Verse* was published in 1997, and his Oxford Authors edition of Rudyard Kipling's stories and poems was published in 1999.

Jacqueline M. Labbe is a Reader in nineteenth-century poetry at the University of Warwick. Her past publications include *Romantic Visualities: Landscape, Gender and Romanticism* (Macmillan – now Palgrave, 1998), *The Romantic Paradox: Love, Violence and the Uses of Romance, 1760–1830* (Macmillan – now Palgrave, 2000), and numerous articles. She is currently working on a study of the culture of gender in the Romantic period, focusing on the poetry of Charlotte Smith, for Manchester University Press.

Jil Larson is an Associate Professor of English at Western Michigan University. She has published articles on Joseph Conrad and Thomas Hardy and her book *Ethics and Narrative in the English Novel 1880–1914* was published in 2001.

Scott McCracken is a Senior Lecturer in English at the University of Salford. He is the editor with Sally Ledger of *Cultural Politics at the Fin de Siècle* (1995) and the author of *Pulp: Reading Popular Fiction* (1998). He is currently researching a book on masculinity and the modernist novel.

Ralph Pite is a Senior Lecturer at the University of Liverpool. He has published on Romanticism, Dante, Victorian masculinity, and modern poetry. At present, he is researching a study of regionalism and the English novel, and revising the Annotated Poets edition of the *Poems of Keats*.

Susan Rowland is a Senior Lecturer in English at the University of Greenwich. She is the author of *C. G. Jung and Literary Theory: the Challenge From Fiction* (Macmillan 1999, reprinted Palgrave 2001), *From Agatha Christie to Ruth Rendell* (Palgrave 2001) and of *Jung: A Feminist Revision* (2001). Her research is particularly directed towards Jung and feminism, women writers and detective fiction.

Trefor Thomas is a Research Associate in the Centre for North-West Regional Studies based in the Department of History, Manchester Metropolitan University. He is the editor of an edition of G. W. M. Reynolds's *The Mysteries of London*, and has written a number of articles on lesser-known Victorian novelists.

1
Introduction

Alice Jenkins and Juliet John

To reread Victorian fiction in the midst of postmodernist scepticism about fiction (or, perhaps more accurately, about anything that claims to be other than fiction) is a paradoxical and contradictory exercise. And yet these contradictions have deterred neither professional nor amateur readers: appetites for Victorian fiction seem to be increasing, if anything, as the centenary of Victoria's death approaches. The commercial success of inexpensive reprints of Victorian texts, mainly novels, published by Wordsworth Classics and Penguin Popular Classics, demonstrates that a demand for such literature thrives outside the academy. The unique and perhaps surprising success of John Sutherland's *Is Heathcliff a Murderer?*, which earned a place *The Times* bestseller list, indicates, among other things, that readings (not just reprints) of Victorian fiction can be popular – a potentially radical discovery for professional readers of Victorian literature.[1]

As film adaptations of Victorian classics continue to prove, the accessibility and cultural kudos of such texts provide material ripe for marketing teams. Clever marketing is not enough, however, to explain the continuing ability of Victorian fiction to appeal to academics and general readers and viewers alike. The Victorian age, in its middle phase particularly, was arguably the first historical period in which fiction as a literary genre was culturally central. No doubt its sense of its own primacy and relevance to the 'real' go some way towards explaining not only its present-day popularity, but also its centrality on current university syllabuses and in academic debate (we are talking here, of course, about 'mainstream' Victorian fiction). That Victorian fiction carries with it a sense of both its own ordinariness and its own importance is just one of the characteristics that continue to intrigue and engage the academic reader today.

1

'Victorian fiction' is of course a troublesome category, convenient but potentially misleading. The adjective 'Victorian' is a loaded term; it is not the main aim of this collection to define a conceptual and historical label which must necessarily be subject to continuous metamorphosis; while most of the essays in the collection confine themselves to fiction of the reign of Victoria (1837–1901), others have not limited themselves to strictly chronological definitions. This diversity of interpretations of the term 'Victorian' is in keeping with one of the main aims of this volume: to undermine some of the totalizing myths which have attached themselves both to academic study of the Victorian period, and to perceptions of that era. The stereotypical idea of the Victorians as repressed, duty-bound and humourless slaves to family values still holds sway among many students of Victorian literature. The revisionist aspect of this collection does not consist in a systematic debunking of this idea, however; our aim is to emphasize the ideological, aesthetic, intellectual and moral diversity of both Victorian fiction and its critical reception.

Our choice of the term 'fiction', rather than 'novel', as the subject for reassessment, is likewise predicated on the recognition that the novel was not the only form of fiction produced by the Victorians, dominant though it may have been. Though the novel was in the generic and cultural ascendancy for much of the period, its literary status was a matter of debate, certainly at the beginning of Victoria's reign, and arguably so at the end. Like some of the most stimulating plots, the history of the Victorian novel evades reassuring closure. Virginia Woolf's essay 'Modern Fiction' (1919) represents perhaps the most systematic and overt criticism of the emphasis on the real – interpreted as the material – which she disliked so much in the writings of contemporaries such as Arnold Bennett.[2] Her relocation of 'the real' in the mind or spirit rather than in the material world is effectively a manifesto for the modernist novel and a rejection of the values of those by implication still working in a pre-'modern', Victorian tradition. Isobel Armstrong has analysed the partisan need of modernist poets to attack the writing of their Victorian predecessors as not 'modern' in order to enhance their own claims to that label, and a similar argument could be made about Woolf and her criticism of Victorian fiction.[3] Henry James is a nodal figure in the history of the novel, wryly conscious of his need to reject his internalized Victorian heritage. The aesthetic distaste he expresses towards the 'large loose baggy monsters'[4] of his predecessors does not preclude his consciousness of his own literary debt; of Dickens, in particular, he remarked ambivalently, 'He did too much for us ever to leave us free'.[5] Less prominent in literary histories, but equally important in the demise or dismantling of the 'large loose baggy monsters' James describes, is the popularity of the short story as a literary form at the *fin de siècle*. The grand narrative had become, by the end of the century, significantly shorter.

The origins of Victorian fiction are just as resistant to definition as is its date of termination. The fact that the rise of the novel as a genre shadows the political and economic rise of the middle class has been securely established by Ian Watt, and more recently by Nancy Armstrong.[6] It is worth remembering, however, that neither the novel nor the middle class was as established when Victoria came to the throne, as blanket accounts of literary history sometimes lead us to believe. In the early 1830s, for example, reviews of biography, criticism and non-fiction prose (not to mention the usual suspects, poetry and drama) were all included in the 'Literature' columns of newspapers, while fiction was included under the headings 'Magazine Day' or 'Miscellaneous'.[7] Indeed, Kathryn Chittick makes the point that *The Pickwick Papers* (1836–7) and *Oliver Twist* (1837–9) were not originally conceived as novels, but in the case of the former as a periodical, and in the case of the latter a serial.[8] The origins of the first Victorian 'novels' by the most well-known Victorian 'novelist' are thus thoroughbred only when viewed through a distorting retrospective lens.

The rise of the novel to become the dominant genre of the Victorian age, likewise, has a more mundane, material rationale than evolutionary metanarratives about its synonymity with the rise of the middle class sometimes emphasize. Though histories of early Victorian literature commonly and rightly chart those momentous social and political changes which shaped Victorian and 'modern' Britain (including the 1832 Reform Bill, changes to the criminal law, industrialization and Chartism), the transformation of a nation's structures of power and its literary landscape demands more than political legislation, however radical that legislation may be. In 1837 the country was in the midst of a cultural revolution, quieter perhaps than the political and industrial revolutions afoot, but no less formative in the emergence of the novel as the genre of the age – and formative, further, in the development of a modern state. Literacy was increasing and developments in the publishing trade meant that books and newspapers were expanding their readership, moving further down the social ladder in the early Victorian period than ever before. As Engel and King argue in *The Victorian Novel Before Victoria*, 'Forces outside the court in 1830 [...] were radically reforming the dissemination of fiction so that it began to reach the same class which the Reform Bill enfranchised'.[9] Until

1830, the cheap fiction market had largely been left to small and disreputable publishers like the Minerva Press, but in June 1829 when Tom Cadell issued the Author's Edition of the Waverley novels in five-shilling volumes, 'he inaugurated the vogue of inexpensive recent fiction imprints'.[10] In 1831, Colburn and Bentley's Standard Novels were being published at six shillings each. These developments began a sharp fall in book prices leading to a broader readership, a trend which continued until 1850. The popularity and availability of the new literary form of the novel at the outset of the Victorian period in fact represents the beginnings of a mass readership.

The association of the novel with the middle class is not, then, a simple, monologic story of cultural imperialism. While the 'rise' of the middle class is one of upward social mobility, the 'rise' of the novel is very much bound up with economic and educational developments which allowed literature to move *down* the social ladder. Again, though the novel and the middle class may have dominated the social and cultural scene in the Victorian period, this very domination was itself in some respects a radical feature of Victorian history (though it should be remembered that in many ways the newly empowered middle class brought conservative and bourgeois values into political prominence). The middle class was an agent of change; its favourite genre, the novel, was reflective of that change. Foucault's influential reading of the transition from the eighteenth to the nineteenth century persuasively replaces the humanist myth of history as civilized progress with the idea that the real change was from a 'punitive' to a 'disciplined' society which subtly curtailed individual freedom by systems of 'surveillance'.[11] This theory has undoubted force; but this force makes it even more imperative to emphasize that, for all its faults, the decade that saw Victoria's accession also witnessed the beginning of the process of modern parliamentary reform. Bearing this in mind, then, the history of the novel and the middle class is as much about burgeoning democracy as it is about discipline – though of course these may well be two sides of the same coin. The material beginnings of the Victorian novel are thus bound up with this double narrative of democracy/discipline.

The impure origins of Victorian fiction are also entangled with those of the emerging mass media; as Chittick explains, 'the democratization of politics was not only reported but reflected in the press'.[12] Dickens's novels were, of course, formed by, and formative in, these crucial changes in the distribution of cultural capital. Though serialization in newspapers was never as strong in Britain as in France, many of Dickens's *Sketches by Boz* were originally published in newspapers

(1834–5) and, with his later novels, played a major role in the popular-izing of fiction (and newspapers). *The Pickwick Papers* and *Oliver Twist* were published in monthly numbers, but the practice of 'extracting' passages in newspapers was widespread. In this age before adequate copyright protection, the author did not gain a penny for these extracts, however unquenchable public appetites.

The appetite for fiction in the Victorian period was partly a result of the fact that the middle classes wanted to read texts that seemed to them 'real'. The emergence of the so-called 'classic realist' novel is thus as much a response to consumer demand as it is an imposition of the hegemonic discourse of the middle-class author on the unsuspecting, passive reader. Our language here deliberately echoes that of Catherine Belsey's influential critique of the classic realist novel in *Critical Practice*, where she argues – drawing on Barthes's *S/Z* (1970) – that the classic realist text constructs the reader as a passive consumer of the novel's ideologies and is consequently a conservative genre:

> The strategies of the classic realist text divert the reader from what is contradictory within it to the renewed recognition (misrecognition) of what he or she already 'knows', knows because the myths and signifying systems of the classic realist text re-present experience in the ways in which it is conventionally articulated in our society.[13]

While Belsey's attention to the ideological implications of style is helpful in its illumination of author/reader dynamics, the ideological forces operating in Victorian Britain obviously extend beyond the one-to-one author/reader interaction. The socio-historical, economic and material shifts in Victorian Britain make the question of what is con-servative – or what the reader 'already "knows"', to echo the quotation above – a complex one. Belsey's main agenda, of course, is to encour-age a 'new' kind of critical practice, to encourage readers to be active producers, rather than passive consumers of meaning. It is perhaps debatable whether the binary opposition between 'active' producers and 'passive' consumers is a stable one in a literary critical context; what is certain is that 'active' interpretations of the ideology of style and genre are at their most relevant to the extra-textual world when placed in dialogue with a consideration of the processes and conditions of production of literary texts.

While some readers today may enjoy reading realist texts because they appear to offer reassurance and confirmation of the *status quo*, stu-dents new to Victorian literature must be aware that the middle class, who were in large part the writers and consumers of such texts, had never before enjoyed such prominence, and their very prominence was in fact the result of radical social changes. Doubtless confirmation of middle-class power is what is partly at stake in the realist novel. This desire to legitimize the middle class is not necessarily the same, however, as legitimization of the *status quo* as it was in the Victorian period – that is, constantly changing. The obsession with definitions and representations of 'the real' in both Victorian fiction and its criticism is a response to the enormity of the social and political changes which had empowered the middle class; it reflects a deep cultural need to make sense of change, to impose order on potential chaos.[14] The 'classic realist' novel is shaped by the anxiety of the middle class as much as by its complacency.

The question of what constitutes the classic realist novel is obviously a vexed one, perhaps even more so since Belsey's critique, which includes texts as early as *Oliver Twist* (1837–9), a 'novel' which did not even consider itself a novel when it began its literary life and which is as allegorical as it is realist.[15] Moreover, without becoming mired in literary historical pedantry, it is perhaps worth pointing out that the term 'realist' was not current as a literary critical term until the 1850s,[16] though the obsession with 'the real' in literature was intense for most of the Victorian period. In early- and mid-Victorian critical writing, 'the real' was often dialectically discussed in relation to 'the romantic'. Traditional histories of Victorian fiction emphasize the gradual victory of 'realism' over 'romance', though as Lyn Pykett has pointed out, the relationship between the two terms and modes was never straightforward.[17] Throughout the Victorian period, a strong taste for the fantastic and the melodramatic existed, and was met by – among other texts – translations of the *Arabian Nights*[18] and Grimms' fairy tales (1812), the sensation novels appearing from the late 1850s onwards, Victorian Gothic, and at the end of the century by the Decadent fantasy of such writers as Wilde. Robert Louis Stevenson, of course, was an outspoken advocate and an outstanding exponent of 'Romance'. Victorian children's fiction is still in demand and the Victorians are as acclaimed for their nonsense as they are for their sense. If realism as an aesthetic mode looms large in twentieth-century discussions of the Victorians – and there is no doubt that it does – this perhaps says as much about our need to create straw 'men' against which to measure ourselves as it says about the Victorians themselves. The Victorian age was an unsurpassed period of innovation in fiction: silver-fork fiction, detective fiction and science fiction are just some of the new forms of writing which emerged along with realist fiction. Further, of course, women fiction writers achieved an unprecedented prominence in this period. It would be incorrect to see realist and anti-realist fiction as starkly oppositional; Victorian fiction renewed itself through an ongrowing process of intertextual 'dialogism', to adapt Mikhail Bakhtin's influential concept.[19]

Post-structuralist accounts of 'realism' have of course encouraged scepticism about the the term 'realism' itself, J. Hillis Miller's essay 'The Fiction of Realism' perhaps epitomizing the school which sees realist texts as creating 'illusion out of illusion and the appearance of reality out of illusion, in a play of language without beginning, end, or extra linguistic foundation'.[20] Miller's essay, unsurprisingly, says as much about the deconstructive movement of the 1970s as it does about realism, just as Belsey's text, with its utopian suggestion that the reader can ever be other than consumer, is paradoxically of the 1980s in its insistent emphasis on freedom of choice for the reader/consumer. Those writing Victorian fiction often had none of the coyness of a modern liberal in a television age about the power of their medium; for the newly empowered middle-class writer, it was arguably a proactive political act to exploit the novel as an ideological vehicle, to consciously exert 'influence' on the reader. What Belsey, Miller and critical theory more generally are reacting against, of course, is the kind of criticism of Victorian literature which avoids talk of politics or textuality and sublimates all criticism into ethical discourse alone. Though this type of criticism has lost much of its force in the face of more politicized and theorized writing on literature, nonetheless it should be remembered that with F. R. Leavis at its forefront, humanist criticism did as much to legitimize the study of English in the 1950s and 1960s as literary theory has done to ensure its survival in more recent decades. Partly as a result of the impact of Leavis's work, the humanist tradition in literary criticism, which stretches back to the Victorian Matthew Arnold, has perhaps permeated Victorian studies longer than it has the study of other literary periods.

But as we approach a hundred years of reading Victorian fiction, a new eclecticism of approaches and canons is becoming apparent. The diversity of approaches captured in this collection will perhaps be viewed as an expression of the postmodern multiplicity of our own time, but the collection as a whole hopes to provide an important stock-taking of criticism of Victorian fiction as it is today and as it has been. We hope that this anthology will make a contribution to the revisionist project in Victorian studies. However, the lack of aesthetic or ideological uniformity in the collection is testimony to our belief that revisionism can take many forms; definitions of what it is to be revisionist are largely dependent on perceptions of the prevailing academic context: these perceptions, quite rightly, differ. The essays in this volume are written from a number of theoretical and methodological standpoints; these reflect differing assessments of the current state of Victorian literary studies. This anthology thus presents not an organic vision of the Victorians (not all contributors, for example, would subscribe to the views expressed in this introduction), but a collection of voices committed to a process of debate and dialogue which will help to ensure that the reputation of Victorian fiction is protected from the deadening, mythologizing weight of historical distance. The project of rereading Victorian fiction shows no sign of reaching closure. Despite the differences within Victorian studies which this volume will make apparent, there is a strong sense that evasion of closure in this particular story is a good thing.

The first essay in this volume, Philip Davis's reassessment of the role of sentiment in reading Victorian fiction, explores the temporality of both the Victorian novel as a form and the experience of reading a novel. His argument uses close readings of texts by Dickens, Gaskell and Eliot to develop a poetics of realist fiction, in which reiteration and sequentiality of elements within the text link the reader in a chain of remembrance of events both inside and outside the temporal scope of the narrative. Davis's essay undermines the association of 'sentimentalism' with emotion, and re-evaluates it as a form of thought. Daniel Karlin's essay also explores the notion of realism, focusing on Eliot's discourse of hands and hand-work in *Middlemarch*. Karlin discusses the gendered nature of hand gestures and hand-held implements, and considers the connections Eliot's use of this discourse creates between different types of work, from the ladylike piano-playing of Rosamund Vincy to the labouring and navvying of the fieldworkers and railwaymen. Through a comparison with Henry Fielding's semi-serious dramatization of himself as a writer of histories rather than fictions, Karlin argues that Eliot's realism presents itself as within the spectrum of work done by hand, and that this constitutes part of its authority and determines part of its address.

In his essay on *Sartor Resartus* and *Great Expectations*, Bernard Beatty is, like Daniel Karlin, concerned with the body and apparatus surrounding it. Beatty discusses a symbolic language based on clothing and reads in it a figuration of the difference between symbolist and allegorical writing. His essay explores the metaphorical and liturgical associations of clothing for Victorian writers, and relates Dickens's use of symbol to that of the Gospels. Beatty provides an account of the varying relationship between eros and agape in *Great Expectations*.

Trefor Thomas's essay on the novel-series *The Mysteries of London* rereads a part of the story of the novel that has been under-represented in previous academic study of Victorian fiction. Thomas indicates how the immensely popular, cheap and thrilling fiction of G. M. W. Reynolds can be read with regard to the critical concerns of the present day – he gives examples of the series' preoccupation with cross-dressing, crime and radical politics, for example. Further, Thomas's essay broadens the discussion of Victorian narrative to include consideration of the illustrations which were a key part of these texts, and of their public appeal.

With Gary Day's essay the focus of the collection shifts towards the fantastic in Victorian fiction. Day rereads *Dracula* in the light of the development of a state bureaucracy in Britain during the last decades of the nineteenth century. He sees the continuing potency of *Dracula* – both as novel and as object of cultural consumption – as reflective of the increasing power of administrative surveillance in our own century. Examining previous *Dracula* criticism in the light of Marxist sociology and Foucauldian analyses of sexuality, Day reads the novel as enacting the repression of selfhood in favour of citizenship. He argues that the novel's central concern with textual form and narrative materiality is part of a wider attempt to purge language of its personal and expressive possibilities in order to create a style more suited to the regulatory discourses of citizenship.

Jacqueline M. Labbe's essay is concerned, like Day's, with themes of gender and religion as they appear in Victorian fantasy. Labbe examines the development in children's fiction of a feminized Christian theology, which presented readers with female embodiments of the figures of the Trinity. Labbe explores the relationship between gender anxiety and loss of faith in orthodox Christianity through the fiction of George MacDonald and Charles Kingsley. Such children's literature, Labbe argues, used female characters to develop a kind of Christianity that was less threatening and more comforting to its adherents than had been the wholly male Trinity of other discourses.

In his essay, Michael Irwin uses the *Alice* books to examine the nature of originality and derivativeness in literature. Discussing the role of sources both literary and oral, personal and public, in the composition of various of Carroll's texts, the essay emphasizes the self-reflexivity and intertextuality of *Alice*. Irwin's essay resists conventional Freudian analyses of the narratives, and observes that, particularly in our own time, the *Alice* books succeed in deconstructing the sexual attitudes of those who attempt to deconstruct them.

Moving towards fiction written during the later part of the nineteenth century, Ralph Pite's essay draws on discourses of postcolonialism and class to give a reading of Gissing's novel *Born in Exile*. Pite examines the relations of identity and place within this novel, seeing its central protagonist as occupying a similar position to that of the colonial subject. Pite's argument sees the novel's discourse of exile and homecoming as responsive to an increasingly divided British society in the last decades of the nineteenth century.

In its interest in the importance of location in the construction of identity, Pite's analysis of Gissing's novel shares a thematic concern, though not a methodology, with Scott McCracken's account of Olive Schreiner's allegorical fiction. McCracken's essay is the first of two in this collection that deal with late-Victorian feminist fiction, particularly the texts that have come to be known as 'New Woman' writing. He compares Brecht's writings on theatre with Judith Butler's work on the performativity of gendered identity, and develops a rereading of Olive Schreiner's colonial allegories. McCracken reminds us of the importance of the setting of Schreiner's stories, and examines her use of the desert as a stage for fictional action in the light of her colonial background and her increasingly, but ambiguously, anti-imperialist politics.

Jil Larson's essay also considers New Woman fiction, but from a different perspective. Larson examines the work of Olive Schreiner, Thomas Hardy and Sarah Grand, and discusses their deconstructions of the rigid, gendered distinction between reason and emotion. She shows how these writers questioned stereotypical devaluation of emotion as 'feminine' and valorization of reason as 'masculine', and argues that novels such as *Jude the Obscure* and *The Story of an African Farm* sought to demonstrate a synthesis between thought and feeling that could be shared by both men and women.

Angus Easson's essay on *The Pickwick Papers* and *Don Quixote* is the first of several in this collection which transgress the chronological boundaries set by the term 'Victorian'. Further, it puts into play the definition of the 'novel' as a form. *The Pickwick Papers* was not originally conceived as a serialization, but as a serial – that is, it had at first no intended unity of characterization or story-line, but could, as far as structure and conception went, have run on indefinitely. Easson's essay rereads Dickens's reading of Cervantes, and places *The Pickwick Papers* in a long tradition of English reinventions of Cervantes's text; the essay traces the development of Pickwick as 'hero' through the serial episodes, and considers Dickens's narrative in the context of eighteenth-century reworkings of the Quixotic tale.

The last two essays in this volume demonstrate that rereading of Victorian fiction can itself take place through the medium of fiction. Whereas Angus Easson's essay moves backwards and forwards in time between the nineteenth century and the seventeenth, Robin Gilmour's offers a consideration of twentieth-century novelists' fictional readings of Victorian narratives. Gilmour compares the novels of a range of modern writers, including John Fowles, A. S. Byatt and Graham Swift, and distinguishes six major categories of novel dealing with or in the literature of the Victorian period. He examines the apparent paradox that Victorian novels are at once highly successful among modern readers in search of unproblematic narratives with recognizable characters, and a fertile source for contemporary writers working in experimental forms, or in forms which emphasize the problematics of narrative and character.

Susan Rowland focuses this debate on one particular twentieth-century novel, Michèle Roberts's *In the Red Kitchen*. Using concepts derived from Jungian analysis, Rowland compares nineteenth-century accounts of the relationship of gender and spiritualism in the Victorian period with Roberts's 1990s feminist reimagining of it. Rowland's essay takes up themes of hysteria, the absence from history of a female account of events, and the fictionality inherent in theorizing.

Notes

Short extracts from this introduction are also included in the introduction to Juliet John (ed.), *Cult Criminals: the Newgate Novels*, 6 vols (London: Routledge, 1998), I, pp. v–lxxi.

1. John Sutherland, *Is Heathcliff a Murderer? Great Puzzles in Nineteenth-Century Literature*, The World's Classics (Oxford: Oxford University Press, 1996).
2. In David Lodge (ed.), *Twentieth Century Literary Criticism: a Reader* (London: Longman, 1972), pp. 86–91.
3. Armstrong, *Victorian Poetry: Poetry, Poetics and Politics* (London: Routledge, 1993), pp. 1–4, 7–8.
4. James uses this phrase in his Preface to *The Tragic Muse* (1890) to describe the formlessness of nineteenth-century novels like Thackeray's *The Newcomes* (1853–5), Dumas's *The Three Musketeers* (1844) and Tolstoy's *War and Peace* (1863–9): *The Art of the Novel: Critical Prefaces*, ed. R. P. Blackmur (New York: Scribner's, 1935), pp. 70–97 (p. 84).
5. From Henry James, *A Small Boy and Others* (New York, 1913); quoted in Philip Collins, *Dickens: The Critical Heritage* (New York: Barnes & Noble, 1971), pp. 612–14 (p. 613).
6. Ian Watt, *The Rise of the Novel: Studies in Defoe, Richardson and Fielding* (London: Chatto and Windus, 1957; repr. 1974); Nancy Armstrong, *Desire*

and Domestic Fiction: A Political History of the Novel (Oxford: Oxford University Press, 1987).

7. Kathryn Chittick, *Dickens and the 1830s* (Cambridge: Cambridge University Press, 1990), p. x.
8. *Ibid.*, pp. 64, 87.
9. Elliott Engell and Margaret F. King, *The Victorian Novel before Victoria: British Fiction during the Reign of William IV, 1830–37* (London: Macmillan, 1984), p. 5.
10. *Ibid.*
11. See Michel Foucault, *Discipline and Punish: The Birth of the Prison* (Harmondsworth: Penguin, 1991) (first publ. as *Surveiller et punir: naissance de la prison*, by Editions Gallimard, 1975; this transl. first publ. by Allen Lane, 1975; published in Peregrine, 1979; repr. Penguin, 1991).
12. Chittick, *Dickens and the 1830s*, p. 24.
13. Catherine Belsey, *Critical Practice* (London: Methuen, 1980; repr. London: Routledge, 1994), pp. 125–29 (p. 128).
14. The French Revolution and the war with France (1793–1815), as well as the working-class Chartist movement of the 1830s and 1840s, meant that the fear of chaos was particularly prevalent in the early part of Victoria's reign.
15. See Belsey, *Critical Practice*, pp. 67–84; Belsey's assortment of so-called classic realist texts also includes *Bleak House* (1852–3), a text whose avowed intention, at least, is to emphasize 'the romantic side of familiar things' (Preface). The fusion of the fantastic and the real in all Dickens's novels seems to us to exclude Dickens from unproblematic treatment as a 'classic realist' writer.
16. Ian Watt, one of the few critics to try to date the use of 'realism' as a literary critical term, claims that '"Réalisme" was apparently first used as an aesthetic description in 1835 to denote the "verité humaine" of Rembrandt as opposed to the *"idéalité poétique"* of neo-classical painting; it was later consecrated as a specific literary term by the foundation in 1856 of *Réalisme*, a journal edited by Duranty': *The Rise of the Novel*, p. 10. Watt's source is Bernard Weinberg's *French Realism: The Critical Reaction, 1830–1870*, MLA of America General Series (London: [n. pub.], 1937), p. 114. See also Lilian R. Furst (ed.), *Realism* (London: Longman, 1992).
17. Lyn Pykett, 'The Real versus the Ideal: Theories of Fiction in Periodicals, 1850–1870', *Victorian Periodicals Review*, 15 (1982), 63–74.
18. Though translations of the *Arabian Nights* have been available in English since the early eighteenth century, the best known English translation is that of Sir Richard Burton, published 1885–88.
19. See Mikhail Bakhtin, *The Dialogic Imagination*, ed. Michael Holquist, trans. Caryl Emerson and Michael Holquist (Austin: University of Texas Press, 1981).
20. See 'J. Hillis Miller on the Fiction of Realism', in *Realism*, ed. Lilian R. Furst, pp. 287–318 (p. 315); repr. from 'The Fiction of Realism: Sketches by Boz, Oliver Twist, and Cruikshank's Illustrations', in *Dickens Centennial Essays*, eds Ada Nisbet and Blake Nevius (Berkeley: University of California Press, 1971), pp. 85–126. The quotation is specifically about *Oliver Twist*, which Miller, like Belsey, uses questionably as an example of a realist text.

2
Victorian Realist Prose and Sentimentality

Philip Davis

For all his intellectual reservations about the work of Dickens, George Henry Lewes wrote of the irresistible nature of its immediate appeal to the feelings: 'If an author makes me laugh, he is humorous; if he makes me cry, he is pathetic. In vain will any one tell me that such a picture is not laughable, is not pathetic; or that I am wrong in being moved.'[1] If at the time of reading, you are personally moved, argues Lewes, you cannot simply get away from the sheer fact of that experience.

But of course you can deny its force, afterwards. Indeed, although Lewes argued that it is impossible to resist feeling, it has become our defence in the sceptical late twentieth century to argue against it instead. Critics often say, not 'I have been moved', but 'I have been manipulated'. I want to defend what has been mis-described as Victorian sentimentality – in particular with relation to the pathos and sad kindness of the ordinary in prose. I shall argue that there are structures of emotion here which are to be valued not just for the sake of feeling but as a tool for implicit thinking.

Carlyle himself dismissed his age, early on, as 'the reign of Sentimentality'.[2] But what Carlyle meant by sentimentality was auto-biographical self-consciousness: the conscious *idea* of one's own senti-ments voluntarily cultivated, their spectacle relished in the self's own mental looking-glass. Reviewing one such example of Rousseauist introspection in 1838, Carlyle protests: ' "One thing above all others," says Goethe once; "I have never *thought about Thinking.*" [...] How much wastefuller is it to *feel about Feeling*! One is wearied of that; the healthy soul avoids that. Thou shalt look outward, not inward.' The very space of the world is distorted by subjective egoism: 'Every mortal is a microcosm; to himself a *macro*cosm, or Universe large as Nature; universal Nature would barely hold what he *could* say about himself'.[3]

Such falsely articulate self-consciousness speaks only of the mere surface ideas of life, argued Carlyle: 'The sign of health is Unconsciousness'.[4] Carlyle wanted not those superficial mechanical ideas of consciousness that, befitting an age of machinery, were put together slowly and vainly in the head, but an earlier form of life-thought, of 'dynamical' thinking working below the level of voluntary arrangement.

I want to propose a different model of sentimentality and its relation to consciousness, which I shall offer as a vulnerable but indeed truly dynamic form of thought: a later account of what it means to 'feel about Feeling', offered in terms of the Victorian novel rather than Romantic autobiography. The so-called sentimentality I value exists not so much in the feelings of the characters as in *our* feelings of their feelings, our vicarious consciousness of their unconsciousnesses, and the thoughts that are saved by us as a result.

I want to take a substantial example from Elizabeth Gaskell's *Cranford* (1851–3), which first appeared in Dickens's own *Household Words*. Here the old spinster Miss Matty, last surviving member of her family, goes through old letters with her young friend and our intermediary-narrator, Mary Smith – remembering how as a result of a terrible family row, long ago, her young brother Peter had run away to sea. Here is an image of vicarious reading and feeling, reaching back into the very origins of the novel in its relation to the writing of letters and biographical histories:

> We lighted the candle, and found the captain's letter and Peter's too. And we also found a little simple begging letter from Mrs Jenkyns to Peter, addressed to him at the house of an old schoolfellow, whither she fancied he might have gone. They had returned it unopened; and unopened it had remained ever since, having been inadvertently put by among the other letters of that time. This is it:
> 'MY DEAREST PETER, You did not think we should be so sorry as we are, I know, or you would never have gone away. You are too good. Your father sits and sighs till my heart aches to hear him. He cannot hold up his head for grief; and yet he only did what he thought was right. Perhaps he has been too severe, and perhaps I have not been kind enough; but God knows how we love you, my dear only boy. Dor looks so sorry you are gone. Come back and make us happy, who love you so much. I *know* you will come back.'
> But Peter did not come back. That spring day was the last time he ever saw his mother's face. The writer of the letter – the last – the only person who had ever seen what was written in it, was dead

long ago – and I, a stranger, not born at the time when this occurrence took place, was the one to open it.[5]

If we are to read what it is all too easy to dismiss as merely sentimental, we need the equivalent of those two framing paragraphs on either side of the vulnerable old letter with its defensive perhapses and onlys. It is not as though even in 1851 Gaskell could rely upon a reader's kindness or reverence, without establishing the protective context and ritual that called for it. Thus, 'This is it' is not just a prose fact, but within that mechanical device dynamically signals the crossing of a threshold of both time and imagination. It is matched on the other side of the letter by a return to the reality of the present, in that other more-than-factual statement: 'But Peter did not come back.'

There was neither goodbye nor reconciliation. Somewhere along the line what had seemed a terrible but temporary family row had become formalized into a permanent parting. That is why this passage has become hardened into a little history, a narrative of the past, despite the present feelings recalled within it; its incompleteness now turned by death into a completed life-story. For this is a letter seen in the light not only of retrospect but of death, when as in Dickens's *A Christmas Carol* (1843) the shadow of last things is thrown into the midst of things. So-called sentimentalism is always, finally, to do with mortality, with 'things now' being both shadowed by and shielded from 'things to come'.

For though the sorrows of Miss Matty's mother are, like her, all in the past now, there is still emotion here. And for Victorians such as Dickens and Gaskell, where there is still emotion, it is a sign that something simply does continue to matter in the world, though we may not know rationally why it should. Yet that instinctively it *does* still matter means that somewhere in the world that emotion must be picked up. It is picked up here, via Miss Matty and the narrator, by the reader. The reader's vicarious sadness does for the writer of that letter what she could not do for herself and what her son was unable to do for her either: it does something, from outside the situation both in space and time, to rectify all that is signalled by that word 'inadvertently', the out-of-date letter having been inadvertently put by among the other letters of that time. Vicarious feeling values her, even though that feeling, in terms of the language of Benthamite utility, is both useless and too late, just as the mother's own begging letter was misplaced and ineffective too. 'The writer of the letter – the last – the only person who had ever seen what was written in it, was *dead* long ago – and I, a stranger, not *born* at the time when this occurrence took place, was the one to open it.' Mary Smith turns *back* to that letter as if for Gaskell this was an image of how through suspended animation even the ineffective stuff of life could become the human documents of literature. A family failure reaches, via the sympathetic 'stranger', the wider human family. It is what Dickens's Dombey resists receiving from his daughter Florence: something felt in the charged atmosphere with a matching thought deeply implicit within it. The right name for the misnomer of sentimentality is, therefore, literary emotion, on behalf and in memory of emotion and buried thought in life.

Literary emotion, aesthetic emotion, is here in place of religious redemption: 'dead long ago, and I, a stranger, not born'. For in the midst of life, in the middle of the situation, with the outcome still uncertain and awaited, the feelings of Peter's mother were obviously anxious; only afterwards, when death formally closes a situation otherwise incomplete or unsatisfactory, does the feeling of that feeling transform the emotion of anxiety in the midst of things to sadness after their end, offering a value to that anxiety not in terms of outcome but in place of it. And although that sad vicarious emotion might be said to redeem the mother's feelings, the mother is dead, the feelings went unanswered at the time, and vicarious emotion is further moved by the thought that of itself it cannot redeem what it is affected by. 'I *know* you will come back' is answered only by 'But Peter did not come back'. That is how proper vicariousness is not just a voluntary emotional self-indulgence or parasitic emotionalism, but, as consciously human and not divine, it has implicit painful *knowledge* of what it can do and what it cannot; it has a formal condition and a generic shape, for it is a secular bearing of witness that exists of necessity both outside the person suffering and after the event. In its heart of hearts it knows this paradox: that emotions which do no good to those to whom they are directed and even cause pain to those who hold them, may yet be good and bespeak goodness. And yet at the time we have them we cannot value those cares, or value ourselves for feeling them, especially when they are unvalidated by successful outcomes. Thus in feeling for others what they – and what we in their place – could not do for themselves, the secondary act of vicarious feeling does something but does not do everything. That incompleteness is what is moving about the mother in the sentence 'Your father sits and sighs till my heart aches to hear him': 'till' there is not a temporally saving word; it does not mean 'your father sighed till I was able to relieve him of his pain by my sympathetic action – end of problem'; 'till' means only 'to the point at which' my heart ached to hear him, and still he went on sighing, and still vicariously I went on aching. There is still, there is always something unresolved by action and by passion alike:

> 'And she was too late,' said Miss Matty; 'too late!' We sat in silence, pondering on the full meaning of those sad, sad words. At length I asked Miss Matty to tell me how her mother bore it.

There is always a residue: emotion cannot be wholly translated into either thought or action. The residue here lies in the implicit and never exhausted meaning of 'too late' when it is fully felt at the personal level. That is why 'sad, sad' is unashamedly repeated as well as 'too late, too late'. The ordinary reader recognizes here an image of how emotion marks and preserves the left-over wastes of experience: emotion becomes memory, released in the form of recognition by equivalent moments in life or literature.

The release into literary emotion is important not least because in life itself feeling is never fully synchronized with the events that provoke it, but always comes a beat too late. Literature combats this lack of synchronization, but we have also seen how realist prose, at the same time, reproduces it, and thus both does and does not redeem the time. For in that movement 'We sat in silence, pondering on the full meaning of those sad, sad words. At length I asked Miss Matty to tell me how her mother bore it', look how that sentence beginning 'At length' both retrospectively throws more time onto the sentence preceding it, by stressing the delaying effort required to quit it, and yet still goes on past it into renewed normality. Realist prose is like the world: hidden amidst the banal and the on-going in small places, there exists what is not really small yet goes for the most part formally unrecognized and unredeemed.

Realist prose is, therefore, emphatically not like the dream-world briefly offered at the beginning of Chapter 45 of Gaskell's *North and South* (1855) – a world in which 'time and space were not, though all other things seemed real' or where 'every event was measured by the emotions of the mind, not by its actual existence'.[6] In realism, the emotions have to go on vulnerably inside the actual world of time and space. If in dreams the emotions are absolute, in the medium of Victorian prose-realism, emotion has to survive more relativistically, more temporizingly within the bearable compromises of ordinary life.

It is therefore a prose which, in sober memory of life, is closer to the *Autobiography* of the novelist Margaret Oliphant, published posthumously in 1899, than to the *Confessions* of Jean-Jacques Rousseau of 1782 and 1789. Thus Oliphant recalling how in 1854 she learnt from the doctor that her mother is to die:

> He shook his head, and I knew – the idea having never entered my mind before that she was to die. I recollect going away, walking away as in a dream, not able to go to her, to look at her, from whom I had never had a secret, with this secret in my soul that must be told least of all to her; and the sensation that here was something which would not lighten after a while as all my troubles had always done, and pass away. I had never come face to face with the inevitable before. I was well enough used to sounding all the depths of miserable thought and then with a spring getting up from this very deep and seeing daylight again – but there was no daylight here – no hope – no getting over it. Then there followed a struggle of a month or so, much suffering on her part and a long troubled watch and nursing on mine.[7]

Encapsulated in the unconscious ambiguity of that phrase 'pass away', this is the language of 'never before' struggling with the realization of 'never again'. Syntactically there are final sentences here, short sentences of realization which lead nowhere: 'I had never come face to face with the inevitable before'. But these absolutes still have to exist in the midst of a mundane relative situation, in which the sentence 'Then there followed a struggle of a month or so' does not begin a fresh paragraph but merely carries on, has to keep going – in time, within the situation – regardless of the emotional and intellectual realization preceding it. But especially fine is that sequence trapped in the middle of the long second sentence that tries to get used to the idea – 'not able to go to her, to look at her, from whom I had never had a secret, with this secret in my soul that must be told least of all to her'. For a second there is telegraphic poetry in the midst of this prose, like a dynamic shorthand within the syntax: 'from whom I had never had a secret – with *this* secret'. By putting those two clauses together, whilst their emotional meaning speaks of their having to be kept painfully apart, the line for a second goes backwards, against the prosaic grain of time, before it goes forwards again into what was already implicit in it like a pre-echo: 'her, from whom I had never had a secret, with this secret in my soul that must be told *least of all* to her'. For all the apparent linearity, it has ended in a circle. Thus, prose here shows drama trapped within the compromised jumble of experience, without time, place or person to give it full emotional relief. *We* feel for Oliphant, from outside, what she can hardly bear on her own in the midst of life. That is not just about reading but is ontological biology: it is about the fact that as constrained creatures we all live immersed inside a thing which we call life, and yet we suspect or hope or believe that there is simultaneously a view to be had of it from elsewhere, from outside or above it – whether or not there is anyone or anything there to do the viewing. For once, the reader here is that someone or something outside life, as well as identifying with the limited creatures struggling within the embroiled medium.

That is to say, we misunderstand the nature of emotional vicariousness if we suspiciously attribute it to nothing more than a voluntary collusion between a writer's manipulativeness and a reader's appetitiveness. There is something more to be said about the formal requirement of vicariousness.

Thus, in Marian Evans's translation of *The Essence of Christianity*, Ludwig Feuerbach argues: 'The Greeks and the Romans deified accidents as substances: virtues, states of mind, passions, as independent beings'. 'In Rome,' he goes on, 'even the passions of fear and horror had their temples': the Romans isolated and dramatized feelings that existed *within* the human situation into independent forces, powers and gods presiding *over* it. 'The Christians,' he adds, 'also made mental phenomena into independent beings' – projected inner nature outwards as God and His attributes, as angels or as devils.[8] Yet, said Feuerbach, in the secular grammar of the modern world, what used to be seen as divine powers are no longer the dominant subjects of sentences. Instead, translated back down from above to within the human condition, those formerly high powers are manifested now as smaller undeified 'accidents', trying to find a proportionate place for themselves within the crowded context of indiscriminate modern life.

Here is an example of what such a world might feel like. At the end of Chapter 4 of *Adam Bede* (1859), Adam on the sudden death of his father feels an equally sudden regret at his harshness to his father in his latter days, and George Eliot closes the chapter by saying, formally: 'When death, the great reconciler has come, it is never our tenderness that we repent of, but our severity.'[9]

Compare that vain hindsight with the scene, a chapter later, in which Mr Irwine goes upstairs to pay his habitual visit to the tiresome invalid, his sister:

> Anne's eyes were closed, and her brow contracted as if from intense pain. Mr Irwine went to the bed-side, and took up one of the delicate hands and kissed it; a slight pressure from the small fingers told

him that it was worth while to come up-stairs for the sake of doing that. He lingered a moment, looking at her, and then turned away and left the room, treading very gently – he had taken off his boots and put on slippers before he came up-stairs. Whoever remembers how many things he has declined to do even for himself, rather than have the trouble of putting on or taking off his boots, will not think the last detail insignificant.

Adam Bede, pp. 109–10

Irwine does for his sister something equivalent to what Adam now vainly regrets not doing for his father. It is only in the light of death that, too late, Adam sees the value of what otherwise might well seem sentimental and insignificant. Only the very end of life, in the form of death, gives belated importance to the embedded medium of life in which little, unremembered and barely appreciated acts of kindness go on without any proud claim or extrinsic support for their significance. In Victorian realist prose the apparent unimportance of things is inseparably connected to how secretly powerful they are: only that sudden and momentary burst of vicarious emotion can dynamically recognize, as if from outside, the implicit importance of things which inside the human system are important precisely by their not claiming to be so at the time. Vicariousness bespeaks what we cannot claim for ourselves and yet belongs to us.

The failure of prose to provide a *visibly* distinct form for itself on the page, in the way that poetry so manifestly does, is intrinsic to its strength as a vehicle of Victorian realism. For prose is a medium which seems indiscriminate and non-hierarchical; it has no apparent form external to itself, but goes on and on, along the line, across the page, very much in the line of mundane time. It is the very medium for the barely visible, the hidden and the momentary, or the under-rated. Just two sentences from Chapter 15 of *Bleak House* (1852–3) may serve as example:

'Go into the Court of Chancery yonder, and ask what is one of the standing jokes that brighten up their business sometimes, and they will tell you that the best joke they have, is the man from Shropshire. I,' he said, beating one hand on the other, passionately, 'am the man from Shropshire.'[10]

Hidden within the humdrum mechanism of its apparently formless linearity, there is in such prose the secret dynamic of the invisible existence of different *levels* along the self-same *line*. Thus this prose realistically mimes the way in which, within time's mere on-going linear indifference, there are hidden in the world itself neglected human differences important only to those who feel them when they can barely be seen. So here one sentence says: They laugh at the man from Shropshire; and almost immediately the next goes on: I am the man from Shropshire. There is no formal recognition of the difference which my being the man from Shropshire makes: the view from inside is laid with vulnerable pain alongside the view from outside it, like one thing merely succeeding another in time – whilst really we move from comedy to something that is not funny, although it knows that it is seen as being so. All that Dickens does magnificently is to insert that 'he said, beating one hand on the other, passionately', less for its own sake as mere stage-direction, but more as a minute indicator of the need for extra time, momentarily highlighting the hidden poetic shifts in level from 'they' and 'the man from Shropshire' outside to 'I' within; or, as if across a lost poetic line-ending, from the lonely 'I' to the vulnerably emphatic '*am* the man from Shropshire'. Prose offers no apparent distinction and very little time between the world's view and the man's. But it tacitly asks a reader to register – fleetingly but deeply because there is so little time and so little room – a sense of emotional difference within that formal lack of distinction which it also nonetheless realistically preserves.

Thus, without creating the distortion of which Carlyle complains, these sentences confirm the fact that, as Carlyle put it, 'Every mortal is a microcosm; to himself a *macro*cosm'. Emotion *is* that felt disproportion between the indifference outside and the sense of overwhelming meaning within. Hurt by the discrepancy, emotion constitutes of itself a compensation for it. That protective feeling offers via the readers an alternative society, an alternative secret family, compared to the laughter in the Courts. It is, tenderly, both comic and sad, together.

And comic and sad is what it is when the man from Shropshire finally through his own force of opposition exhausts himself to death. Even his old adversary, Inspector Bucket, is upset:

'Worn out, Mr Gridley? After dodging me for all these weeks, and forcing me to climb the roof here like a Tom Cat, and to come to see you as a Doctor? That ain't like being worn out. *I* should think not! Now I tell you what *you* want. You want excitement, you know, to keep you up; that's what *you* want. You're used to it, and you can't do without it. I couldn't myself. Very well, then; here's this warrant got by Mr Tulkinghorn of Lincoln's Inn Fields, and backed into half-a-dozen counties since. What do you say to coming along with me, upon this warrant, and having a good angry argument before the Magistrate? It'll do you good; it'll freshen you up, and get you into training for another turn at the Chancellor. Give in? Why, I am surprised to hear a man of your energy talk of giving in. You mustn't do that. You're half the fun of the fair, in the Court of Chancery. George, you lend Mr Gridley a hand, and let's see now whether he won't be better up than down.'

'He is very weak,' said the trooper, in a low voice.

'Is he?' returned Bucket, anxiously. 'I only want to rouse him. I don't like to see an old acquaintance giving in like this. It would cheer him up more than anything, if I could make him a little waxy with me. He's welcome to drop into me, right and left, if he likes. I shall never take advantage of it.'

Bleak House, Chapter 24, p. 373

This is a restricted view of life that can only seek to transform everything from within by changing nothing from without. It is through sheer dogged habit and coaxing familiarity that the hurt of 'They will tell you that the best joke they have, is the man from Shropshire' becomes the appreciative 'You're half the fun of the fair, in the Court of Chancery'. There is a benign comedy and a vitality offered in continuing to play the parts: I'll chase you, you get angry; under cover of the mechanical form that keeps us both going, there is hidden sympathy as well as willed pretence. For what Inspector Bucket wants is a response from Gridley that acknowledges the transformation of a still-continuing sense of injustice into a sheer way of life that itself helps keep him alive. And when you know ('in a *low* voice') that in fact this way of life has killed Gridley, it makes you also feel sorry for Bucket. It is not that we, as would-be intellectuals, have access to knowledge that the characters do not have; it is just that the characters cannot afford that knowledge if they are to carry on living, and so they live despite their implicit knowledge until the two – death and knowledge – finally surface together. Only when she is dying does Dora admit that she has always felt that she was not the right wife for David Copperfield: in life she still had to continue to be that unsatisfactory wife as well as possible. It is as if thought cannot change everything, and everything cannot be changed into thought. Emotion speaks of the continuing human residue.

But when a rationalist such as Spinoza described emotion as no more and no less than 'a confused idea', he was proposing to abolish confusion by transforming that passive residue within emotion into active consciousness.[11] Much translated within the Victorian period – witness

George Eliot, Matthew Arnold, Froude, Hale White – Spinoza was himself, like Feuerbach, a translator – from the religious to the secular, from the emotional to the rational. Although to Spinoza emotion was not meaningless but thought-bearing, still it bore thoughts only confusedly, inadequately and passively. When the thought behind an emotion was translated into conceptual terms, then it was no longer the case that we suffered the thought – that the thought had us emotionally, passionately, passively – but that we had the thought, instead, adequately and actively. The children of Israel obeyed the law of God emotionally, not rationally, not realizing that the precepts of God were really ideas of eternal reason. By implication, an adult, a secular nineteenth-century adult, should put away childish things and wholly translate passive feelings into the active ideas distortedly concealed within them.

Is that what I have been defending – sentimentality as a childish holding-on to emotions? So often Victorian sentimentality seems to exist defensively and protectively, putting women and children first, and if men thereafter, only little, weak, foolish, childish, or underprivileged men from the lower order. This may suggest that sentimentality is not truly active, as Spinoza might have wished, but merely the re-active product of the harsh masculine world of the urban Industrial Revolution. When people moved from the countryside to the towns and hardly knew where they were any more in that harsher and faster world, at least they still knew the communal heart was in its right place. Is not that what Victorian sentimentality is: a defensive part of urban social history, democratizing inarticulate good feeling, offering family feeling a place in the new world? Yet I want to argue that this reassuring emotional vicariousness had something more to it than the externalized perspective that historical explanation offers. David Copperfield, thinking of Mr Dick's sensitivity to the troubles of the Strongs, says this: 'There is a subtlety of perception in real attachment, even when it is borne towards man by one of the lower animals, which leaves the higher intellect behind. To this mind of the heart, if I may call it so, in Mr Dick, some bright ray of the truth shot through'.[12] Admittedly, even this is not without the danger that in the post-Romantic period attends upon people of intellect patronizingly claiming moral credit for themselves by sacrificing that intelligence to an alleged preference for sentimental feelings. But I am not saying that I, any more than David Copperfield, want to be one of those 'lower animals'. To put it harshly, like Pip in *Great Expectations* (1860–1) I do not want to be Joe Gargery however much I may think (in part through guilt) that I admire him. What I am saying is that those lower creatures are something residually in us, whatever further intelligence is developed above. And that involuntary emotion biologically recognizes and recalls this. When Mr Peggotty is smitten with the loss of little Emily and Mrs Gummidge suddenly, comically, movingly, stops being a moaning widow and says actively from outside herself: 'If any *should* come nigh, they shall see the old widder woman true to 'em, a long way off' (*David Copperfield*, Chapter 32, p. 375) – Dickens is not saying: Become simple and be like her; but rather that she is a part of the language, and not so much here a separate character as a disposition that needs other elements, other characters, including Steerforth, alongside it to make a whole; that she is an emotion that needs a thought.

The mind of the heart is where mind begins. There is a biological need to start from feelings; they are the evolutionary source of ordinary intelligence, the link between the physical and psychical realms.

Finally, feelings are the stuff that show the human value of those thoughts that try to grasp our condition. Often such feeling is felt only *en passant*, as an intrinsic part of the excited energy of a thought registered implicitly in the very midst of life. So it is in a sentence from *Cranford* I have already quoted, concerning the undelivered letter: 'They had returned it unopened; and unopened it had remained ever since […]' – where something is lodged, like poetry, in its very midst ('it unopened; and unopened it'). But occasionally, and often in relation to loss and death, Victorian realist prose can literally find the time to bring to light that transient life-content which lies latent within and between its sentences or half-buried behind its appearances. Here from *The Old Curiosity Shop* (1841) is an old woman at the grave of a twenty-three-year-old man: 'Were you his mother?' asks Little Nell (terrible past tense that); 'I was his wife, my dear':

> And now that five-and-thirty years were gone, she spoke of the dead man as if he were her son or grandson, with a kind of pity for his youth, growing out of her own old age, and an exalting of his strength and manly beauty as compared with her own weakness and decay; and yet she spoke about him as her husband too, and thinking of herself in connection with him, as she used to be and not as she was now, talked of their meeting in another world as if he were dead but yesterday, and she, separated from her former self, were thinking of the happiness of that comely girl who seemed to have died with him.[13]

This is a woman who has had to live on, for a long time, after so much of her life has ended. Consequently, this is *one* sentence precisely because in one lifetime so many times, so many varied points of view and shifting centres of being, so many differing relations, have to be held in one person. Yet the sentence is loose and flexible because those differing times cannot possibly be held together at quite the *same* time, simultaneously. These varied mental movements bespeak a life-time's intelligence acting within and between time's changes of feeling. It is not only that there are two different modes here – mother or grand-mother in the first half, wife or bride in the second. In each half there are different movements, too: in the first half, that Wordsworthian sense of age as a source of both growing and of decaying, resulting in pity and admiration respectively for the dead young man; in the second, that shift from the thought of future reunion with the dead beloved, to the thought of the death not only of the husband but with him of the young girl she used to be. The life-separations and life-connections made here for once within one person are part of the same genetic dynamic that often we have seen requiring two people – the sufferer and the witness. Such movements imply a law, a law that requires that sometimes we should be so emotionally immersed in a situation as hardly to know what we are feeling, while at other times, correspondingly, we should feel vicariously for other people, from outside the situation, what we could hardly afford to feel were we, like they now, within it.

That old woman already has within her what Scrooge must achieve in *A Christmas Carol* if he is to live in the present, past and future together and not just in the linear flight of a life. Indeed, this essay is really an introduction to reading *A Christmas Carol* as a central Victorian work. For what *A Christmas Carol* offers is the impossible but also most needful thing: the opportunity to have feelings about your own feelings, vicariously, as if you were looking back at yourself as another person who was also you. Scrooge has to learn to look both ways: at the past scenario before his eyes and at the person who is doing the seeing. From this double perspective, normally impossible to us and displaced, he feels his own feelings: at one time he feels the same again as he did in the past and forgets his present self; at another, he has feelings excluded from those expressed in what he sees, in regret for what became of him.

Above all, Scrooge witnesses his own self, his own history and his own life not just confusedly and uncertainly within his own head, as though the past were unreal or over or ignorable, but objectively,

externally, in time again, as though the Rousseauist introspective sentimentality that Carlyle detested was itself miraculously turned inside-
out. For the book is a warning against the misuse of feeling that comes
about at a second defensive stage of development. I mean the second
stage that results in Scrooge opening the story by edging his way along
the crowded paths of life, 'warning all human sympathy to keep its distance'.[14] It is of course his own human sympathy that he is defensively
trying to keep at a distance, and signs of this inversion are discernible
in the way Scrooge speaks to his nephew: 'What reason have you to be
merry? You're poor enough' – or, again, in the way he thinks of Bob
Cratchit: 'My clerk with fifteen shillings a week, and a wife and family,
talking about a merry Christmas' (*A Christmas Carol*, pp. 48, 50). It is
like sympathy turned back-to-front. For Scrooge himself has been
turned, skewed, back to front: as his fiancée told him, when it was
already happening, it was his fear of poverty that led him to his love of
wealth. Not daring to feel his weakness as weakness, or to remember
the vulnerable origin of his strong and hardened defences, Scrooge
finds that feelings themselves have led him not to want to feel. That is
the second-order state, when the emotions that first refer outward
begin to form a tangle of internal and indirect relations amongst themselves instead.

But it is to the first heart that the Spirit, like a therapist, must
return Scrooge, making him remember and feel again what insecur-
ities, repressed, led him to his apparent lack of feeling. Here Scrooge
is taken back to see himself left behind at school – in the Christmas
holidays:

> 'The school is not quite deserted,' said the Ghost. 'A solitary
> child, neglected by his friends, is left there still.' Scrooge said he
> knew it. And he sobbed.
>
> *A Christmas Carol*, p. 71

For a moment he becomes that boy again, and then with 'a rapidity of
transition very foreign' to what has become his usual character, he
finds himself saying in something other than mere self-pity, 'Poor boy!'
– which immediately leads him to make another connection of more
recent memory:

> 'I wish,' Scrooge muttered, putting his hand in his pocket, and
> looking about him , after drying his eyes with his cuff: 'but it's too
> late now.'

'What is the matter?' asked the Spirit.

'Nothing,' said Scrooge. 'Nothing. There was a boy singing a Christmas Carol at my door last night. I should like to have given him something: that's all.'

A Christmas Carol, p. 73

That is the beginning, at least, of fast thought arising out of renewed feeling, action from passion, but thought at this stage still felt as too late, too complicated in its tense ('should like to have given'). 'Real remembering', says Doris Lessing in her autobiography, 'is – if even for a flash, even a moment, being back in the experience itself. You remember pain with pain, love with love, one's real best self with one's best self'.[15] That is what *A Christmas Carol* is after – real dynamic remembering, *when what has happened to you is felt by you*, in terms of the direct feelings themselves and not just their indirect effects on you ever after. Nothing – no mere idea of life – is more vital.

Most of the prose I have been considering in this essay has been locked into the line of time, its realistic messages hidden there, entrapped in relativism, still in the process, even whilst trying to think about it. But *A Christmas Carol* offers a different space-time, a form of getting outside the self before returning back inside it again. And that is why it is massively important that at the end of *A Christmas Carol*, Scrooge awakes to find that it is still Christmas Day, that by recalling and feeling (and not merely dreaming) no time has been wasted, after all. 'I haven't missed it', says Scrooge (*A Christmas Carol*, p. 128). Ideas, abstracted, seem big things. For Scrooge, ideas have been worked back inside the situation that needs them, so quickly and so utterly, that no time has been lost.

In the reality which nineteenth-century prose so powerfully images in its very syntax, there is barely space or time to register ideas as anything other than small and momentary when they are almost invisibly ploughed back again into the life-situation that needs them. But we are not missing ideas if we find and use them in the midst of feeling; we are not belittling ideas if we have them not in apparently large abstraction but, quickly and emotionally, in time. So-called Victorian sentimentality, at its most powerful, is a normalized form of implicit or displaced or re-immersed *thinking*. Going on in the very midst of common life, it is – as Wordsworth put it in the great 'Preface' to *Lyrical Ballads*, which stands as a founding text for Victorian fictional prose rather than Victorian poetry – thinking *in* the spirit of human passions.[16]

Notes

1. *Versatile Victorian: Selected Writings of George Henry Lewes*, ed. Rosemary Ashton (London: Bristol Classical Press and Duckworth, 1992), p. 68.
2. Thomas Carlyle, 'Characteristics', in *Critical and Miscellaneous Essays*, 5 vols (London: Chapman and Hall, 1899), III, 1–43 (p. 9).
3. Thomas Carlyle, 'Varnhagen Von Ense's Memoirs', in *Critical and Miscellaneous Essays*, IV, 88–119 (pp. 108–9).
4. Carlyle, 'Characteristics', pp. 4–5.
5. Elizabeth Gaskell, *Cranford*, ed. P. Keating (Harmondsworth: Penguin, 1976), Chapter 6, p. 100.
6. Elizabeth Gaskell, *North and South*, ed. M. Dodsworth (Harmondsworth: Penguin, 1970), p. 468.
7. *The Autobiography of Margaret Oliphant*, ed. Elisabeth Jay (Oxford: Oxford University Press, 1990), pp. 37–8.
8. Ludwig Feuerbach, *The Essence of Christianity*, trans. Marian Evans (London: Chapman, 1853), p. 21.
9. George Eliot, *Adam Bede*, ed. Stephen Gill (London: Penguin, 1985), Chapter 4, p. 97.
10. Charles Dickens, *Bleak House*, ed. Stephen Gill (Oxford: Oxford University Press, 1996), Chapter 15, p. 230. Further references will be given in the text by page number in this edition.
11. Benedict de Spinoza, *Ethics*, trans. George Eliot, ed. T. Deegan (Salzburg: University of Salzburg Studies in English Literature, 1981), p. 151, end of Part 3, 'General Definition of the Emotions'.
12. Charles Dickens, *David Copperfield*, ed. Nina Burgis (Oxford: Oxford University Press, 1983), Chapter 42, p. 509. Further references will be given in the text by page number in this edition.
13. Charles Dickens, *The Old Curiosity Shop*, ed. Paul Schlicke (London: Everyman, 1995), Chapter 16, pp. 134–5.
14. Charles Dickens, *A Christmas Carol*, ed. Michael Slater (Harmondsworth: Penguin, 1985), Stave 1, p. 47. Further references will be given in the text by page number in this edition.
15. Doris Lessing, *Under My Skin* (London: HarperCollins, 1994), p. 218.
16. William Wordsworth, *Prose Works*, eds W. J. B. Owen and Jane Worthington Smyser, 3 vols (Oxford: Oxford University Press, 1974), I, 142.

3
Having the Whip-Hand in *Middlemarch*

Daniel Karlin

I begin with an incident which takes place in Chapter 12 of *Middlemarch*.[1] The scene is Stone Court, the residence of the old miser and misanthrope Peter Featherstone, and the occasion is the first meeting between Rosamond Vincy and Lydgate. Lydgate comes in just as Rosamond is about to leave, and Featherstone mentions that she has been singing to him: she is, he boasts, the best in Middlemarch.

> 'Middlemarch has not a very high standard, uncle,' said Rosamond, with a pretty lightness, going towards her whip, which lay at a distance.
> Lydgate was quick in anticipating her. He reached the whip before she did, and turned to present it to her. She bowed and looked at him: he of course was looking at her, and their eyes met with that peculiar meeting which is never arrived at by effort, but seems like a sudden divine clearance of haze.
>
> (Chapter 12, p. 117)

The meeting of Rosamond's and Lydgate's eyes may be unpremeditated, but the same cannot be said of the narrative of that meeting, or the dramatic irony which it enfolds. It is all about anticipation: the physical gesture on the part of the character is made to coincide with the writer's employment of prolepsis, the rhetorical figure of anticipation: power is to be an issue in Lydgate's relations with Rosamond, and in handing her the whip he is making a rod for his own back. She goes on to make use of the whip, mastering him in ways which he precisely does not anticipate; indeed, his quickness in anticipating her here is deceptive, just as her pretty lightness turns out to conceal an unbending will and grip. We can trace the figure all the way to the other end of the novel, to the moment in Chapter 78 when someone – but not Lydgate – finally gets the whip-hand of Rosamond. This person is Will Ladislaw, and he does it with a metaphorical whip, with his voice, when he rejects the touch of her hand:

> She put out her arm and laid the tips of her fingers on Will's coat-sleeve.
>
> 'Don't touch me!' he said, with an utterance like the cut of a lash [...]. He wheeled round to the other side of the room and stood opposite to her, with the tips of his fingers in his pockets and his head thrown back.
>
> (Chapter 78, p. 777)

In the care with which the tips of Rosamond's fingers are opposed to the tips of Ladislaw's, the realism of both gestures (disposing us to believe them 'in character') is subsumed by a different design. This design is the subject of my essay. When Lydgate hands Rosamond her whip, he, too, is acting in character, yet his action has another quality. The 'touch' of the passage – spectral, disembodied, yet palpable and powerful – is that of the writer's hand.

I want to connect the fact that *Middlemarch* is George Eliot's handwork with the predominance, in the novel's system of representations, of hands and everything associated with them. I have seventy pages of extracts, a Casaubon-like heap of material, in which hands are mentioned: either directly, or by association with the actions and gestures they perform, or in a multitude of figurative expressions.[2] Naturally the novel provides a fine collection of whips, Rosamond's being in every way exceptional, since all the others belong to men; moreover they are singularly ineffectual in their use of them, except in one instance. Sir James Chettam, in Chapter 6, beats his whip nervously against his boot and then drops it when Mrs Cadwallader informs him of Dorothea's engagement to Casaubon (p. 58); Fred Vincy also beats his boot with his whip, in Chapter 12, as he is being tormented about money by his uncle Featherstone (p. 111), and sulkily takes up his hat and whip in Chapter 14, when Mary Garth rebuffs him (p. 140); in Chapter 24, in the Garth family kitchen, his whip becomes a toy and he is embarrassed by one of the Garth children asking to be taken out riding, since it is because of his ill-advised dealings in horse-flesh that he has got into debt and involved Mr Garth in difficulty (p. 246). Later on, however, Fred uses his whip to good effect, when he chases the labourers in the field who have been harassing the railway men. (It is hard to take Fred seriously as a class warrior, and in fact George Eliot does not intend us to: she does the whole episode as burlesque, and its function in the plot is, paradoxically, to get the genteel Fred off his horse and into Caleb Garth's employment, where he works for a living with his hands.) Fred's sinking down the social scale is matched by Rosamond's rise, and she stigmatizes the vulgarity of the young men she is forced to frequent as 'Middlemarch gentry, elated with their silver-headed whips and satin stocks, but embarrassed in their manners, and timidly jocose' (Chapter 27, p. 267). The last (literal) whip in the novel, like the first, belongs to the unlucky Sir James, who hopes that scandal about Ladislaw being Rosamond's lover will put Dorothea off him; he sets up Mrs Cadwallader to mention this item of gossip, as though by accident, in the course of a walk, but he is embarrassed at his own underhand methods, and we see him 'turning aside to whip a shrub' when Mrs Cadwallader begins her story (Chapter 62, p. 626).

The psychological acuteness of this last example, its concise rendering of embarrassment mixed with frustrated aggression (the 'shrub' is an image of Ladislaw himself in Sir James's mind as an upstart of no account) is what the novel is famous for, and is one of the defining elements of realist fiction. The episode in which Lydgate hands Rosamond her whip differs from this kind of realism, but is only enabled to do so by the mass of instances which conform to type. The same is true of other gestures: holding, clasping, pressing, shaking, and releasing hands, for example, which occur dozens of times, from St Teresa holding hands with her little brother in the 'Prelude' (p. 3) to Fred grasping Mary's hand 'till it rather hurt her' in Chapter 86 (p. 830). Some of the novel's most heightened or poignant passages are marked by the touch of hands, such as the one at the end of Chapter 42 when Dorothea and Casaubon are momentarily and precariously reconciled ('She put her hand into her husband's, and they went along the broad corridor together', p. 427), or in the meeting of Dorothea and Rosamond in Chapter 81 ('Rosamond [...] could not avoid putting her small hand into Dorothea's which clasped it with gentle motherliness', p. 793), or during the culminating scene in Chapter 83 between Dorothea and Will, each of whose stages is marked by the holding or releasing of hands. A sub-set of this group concerns moments in which characters lay or put their hands on the hands of someone else. Almost always such moments represent ambivalent impulses, in which affection or even apology co-exists with the desire to dominate. Several times Dorothea lays her hand on Mr Casaubon's in this way, and he is stiffly sensitive to its implication: when she is talking of Will Ladislaw's decision to throw off his dependence on her husband, for example:

> 'I told him I was sure that the thing you considered in all you did for him was his own welfare. I remembered your goodness in what you said about him when I first saw him at Lowick,' said Dorothea, putting her hand on her husband's.
>
> 'I had a duty towards him,' said Mr Casaubon, laying his other hand on Dorothea's in conscientious acceptance of her caress, but with a glance which he could not hinder from being uneasy.
>
> (Chapter 22, p. 225)

When, right at the end of the novel, Will lays his hand on Dorothea's, her hand 'turns itself upward to be clasped' (Chapter 83, p. 811), her will corresponding to his, so that she is not claimed or imposed on.[3] The precision of the physical notation in such passages, and the energy of mind and feeling with which it is charged, are typical of the novel's treatment of hands, and contrast with its relative lack of interest in, for example, the tones of the voice, or the movement and expression of other parts of the body.[4] In turn, the characters notice and are interested in hands: when Sir James Chettam is paying unwanted court to Dorothea, she finds his 'dimpled hands [...] quite disagreeable' (Chapter 3, p. 30), while Lydgate's large white ones are attractive to Rosamond; she has already heard about them from Mary Garth, who mentions the new doctor's 'large solid white hands' in her description of him in Chapter 12 (p. 114). The whiteness of Lydgate's hands is a mark of social difference, almost of otherness: Rosamond contrasts them with the red hands of her other suitor, young Ned Plymdale, who belongs to the stratum of Middlemarch society from which she is determined to escape (Chapter 27, p. 269). The painter Naumann notices Dorothea's 'beautiful ungloved hand' in Rome (Chapter 19, p. 189); but we already know that Dorothea's hands would attract a painter, because that is the first definite thing which George Eliot tells us about her, in the second sentence of Chapter 1: 'Her hand and wrist were so finely formed that she could wear sleeves not less bare of style than those in which the Blessed Virgin appeared to Italian painters' (p. 7). In Chapter 4 we learn that these hands have a metaphysical as well as an aesthetic quality: 'They were not thin hands, or small hands; but powerful, feminine, maternal hands. She seemed to be holding them up in propitiation for her passionate desire to know and to think,' (Chapter 4, p. 38).

Rosamond's hands, needless to say, *are* thin and small, in a feminine but un-maternal way, and she is seen using them in the novel for three main purposes: to sew, to play the piano, and to touch herself, especially her 'wondrous hair-plaits – an habitual gesture with her as pretty as any movements of a kitten's paw' (Chapter 16, p. 160).[5] Rosamond's skill in music, by which the 'hidden soul' of her old music-master seems to be 'flowing forth from her fingers' (Chapter 16, p. 161), raises some interesting questions about aesthetics and the body, but these are of limited significance in the novel; the portrayal of her narcissism is, as Rosemary Ashton remarks, too insistent, and is in danger of seeming as stereotyped as the gestures given to minor characters, such as the auctioneer Mr Trumbull, who is always seen 'trimming' himself with his forefinger and playing with his watch-seals.[6] Rosamond's sewing, on the other hand, connects her to one of the book's central subjects. I am interested here not so much in the web as a governing metaphor as in the 'work' which the middle-class women characters are shown habitually doing with their hands.[7] The constant references to women carrying, holding, picking up, laying down, getting on with or neglecting their 'work' are part of the novel's realism, its verisimilitude; moreover, George Eliot is attentive to the ways in which this habitual, almost necessary and unconscious activity of the hands becomes infused with individual and social character, so that when Mrs Garth lays down her knitting and folds her arms it is described as 'an unwonted sign of emotion in her that she should put her work out of her hands' (Chapter 57, p. 575), and the excitement of a fresh subject of gossip in Middlemarch is signalled by 'wives, widows, and single ladies [taking] their work and [going] out to tea oftener than usual' (Chapter 71, p. 719). Women use their sewing as a weapon in conversation: Fred is on the receiving end of this from Mary Garth in Chapter 14 ('Mary was sewing swiftly, and seemed provokingly mistress of the situation', p. 138), and from her mother in Chapter 57 ('She was knitting, and could either look at Fred or not, as she chose', p. 573). But, as with the whip, the close notation of women's sewing is, at certain crucial moments, overdetermined, and bears the mark not of something observed to happen, but something made. It is important for the novel's purpose that these visionary interventions or intrusions should be disguised, so to speak, as contingent and probable, and so they seek safety in numbers. Since there are so many references to women sewing, it is unsurprising to find such a reference in the scene of Lydgate's involuntary proposal to Rosamond in Chapter 31, even if it turns out to repeat the episode of his handing her the whip and to mark his entry into servitude:

> Miss Vincy was alone, and blushed so deeply when Lydgate came in that he felt a corresponding embarrassment, and instead of any playfulness, he began at once to speak of his reason for calling, and to beg her, almost formally, to deliver the message to her father. Rosamond, who at the first moment felt as if her happiness were returning, was keenly hurt by Lydgate's manner; her blush had departed, and she assented coldly, without adding an unnecessary word, some trivial chain-work which she had in her hands enabling her to avoid looking at Lydgate higher than his chin. In all failures, the beginning is certainly the half of the whole. After sitting two long moments while he moved his whip and could say nothing, Lydgate rose to go, and Rosamond, made nervous by her struggle between mortification and the wish not to betray it, dropped her chain as if startled, and rose too, mechanically. Lydgate instantaneously stooped to pick up the chain. When he rose he was very near to a lovely little face set on a fair long neck which he had been used to see turning about under the most perfect management of self-contented grace. But as he raised his eyes now he saw a certain helpless quivering which touched him quite newly, and made him look at Rosamond with a questioning flash.
>
> (Chapter 31, pp. 300–1)

The two episodes of whip and chain resemble each other not just in their external features (Lydgate hands something to Rosamond and their eyes meet) but in their production – by effort and intention – of a moment of unintended consequences. Although, in the first episode, the sense of being precipitated into something unforeseen is as strong in Rosamond as in Lydgate, in the second it is Lydgate's sensation which predominates, and it is of him that George Eliot remarks, in the next paragraph: 'He did not know where the chain went' (Chapter 31, p. 301). Lydgate's ignorance, which of course implies the author's knowledge, is based on a delusion about what Rosamond is like; and this delusion is not particular and contingent, but the necessary product of a general idea. In demonstrating 'where the chain goes', the novel ironically echoes Lydgate's desire, as a scientist, to 'work out the proof of an anatomical conception and make a link in the chain of discovery' (Chapter 15, p. 146) and juxtaposes this project with its own providential narrative, whose conception is there to be 'discovered' only in the sense of being revealed.

This pressure of the writer's hand on the representation of character can be illustrated by following a sequence of gestures in which Lydgate and Rosamond are made, as it were, to collaborate in the unravelling of their lot. Rosamond's 'perfect management of self-contented grace' is what Lydgate has admired and found attractive in her, yet what *touches* him is not her management of her body, but her failure to manage it, the 'helpless quivering' which is the sign, as he believes, of her passionate dependence. In fact it is nothing of the sort: Lydgate is deceived first by Rosamond's self-control and then by her loss of it. The point is that both these things are aspects of a false consciousness which is predicated on the body and its appearances. There is something odd about Lydgate's professional passion for the body, his desire to understand its material principles, his explorations and experiments on the flesh, when it is combined with with his ignorance of how the personal and social body actually works. In particular Lydgate does not understand how human beings exercise power over each other, a lack of understanding which costs him as dearly in his professional dealings with his male colleagues as it does in his personal relations with women.

From the moment he hands her the whip, the erotic charge in Lydgate's relationship with Rosamond is connected with the movement of his hands, whether he is scornfully turning the pages of the *Keepsake* and 'showing his large white hands to much advantage, as Rosamond thought' (Chapter 27, p. 270), or 'bending his head to the table and lifting with his fourth finger her delicate handkerchief which lay at the mouth of her reticule, as if to enjoy its scent' (Chapter 31, p. 293). But the erotic also implies the social, in ways which Lydgate does not appreciate, but which George Eliot pressingly invites her readers to take into account. Let us look again at the handkerchief incident, and bring in the surrounding context. Rosamond compliments Lydgate on the growth of his practice:

'How your practice is spreading! You were called in before to the Chettams, I think; and now, the Casaubons.'

'Yes,' said Lydgate, in a tone of compulsory admission. 'But I don't really like attending such people so well as the poor. The cases are more monotonous, and one has to go through more fuss and listen more deferentially to nonsense.'

'Not more than in Middlemarch,' said Rosamond. 'And at least you go through wide corridors and have the scent of rose-leaves everywhere.'

'That is true, Mademoiselle de Montmorenci,' said Lydgate, just bending his head to the table and lifting with his fourth finger her delicate handkerchief which lay at the mouth of her reticule, as if to enjoy its scent, while he looked at her with a smile.

(Chapter 31, p. 293)

Seen in this light, Lydgate's gesture is a humorous one, paying mock-homage to Rosamond's taste for gracious living. The fourth, or little, finger is the least used, the least needed: it suggests that Lydgate would handle Rosamond as he does her handkerchief, taking pleasure in her delicacy, frivolity and superfluous luxury, but not taking her seriously, and not peering further into the reticule than its mouth. He does not understand the import of Rosamond's comment about his aristocratic patients, and certainly does not appreciate the effect of his own aristocratic connections on her view of him.

The next time this subject comes up, at the end of Chapter 43, Lydgate and Rosamond are married. Rosamond teases Lydgate with his preoccupation with his work:

[']You are always at the Hospital, or seeing poor patients, or thinking about some doctor's quarrel; and then at home you always want to pore over your microscope and phials. Confess you like those things better than me.'

'Haven't you ambition enough to wish that your husband should be something better than a Middlemarch doctor?' said Lydgate, letting his hands fall on to his wife's shoulders, and looking at her with affectionate gravity.

(Chapter 43, p. 437)

Lydgate uses both hands here, not just his fourth finger. I am interested in the phrase 'letting his hands fall', which I connect with Lydgate's affectionate gravity: Lydgate is in earnest, and expects his earnestness to act on Rosamond as though it were, like gravity, an impersonal and necessary force. Suppose we move on to Chapter 58: we are in the first period of Lydgate's disillusionment with Rosamond, his realization that she has a will of her own. The differing value which he and Rosamond place on social rank has now become a matter of real dispute, focusing on Lydgate's contempt for his cousin, Captain Lydgate, the third son of a baronet and in Lydgate's opinion a 'conceited ass' (p. 582). But Rosamond rebukes him: '"I cannot conceive why you should speak of your cousin so contemptuously,"said

Rosamond, her fingers moving at her work while she spoke with a mild gravity which had a touch of disdain in it' (p. 583).

Gravity is now on Rosamond's side: the movement of her fingers and the 'touch of disdain' increase the sense of its being a physical force. When Lydgate, soon after, urges her not to go out riding with Captain Lydgate because of the risk to her pregnancy, Rosamond responds with a revisionary gesture to the one in which Lydgate had let his hands fall on her shoulders:

> Rosamond was arranging her hair before dinner, and the reflection of her head in the glass showed no change in its loveliness except a little turning aside of the long neck. Lydgate had been moving about with his hands in his pockets, and now paused near her, as if he waited some assurance.
>
> 'I wish you would fasten up my plaits, dear,' said Rosamond, letting her arms fall with a little sigh, so as to make a husband ashamed of standing there like a brute. Lydgate had often fastened the plaits before, being among the deftest of men with his large finely-formed fingers. He swept up the soft festoons of plaits and fastened in the tall comb (to such uses do men come!); and what could he do then but kiss the exquisite nape which was shown in all its delicate curves? But when we do what we have done before, it is often with a difference.
>
> (Chapter 58, p. 585)

By 'letting her arms fall', Rosamond compels Lydgate to take his hands out of his pockets, and to touch her in a way which she, and not he, has designed. George Eliot is suggesting, not that Lydgate takes no pleasure in fastening up Rosamond's plaits and kissing her exquisite nape, but that he is being compelled to substitute this pleasure for the 'assurance' he wanted of her compliance. In fact the service which Lydgate performs for Rosamond with his hands is an emblem of his having no hold over her. As the marriage decays, the struggle for power becomes the preoccupation of both husband and wife, and, in Chapter 64, we see Lydgate moving rapidly from tender condescension to a violent assertion of his authority. Attempting to persuade Rosamond that they must live more cheaply, he begins by cajoling her:

> he held her waist with one hand and laid the other gently on both of hers; for this rather abrupt man had much tenderness in his manners towards women, seeming to have always present in his

imagination the weakness of their frames and the delicate poise of their health both in body and mind.

(Chapter 64, p. 649)

Lydgate's actions, of holding Rosamond by the waist and laying his hand on both of hers, are prompted by a fundamental misconstruing of female nature in general, and Rosamond's in particular. The bitter pill he is asking her to swallow is to give up their house and furniture to Ned Plymdale, her old suitor – he of the red hands – who is prospering in trade and has married a lesser Middlemarch beauty. Lydgate is as ignorant of the nature of this humiliation as Rosamond is of the one she enjoins on him, to ask his family for money, to affirm his loyalty to the social rank into which she thought she was rising when she married him:

> 'You will not behave as you ought to your own family. You offended Captain Lydgate. Sir Godwin was very kind to me when we were at Quallingham, and I am sure if you showed proper regard to him and told him your affairs, he would do anything for you. But rather than that, you like giving up our house and furniture to Mr Ned Plymdale.'
>
> There was something like fierceness in Lydgate's eyes, as he answered with new violence, 'Well then, if you will have it so, I do like it. [...] Understand then, that it is what *I like to do*.'
>
> There was a tone in the last sentence which was equivalent to the clutch of his strong hand on Rosamond's delicate arm. But for all that, his will was not a whit stronger than hers.
>
> (Chapter 64, p. 651)

The relationship between Lydgate and Rosamond has come down to this 'clutch of his strong hand', which is a sign not of power but of impotence. In fact it is Rosamond who clutches Lydgate to real purpose: in one of the novel's starkest reversals, Lydgate discovers that 'the need of accommodating himself to her nature, which was inflexible in proportion to its negations, held him as with pincers' (Chapter 65, p. 666). These pincers, figurative and mechanical hands, extend Rosamond's power into the operations of Lydgate's mind. At the end of this chapter, when Rosamond breaks down in tears, Lydgate's surrender to her is signalled by the very gestures with which he had earlier tried to bend her will.

> Lydgate drew his chair near to hers and pressed her delicate cheek against his cheek with his powerful tender hand. [...] He wished to

excuse everything in her if he could – but it was inevitable that in that excusing mood he should think of her as if she were an animal of another and feebler species. Nevertheless she had mastered him.

(Chapter 65, p. 667)

Reminding us at this moment that Lydgate's hand is physically power-ful exactly measures his lack of power, a lack which is once again, and decisively, attributed to his defective understanding. He holds Rosamond's body as close as he likes, he continues to manipulate her, but she is beyond his grasp. This is where the chain goes, the chain which Lydgate did not perceive at the beginning, but which the writer had already forged.

It could be argued that mastery in the novel belongs not to the charac-ters who struggle for it, but to the writer whose grasp exceeds their reach. Yet the book is very anxious about power, and tells us that no good comes of trying to exercise it. It is especially anxious about writing. The figure of Mr Casaubon stands as a warning of what happens to the writer who both appeals to authority and tries to impose it by means of a systematic, monumental and abstract text. Dorothea, when she replies to Mr Casaubon's proposal, writes out her answer three times:

not because she wished to change the wording, but because her hand was unusually uncertain, and she could not bear that Mr Casaubon should think her handwriting bad and illegible. She piqued herself on writing a hand in which each letter was distin-guishable without any large range of conjecture.

(Chapter 5, p. 45)

Dorothea wants to put this clear and unambiguous handwriting at the service of Mr Casaubon; on their honeymoon in Rome, she presses him to 'begin to write the book which will make your vast knowledge useful to the world', and promises to 'write to your dictation, or I will copy and extract what you tell me' (Chapter 20, p. 200). But the 'Key to all Mythologies' turns out to consist of 'mixed heaps of material, which were to be the doubtful illustration of principles still more doubtful' (Chapter 48, p. 478). Mr Casaubon has managed the feat of devising a text which is dogmatic, oppressive, and yet without authority. Nor is the 'Key to all Mythologies' the only such text: there is also his will. Book 5 of the novel is called 'The Dead Hand', a title which alludes both to Mr Casaubon's attempt to make Dorothea complete his futile work of schol-arship after his death, and also to the codicil which he adds to his will and which disinherits her if she marries Ladislaw. By such means, we are told, Casaubon seeks 'to keep his cold grasp on Dorothea's life' (Chapter 50, p. 493): the use of the word *keep* ironically suggests that she would not notice the difference. Mr Casaubon's hand has always been dead, just as the texts he studies are 'shattered mummies, and fragments of a tradition which was itself a mosaic wrought from crushed ruins' (Chapter 48, p. 478).[8] By his own admission he 'live[s] too much with the dead' (Chapter 2, p. 18), and the task he wants Dorothea to perform is to 'erect a tomb with his name upon it' (Chapter 50, p. 493). Mr Casaubon is worse off than Dorothea, whose obscure life is recuperated in the last words of the novel: she may rest in an unvisited tomb, but Mr Casaubon's textual tomb will not even be built.

The contrast with the novel itself is striking. If it is a tomb with George Eliot's name upon it, then it looks likely to be visited for as long as we can imagine. In this sense Eliot has avoided the fate of both Casaubon and Dorothea. She has also eschewed Lydgate's scientific researches. Lydgate is not the answer to Casaubon; if anything he is his mirror-image. He, too, lives among the dead – as is comically brought home by the scandal spread by Mrs Dollop, the landlady of the Tankard in Slaughter Lane, who firmly believes that 'Doctor Lydgate meant to let the people die in the Hospital, if not to poison them, for the sake of cutting them up without saying by your leave or with your leave'; and, Mrs Dollop shrewdly adds, it was 'a poor tale for a doctor, who if he was good for anything should know what was the matter with you before you died, and not want to pry into your inside after you were gone' (Chapter 45, pp. 442–3). Perhaps such knowledge belongs to the novelist – especially the kind of novelist George Eliot sets out to be. After all the word *life* in the subtitle of the novel – 'A Study of Provincial Life' – quietly makes the point that the book is going to conduct its business among the living.

What limits both Casaubon and Lydgate, and arguably Dorothea as well, is an inadequate knowledge of the conditions of life, whether provincial or not. Lydgate's knowledge of Rosamond is specifically related to this point: he thinks that she has 'just the kind of intelligence one would desire in a woman [...] enshrined in a body which expressed this with a force of demonstration that excluded the need for other evidence' (Chapter 16, p. 164). In the very next paragraph we see him in his bachelor quarters, reading a new book on fever, and

bringing a much more testing vision of details and relations into this pathological study than he had ever thought it necessary to apply to the complexities of love and marriage, these being subjects on which he felt himself amply informed by literature, and that traditional wisdom which is handed down in the genial conversation of men.

Realism is a corrective mode, therefore, bringing a 'testing vision of details and relations' to the study of the social body and the socialized bodies of men and women. But such representation has its limits. It is not such a great thing to represent Middlemarch, either aesthetically or politically – one of the last things we are told in the book is that Dorothea's son inherits Mr Brooke's estate and 'might have represented Middlemarch, but declined, thinking that his opinions had less chance of being stifled if he remained out of doors' (Finale, p. 837). This is an impulse felt also, I think, by the novelist, who fears stifling as a representative writer.

It may therefore make sense to construe the book's realism as a project of escape or evasion of the dead hand of writing, and its providential narrative as the horizon which circumscribes that project. The moments in which this providential narrative makes itself manifest are, as I have suggested, hidden in the book, because George Eliot cannot claim an authority for it, textual or otherwise. She is standing neither on Milton's ground nor on Fielding's: her 'presence' in the narrative, her visibility or palpability as its controlling force, is an issue so fraught with difficulty that she devotes an extraordinary passage of the novel to disavowing it. At the beginning of Chapter 15, and ostensibly to mark the transition from one part of the plot to another, she looks back at the eighteenth-century novel with affection, with envy, with resentment, and with an acute consciousness of her own dilemma:

> A great historian, as he insisted on calling himself, who had the happiness to be dead a hundred and twenty years ago, and so to take his place among the colossi whose huge legs our living pettiness is observed to walk under, glories in his copious remarks and digressions as the least imitable part of his work, and especially in those initial chapters to the successive books of his history, where he seems to bring his arm-chair to the proscenium and chat with us in all the lusty ease of his fine English. But Fielding lived when the days were longer (for time, like money, is measured by our needs), when summer afternoons were spacious, and the clock ticked slowly in the winter evenings. We belated historians must not linger after his example; and if we did so, it is probable that our chat would be thin and eager, as if delivered from a camp-stool in a parrot-house. I at least have so much

to do in unravelling certain human lots, and seeing how they were woven and interwoven, that all the light I can command must be concentrated on this particular web, and not dispersed over that tempting range of relevancies called the universe.

(Chapter 15, p. 141)

This is a passage with its own tempting range of relevancies, but I want to concentrate my light on the contrast between the early and belated writing, and on the very curious and suggestive appeal to historical change as a way of accounting for it. The greater pace and stress of modern life was as much a commonplace for the Victorians as it is for us, and it is their spacious summer afternoons and long winter evenings that we look back on: Eliot would not be surprised by this, since she herself points out that the sense of time is relative. We are accustomed to thinking of our situation, however, in terms of a dwindling of our attention-span, a condition supposedly made worse by television and sound-bite culture, so that we find it hard to take in long novels, whereas Eliot's point is not that she is driven to write shorter books – *Middlemarch* is not in fact much shorter than *Tom Jones* (1749) – but that she is no longer able to write that kind of book – the kind of book in which the author 'seems to bring his arm-chair to the proscenium', in other words draws attention to the fictionality of his/her story and to his/her own command over it. In Fielding's case, this command is expressed not just in the despotic ordering of the plot, but in his freedom to abandon the plot altogether and 'chat' about whatever he likes. He is not subject to his own story, whereas Eliot implies that hers is a task, that she has her hands full and has not the leisure to neglect it. His work is a performance; hers a work that she performs. The greater leisure which Fielding's readers enjoyed is also his own: that is, the long summer afternoons and winter evenings figure a space for writing in which its authority is assumed and exercised without constraint.

But at this point a troubling difficulty enters the argument. For George Eliot begins by reminding us that Fielding, an ancestral figure in the line of realist fiction, 'insisted on calling himself [a historian]' and his fiction a history. She herself, with whatever ambivalence, is affiliated to this tradition – a 'belated historian', perhaps, but one who accepts the designation. Clearly a historian has no business bringing his/her armchair to the proscenium, yet Fielding does so and occupies a position of power, simultaneously enjoining and forbidding his successors to imitate him. George Eliot's image of the task placed in her hands, the 'unravelling [of] certain human lots, and seeing how they were woven and interwoven', transforms the contradiction on which Fielding unselfconsciously depends into a paradox: she achieves mastery over her text by mystifying the source of her authority. The use of the word 'lots' to signify human destinies, the outcomes of human stories, is biblical and providential in its associations, and the task of unravelling them is given to the novelist, who forgets to mention that she has done the original weaving and interweaving with her own hands.

Notes

1. George Eliot, *Middlemarch*, ed. Rosemary Ashton (Harmondsworth: Penguin, 1994). Further references are given in the text by chapter and page number in this edition.
2. By 'figurative' I mean such passages as the following: 'Mr Casaubon seemed even unconscious that trivialities existed, and never handed round that small-talk of heavy men which is as acceptable as stale bride-cake brought forth with an odour of cupboard' (Chapter 3, p. 33).
3. Contrast Celia's 'little hands [...] clasped, and enclosed by Sir James's as a bud is enfolded by a liberal calyx' (Chapter 29, p. 284).
4. This is true even of the face and eyes, though of course these receive what might be called their normal allowance of attention.
5. Rosamond's reaching out to touch Ladislaw in Chapter 78, though not improbable, is unusual for her: on most occasions in the novel she waits to be touched or reached out for.
6. See Rosemary Ashton's introduction to Eliot, *Middlemarch*, p. xv.
7. The strong association between sewing and women's work is, not surprisingly, challenged only by Dorothea: in Chapter 54 she is in her boudoir, and 'had not yet applied herself to her work, but was seated with her hands folded on her lap'; but this 'work' is to do with 'a map of the land attached to the manor and other papers [...] which were to help her in making an exact statement for herself of her income and affairs' (p. 540).
8. Casaubon's writings are the major, but by no means the only, example in the novel of a textual authority which is both oppressive and uncertain. A minor but very telling example is the document which Featherstone requires Fred Vincy to obtain from Mr Bulstrode, supposedly as proof that Fred has not been borrowing money on the expectation of inheriting Featherstone's estate. Fred has to get his father to persuade Bulstrode to write the document, which Featherstone knows perfectly well has no value as evidence: the circle is completed when Featherstone gives Fred permission to burn it.

4

Two Kinds of Clothing: *Sartor Resartus* and *Great Expectations*

Bernard Beatty

In February 1840 Carlyle met Dickens for the first time. This is how he described him:

> clear blue intelligent eyes that he arches amazingly, large protrusive, rather loose mouth, – a face of the most extreme *mobility*, which he shuttles about – eyebrows, eyes, mouth and all in a very singular manner while speaking. Surmount them with a loose coil of common-coloured hair, and set it on a small compact figure very small and dressed *à la D'Orsay* rather than well: this is Pickwick.[1]

Dickens is dressed à la D'Orsay – that is, in the manner of Count D'Orsay, friend of Byron and friend of Dickens who produced a portrait of both. D'Orsay evidently chose the colours of his clothing with great care and first arrived at Carlyle's house in Cheyne Walk in a spectacular glass and gold coach. So the phrase 'dressed à la D'Orsay' suggests stylish ostentation rather than Beau Brummel's stylish restraint. Dickens appears as a version of what Carlyle called 'the dandiacal body' – that is to say, 'Solely, we may say, that you would recognise his existence'.[2] What was Carlyle wearing on this occasion? Dickens does not say, and in general there are not many references to Carlyle's clothing, though everyone mentions that of Dickens. That is because there was nothing remarkable about Carlyle's dress and it did not change much, whereas Dickens loved changing costumes and for readings of his own novels appeared on stage as different characters in rapid succession in different outfits. There are a number of portraits and photographs of Carlyle, however, and it seems that he normally wore a dark, often black, frock coat, light trousers made of a rough material, and a standard shirt and stock. Perhaps this is what he meant

44

by dressing 'well'. His habitually dark clothing may explain Jane Welsh Carlyle's description of her husband as ' the dark man', though, doubtless, it has other resonances too.[3] There is one picture of Jane and him called 'A Chelsea Interior' where he is not dressed like this. He is at home wearing a long dressing-gown.[4] There is nothing to suggest Huysman's Des Esseintes or even Sherlock Holmes in this outfit. It was made for him by his mother who had died four years earlier. That is significant. Carlyle's clothing reveals him as the son of his plain Puritan parents. His plainness is an ostentation of moral life and fidelity to his origins. His own heroes, Luther, Knox, Cromwell and Napoleon – prior to his Coronation – dress plainly. He goes out of his way to tell us that Schiller wore 'plain apparel' and that this is the customary sign of greatness; similarly in his *Life of John Sterling* (1851) he notes that Sterling 'affected dim colours' in his 'apparel'.[5] When he first met Robert Browning, he thought him frivolous because he was wearing a green coat.[6] He was appalled, too, to discover notices all over Edinburgh in 1822 advising the citizens to put on their best clothes for the forthcoming visit of George IV. [7] Similarly, years later, he disliked wearing his gold and purple costume as Rector of Edinburgh University.[8] Unlike Dickens, he disliked and disapproved of dressing up.[9] Dickens's outfits, unlike Carlyle's, separate him from his origin (though his father loved amateur theatricals) and, in particular, are as much distinguished from the appearance of a blacking factory boy as possible.

This is odd, in a way, because it means that Carlyle who writes about the necessity for changing clothes in *Sartor Resartus* (1833) did not himself do so, and that Dickens behaves in the manner which he reproves in Pip (much as he purchases a version of Satis House in Gad's Hill). *Great Expectations* (1860–61) is as much about clothing as *Sartor Resartus* but takes a different view of clothes. Mr Jaggers's announcement of Pip's great expectations is immediately followed by an injunction:

> 'First' said Mr Jaggers, 'you should have some new clothes to come in, and they should not be working clothes. Say this day week. You'll want some money. Shall I leave you twenty guineas?'[10]

The 'first' here is important. Pip's first action in his new life is to go to a Sartor, Mr Trabb, and be reclothed as a gentleman for, as Carlyle has it, 'Man is by the Tailor new-created into a Nobleman, and clothed not only with Wool but with Dignity'.[11] In this way, Pip separates himself from his origins. He belongs, he thinks, in Satis House now and is pleased to go there in his new outfit, unlike Joe Gargery who dresses with Carlyle's consistency.

Dickens can only think through clothes if he is also thinking through other things as well. In a way it is the things that do the thinking. Consider, for instance, that occasion when Joe Gargery is out of his normal costume and in 'his court-suit' in order to appear in Satis House. He does so of his own will because he thinks that it will help Pip, though Pip thinks that Joe 'looked far better in his working dress' (*Great Expectations*, p. 99). Joe's costume change does not signify a change of diction, whereas Pip in his new costume will know to say 'Knave of hearts' rather than 'Jack of hearts'; but yet Joe cannot talk directly to Miss Havisham in his new outfit. Instead he replies to her questions indirectly by talking to Pip. This is Pip's response:

> 'And now, old chap,' said Joe, conveying to me a sensation, first of burning and then of freezing, for I felt as if that familiar expression were applied to Miss Havisham.
>
> *Great Expectations*, p. 101

It is helpful to linger over that phrase 'burning and freezing'. It appears to have nothing to do with clothes but it takes us further than might appear.

Burning and freezing are normally paired in erotic contexts. Leonard Forster's *The Icy Fire* (1969) traced this conjunction from before Petrarch, but principally in Petrarch himself, and then through to modern advertisements.[12] Dickens, notoriously, is not good at depicting Eros. *Great Expectations*, on the other hand, is the one novel where he succeeds, indeed where he deliberately writes Eros into the centre of a novel originally conceived as a tragi-comic story about Pip and the convict.[13] Nevertheless, 'first of burning and then of freezing' does not seem to signify erotically in the Petrarchan fashion. It means firstly that Pip is ashamed of Joe and embarrassed by the idea of addressing Miss Havisham so familiarly as 'old chap'. In the second instance, the phrase marks not an embarrassed alternation of feeling in Pip but a moral discrimination. Joe is warm-hearted, he sits by the fire, he works at the glowing forge. 'Burning' is an appropriate word for him. Miss Havisham sits in a room cut off from sunlight in a faded dress; her hand goes to her cold heart which she has nurtured in Estella. Nevertheless within Miss Havisham's coldness there is a kind of heat. In Chapter 19 of Volume II she upbraids Estella for her 'cold, cold heart' and insists that she has always given her 'a burning love' (p. 302). So burning and freezing are present properties of the room. Dickens has chosen the name 'Estella' for the same reasons that Sidney has chosen the name 'Stella' in *Astrophel and Stella* (1591) though, of course, it is Miss Havisham who chooses the name within the novel. She is the icy rejecting starlight that makes men burn as Dickens burned, we must presume, for Ellen Ternan. It is for that purpose that she has been brought up. Towards the end of the novel, she compares herself to a lighted candle around which hover 'Moths, and all sorts of ugly creatures' and she agrees with Pip that she controls these effects (p. 308). On the very first occasion that Pip visits Miss Havisham, she asks him to summon Estella to the room whilst she herself is looking at herself in a looking-glass:

> 'Call Estella,' she repeated, flashing a look at me. 'You can do that. Call Estella. At the door.'
> To stand in the dark in a mysterious passage of an unknown house, bawling Estella to a scornful young lady neither visible nor responsive, and feeling it a dreadful liberty so to roar out her name, was almost as bad as playing to order. But, she answered at last, and her light came along the dark passage like a star.
> Miss Havisham beckoned her to come close, and took up a jewel from the table, and tried its effect upon her fair young bosom and against her pretty brown hair.
>
> *Great Expectations*, p. 60

Here we are undoubtedly in a Petrarchan world. Later indeed, Miss Havisham says of Estella that 'I stole her heart away and put ice in its place' (p. 397). Pip is beginning to burn and freeze like a sonneteer, as he is intended to, in this opening scene in the house. His Petrarchan reaction to Joe's 'old chap' is a distant echo of this erotic oxymoron. Estella's starlight keeps out the warm light of sun and bright fires but Joe of course brings them in. Joe's brief presence, surprisingly, lingers in Satis House, as a reminder and a harbinger of warmth. Thus Pip sings Joe's own song in the forge – 'Old Clem! Blow the fire, blow the fire' – whilst he pushes Miss Havisham's chair and she, in turn, begins to sing it (p. 96). Conversely Estella's cold image is carried to the forge. Thus when Pip is sitting later with Miss Havisham, who is 'playing with Estella's hair', he finds it impossible to 'dissociate her [Estella's] presence [...] from all those visions that had raised her face in the glowing fire, struck it out of the iron on the anvil, extracted it from the darkness of the night to look in at the wooden window of the forge and flit away' (p. 236). Joe's forge, which normally represents something like Agape, that is to say, the warmth of Christian charity rather than the fires of Eros, is, in that sudden collocation, itself a sign of Eros. This blurred signification is established from the outset for when Pip returns from his second visit to Miss Havisham, having just kissed Estella's cheek, he sees, set against the 'black night-sky', Joe's 'gleaming furnace [...] flinging a path of fire across the road' (*Great Expectations*, p. 93). There are thus two different sorts of burning. And this pattern lies deep in the novel. In Chapter 5 (Volume II), Pip makes a burning declaration of love to Estella as the stricken Miss Havisham looks on. Just before this declaration, Miss Havisham looks at the fire. Again it is a remarkable sentence:

> After watching it for what appeared in the silence and by the light of the slowly wasting candles to be a long time, she was roused by the collapse of some of the red coals, and looked towards me again – at first vacantly – then with a gradually concentrating attention.

Whilst Estella knits on, Pip says plainly 'you know I love you. You know that I have loved you long and dearly' and later moves into an impassioned speech ('You are part of my existence, part of myself' (pp. 359–60; p. 362)). Here the detail of the 'red coals', the only mention anywhere of the colour and warmth of the fire in Miss Havisham's room, is contrasted with the 'wasting candles'– the moth-attracting light of Estella. It is thus connected far more with the birth of Joe's glow of agape in Miss Havisham's heart (this now beats to the tune of 'Old Clem' indeed), than with the erotic fire in Pip. Nevertheless it still, marvellously, represents Eros for her heart is retouched by charity in the same instant that it remembers the vanished erotic warmth of her own feelings still represented in her wedding dress and now renewed in Pip's declaration. She makes this clear herself later: 'Until you spoke to her the other day, and until I saw in you a looking glass that showed me what I once felt myself, I did not know what I had done' (p. 396). On this occasion she kneels at his feet pressing his hand and they remain in a strange tableau with her weeping and he bent over her and holding her. We all know about these kinds of connection in Dickens but we cannot read him without uncovering them. Indeed to read him is to read them. Thus we note that strange detail in Magwitch's description of his childhood, where he says 'I first became aware of myself, down in Essex, a thieving turnips for my living. Summun had run away from me – a man – a tinker – and he'd took the fire with him, and left me wery cold' (p. 344). That phrase 'I first became aware of myself' repeats the opening page of the novel where Pip recalls that his 'first most vivid and broad impression of the identity of things' was that he was a 'small bundle of shivers' (p. 4). This realization is the occasion of, and occasioned by, the appearance of Magwitch himself in the graveyard. The shivering Magwitch and the shivering Pip both seek the fire taken from them. The passage of the entire novel – taking the second ending as the best one – is from cold identity to the warmth of love but there are more gradations and distinctions within love than there are within coldness.[14] That is one of the things the novel shows us. This is a progression made in different ways by Estella, Miss Havisham, Magwitch, Mrs Joe and Pip himself. Pride, Mammon and Eros are the enemies of this progress. Fire, ambivalent sign of Eros and Agape, is also the purgatorial means of stripping false identity away. These are severe thoughts. They might seem to go better with Carlyle's black coat and plain-suited heroes than with one who dresses 'à la D'Orsay', but they are Dickens's thoughts, not Carlyle's.

What has this to do with clothes or with Carlyle? Carlyle certainly talks a lot about clothes but his favourite symbol is fire and his most original symbol is the phoenix which rises anew out of ashes. Except incidentally, however, Carlyle does not connect these things because he does not think through symbols at all though Professor Teufelsdröckh lauds 'the wondrous agency of *Symbols*'.[15] By and large, symbolists do not think through symbols. They contemplate the pro-duction of their own symbols and live in separation. It is allegorists who think through symbols and live in connection. Dickens's imagina-tion is that of an allegorist. Allegorists begin with and have to nurture literal meaning for it is the necessary basis for further signifying. Thus Dickens can connect real fire and real clothes and the connection will be a thought. Carlyle, following Coleridge and German Romantic theory, calls allegory simply 'a poetic sport' and comments 'Not sport but earnest is what we should require'.[16] This earnestness consists in willing into realization a territory which is neither literal nor non-literal but always in between.[17] The effort of this willing is bound into the text as a self-recommending energy which is both forceful and yet instantly and constantly dissipated in its promulgation. In this way, it is an equivalent to sincerity. Thus, though Dickens admired Carlyle and was undoubtedly influenced by him, it is not correct to say with Michael Goldberg that 'the increasing symbolism of [Dickens's] later novels seems obviously derived from *Sartor Resartus* and from Carlyle's general theories of language'.[18]

The most obvious clothes in *Great Expectations* are those of Miss Havisham. Indeed Dickens seems to be at pains to make them stand alone and often reminds us of them. There are no detailed descriptions of clothing in *Great Expectations* apart from Miss Havisham's. Mrs Joe has a coarse apron and a 'square impregnable bib' stuffed with pins and needles but these are emblematic details rather than a set of clothes (p. 8); Estella is once described as wearing a furred travelling dress but we are not told what it looks like; elsewhere we are told that her 'handsome dress had trailed upon the ground' but it is not otherwise specified (p. 239). Magwitch wears a sea-cloak at one point; and Pip's new clothes, significantly, are not described at all. It is common for Dickens to suggest a style of clothing rather than to describe it in detail but, for instance in *Pickwick Papers* (1836–7), *Oliver Twist* (1837–9), and *Barnaby Rudge* (1841), there are very detailed descriptions of dress. It is clear that Dickens wants Miss Havisham's wedding dress to be centrally visible in the book rather than one costume amongst others. When Joe and Biddy marry, we are told by Pip that they both look 'smart' but their clothes are not described (*Great Expectations*, p. 474). How could there be any wedding clothes in the novel apart from Miss Havisham's who, we might say, dresses 'à la D'Orsay rather than well'?

What do Miss Havisham's literal clothes signify? Firstly Eros. Wedding clothes hang attractively on 'the rounded figure of a young woman' for whom they are intended yet Eros is also signed in the spectral disfigurement of that figure now 'shrunk to skin and bone'(p. 59) as it is in Henryson's *Testament of Cresseid* (1532). But then wedding clothes also represent agape insofar as the best image of heaven is that of a wedding feast (as in Matthew 22.8) and those who do not wear a wedding garment cannot enter it. The wedding garment is usually glossed allegorically as charity by Patristic criticism. One should put on, that is dress in, the new man. In this way Miss Havisham's wedding dress is a reversed sign of both kinds of love. Thirdly, Miss Havisham's wedding garment signifies riches and status, that is, Mammon: 'Some bright jewels sparkled on her neck and on her hands, and some other jewels lay sparkling on the table' (p. 58). It is from this hoard that Estella is bedecked. Hence the wedding dress is the visible sign of those new rich clothes of Pip, the false new man that he puts on, which are deliberately not described because they are emblazoned in their archetype. Since riches and status are not the true new self, Miss Havisham functions as a living whited sepulchre who sits without rest in a parody of patience by the monument of her rotting wedding feast. She is like 'a skeleton in the ashes of a rich dress' (p. 59). Yet the eyes of the skeleton glare and burn.

All this is, nevertheless, a real dress which is to be consumed by literal fire. It could not signify unless it was actually worn. The concentration of fire and clothing together in Chapter 10 (Volume III), unlike the spontaneous combustion of Krook in *Bleak House* (1852–3), brings together what we had not envisaged connecting. Dickens insists on the detail, as an allegorist would, that 'every vestige of her dress was burnt, as they told me' (*Great Expectations*, p. 400). The 'as they told me' has, inescapably, something of the character of the gospels for the significant detail 'every vestige of her dress was burnt' is witnessed to by those who do not understand its significance to one who does and who in turn passes it to the attentive and wondering reader. That earlier comparison of Miss Havisham to 'a skeleton in the ashes of a rich dress' which, first time through, did not suggest burning in the word 'ashes' is now literalized in the 'patches of tinder yet alight' which Pip sees floating 'in the smoky air'. This is, he says, all that is left of 'her faded bridal dress' (p. 399). Purged of this old dress, she is laid naked on the now cleared table of the feast and reclothed in the new vesture of white cotton wool which represents both sign of sickness and sign of healing, shroud and christening robe. In this way, Joe's forge fire, presaged so long before in Satis House, transforms its long-awaited recipient who, like Mrs Joe, dies forgiving and under the sign of forgiveness. Pip's clothes, too, are presumably caught up in the fire together with the table cloth and are used also to extinguish it. We are told that he has 'a double-caped great-coat on, and over my arm another thick coat'. Manifestly he is no longer a bundle of shivers but careful of his warmth. Ironically, his task is both to participate in and put out a fire. He holds Miss Havisham fast in an embrace so fiercely protective, almost amorous, that it would not shame or surprise Heathcliff:

> the closer I covered her, the more wildly she shrieked and tried to free herself [...]. Assistance was sent for and I held her until it came, as if I unreasonably fancied (I think I did) that if I let her go, the fire would break out again and consume her.
>
> (p. 399)

This is the most vivid embrace in the entire novel. The baroque chore-ography of it, horrifyingly under the apparent sign of Eros, begins when 'I saw her running at me, shrieking, with a whirl of fire blazing all about her'. There is a sense in which Miss Havisham is the Sleeping Beauty, the Frozen Bride, who is awakened by Pip. The change in her heart from cold to revived heat, goal of Pip and Magwitch, is shown more clearly than that of any other character in the novel. This horrific flaring image, we may say, is where that first intimation of burning and freezing ends up and, once this is seen, we can understand that, after all, even in its first appearance, that was the first referent of Pip's Petrarchan image. The immediate sequence is from Pip's declaration of love in Volume II, Chapter 5 to that remarkable Chapter 10 which moves through the tableau of Miss Havisham kneeling and weeping at his feet to the burning – an embrace of another kind – and finally to Pip's kiss on the dying Miss Havisham's lips which ends the chapter. The kiss is, as H. M. Daleski says, both Eros and Agape, for it is as much 'a kiss of love' as it is a sign of forgiveness.[19] Pip only ever kisses Estella on the cheek and on the hand. The ending of the novel, quite differently toned, shows the lovers Pip and Estella – and they are lovers of a kind – exiting from garden and text 'hand in hand' in 'tranquil light'. There are many reasons for this phrasing but we can suggest that the musical structure of *Great Expectations* itself demands that there could be no fiery embrace at the novel's conclusion because of the privileging of the fiery embrace of Pip and Miss Havisham that is one of the main occasionings of that end – so carefully reminiscent of Adam and Eve leaving Paradise and connected subliminally to the seraphic fire which excludes, and purgatorially includes, those seeking to dwell in the Garden of Love. The fire that burns up Miss Havisham uses up the Eros that it signifies and authorizes that other warmth, hand-in-hand rather than face-to-face, with which the novel concludes. It is Pip who metaphorically ignites the fire and actually puts it out. Normally Dickens is happier in recommending a steady familial glow than a burning Eros. The warmth that Joe tends in the forge is steady, he is himself not on fire with it. This suggests the relationship between Biddy and him and it is this steadiness which is lightly transferred to the last sentence of the novel: 'I saw no shadow of another parting from her'. But the novel is partly about Eros and its rival form of steadiness in the midst of alternation itself which is transferred to Pip and the bride, Miss Havisham, who says 'If she favours you, love her. If she wounds you, love her' (p. 240); transferred, too, is that image of the great leaping flame. The end of the novel, deliberately muted as it is, has to be read in the light, the afterglow, of these energies. The reverberations of the conjunction of fire and clothing multiply throughout the entire novel but Miss Havisham's conflagration has dramatic singularity as a scene. The allegorical imagination connects one thing with another, or better, reads one thing as another, but each thing that it reads remains specific and unblurred.

Carlyle's case is otherwise. What did he see when he gazed on Dickens? He saw, clearly, Dickens's surface : blue eyes, large protrusive, rather loose mouth, and so on. The clothes à la D'Orsay are part of that surface. The writing, loyal to the surface, is natural and vivid. It has its own surface. But Carlyle does not always write like this or see like this. He wishes to follow Professor Teufelsdröckh's advice, which is quite the contrary: 'the beginning of all Wisdom is to look fixedly on Clothes, or even with armed eyesight, until they become *transparent*'. Hence

> 'Happy he who can look through the Clothes of a Man (the woollen, and fleshly, and official Bank-paper and State-paper) into the Man himself; and discern, it may be, in this or the other Dread Potentate, a more or less incompetent Digestive-apparatus; yet also an inscrutable venerable Mystery, in the meanest Tinker that sees with eyes.'
>
> Carlyle, *Sartor Resartus*, p. 50

The text continues after this without inverted commas in the editor's voice which is itself not Carlyle's voice; at least, it is not that voice which describes seeing Dickens for the first time. It is a voice which often invokes and seems to depend upon the likely reaction of the reader to what is presented. One wonders whether that 'meanest Tinker' is the one that ran away from Magwitch. Almost certainly not. The author of *Sartor Resartus* does not see tinkers; here the tinker represents simply the notional transformation of the lowest into the highest. Similarly, Carlyle does not normally see clothes. The closest equivalent to the death of Miss Havisham in the whole of Carlyle's work is his vivid description of the uncovering of the body of St Edmund in *Past and Present* (1843). Curiously Dickens, at least on the evidence of *Pictures from Italy* (1845), which is so hostile to relics and Catholic practices, would have treated such a scene with scorn. The only clothes imaged vividly in *Sartor Resartus* itself are those of the Jewish second-hand clothes dealer who walks around with three hats on (p. 181). But even he is memorable, as Carlyle intends, as an image of clothes-selling, an itinerant Sartor Resartus, rather than as a clothed figure. The point about clothes for him is that they are changeable. We do not see clothed figures but figures who can change their clothing. Dickens, on the other hand, changes clothes but each one of the intermediate clothed figures has presence and signification. That is why clothes, like liturgical vestments, are worn in the first place. They exist to signify. Someone who changes clothes a lot understands this. Someone who, like Carlyle, wore the same clothes regularly, neither could nor would wish to. Similarly, Carlyle's fire is not a symbol which can be seen in its own right but simply a sign of transformation. Hence fire hovers everywhere in Carlyle's *The French Revolution* (1837), and especially in its last chapter, as a 'Fire-Sea' which dissolves the outlines of metal and marble images and has itself no outline, unlike the fire which soars 'as many feet above' Miss Havisham's head 'as she was high' (*Great Expectations*, p. 399). This 'Fire-Sea', like Yeats's gyres, is itself sign only of transformation itself. Thus for Carlyle, France should have accepted the Reformation. This would involve wearing plain clothes like John Knox or Carlyle himself and rejecting significant clothes such as vestments. Vestments are outside Carlyle's sympathy and he does not register or discuss them or this shift. By 'Church Clothes' he means, and he says it in Teufelsdröckh's best pulpit manner, 'infinitely more than Cassocks and Surplices', namely, the ideas and forms 'under which men have at various periods embodied and represented for themselves the Religious Principle' (*Sartor Resartus*, p. 161). Pope put this more succinctly: '*Faith* it self has *diff'rent Dresses* worn'.[20]

Carlyle would not have liked me to say that fire is a sign of a transformation which is itself sign only of transformation itself. But his idea of the phoenix, his only original (because modified) symbol, gives the game away. Carlyle's preferred view is that the multiplicity of his metaphors and the idea of clothing's multiplicity represent 'an inscrutable venerable Mystery'. This is reminiscent of Walter Benjamin's comment on the Romantics' desire for 'a splendid but ultimately non-committal knowledge of an absolute' which therefore turned a symbol simply into 'the manifestation of an idea'.[21] The idea itself has no content. Carlyle plays with the vocabulary and stance of the mystic but never displays the mystic's desire to be actually one with unstateable mystery. The allotted task of 'venerable Mystery' is simply to be an equivalent for the faith of Carlyle's parents and thus sanction, for one who does not believe as they do, what he calls 'the Infinite Nature of Duty' (Carlyle, *On Heroes*, p. 309). Professor Teufelsdröckh's spankingly new idea is, after all, only a version of Psalm 102:

> Of old hast thou laid the foundation of the earth;
> And the heavens are the work of thy hands.
> They shall perish, but thou shalt endure:
> Yea, all of them shall wax old like a garment;
> As a vesture shalt thou change them, and they shall be changed:
> But thou art the same,
> And thy years shall have no end.[22]

Carlyle insists on new symbols for enduring ideas but he does not produce any. He re-uses the old symbols but calls new attention to his use of them. This makes us aware of symbolizing but does not allow us to entrust ourselves to any particular symbol. Since this 'venerable Mystery' cannot be talked about or represented save by symbols which themselves have to be seen through, it is clear that Carlyle's text cannot have a surface. If we look at surfaces 'until they become *transparent*' and this is 'Wisdom', then surface has disappeared. Sections of *Sartor Resartus* cannot have that literal singleness which we found as the location of multiple connections in Pip's embrace of the burning Miss Havisham. As George Levine noted: 'the literal surface of [*Sartor Resartus*] is never whole-hearted and unambiguous'.[23] Not having surfaces, it is also impossible for Carlyle's images to interconnect in the way that they do in *Great Expectations*. Fire and clothes, for instance, other than very incidentally, do not meet. All the effort must go, therefore, into suggesting a surface so ambiguous that we cannot locate it as a surface. It is here rather than in any operation of thought as such or capacity to produce or think through symbols that Carlyle's extraordinary ability lies.

We have already seen how it is done. Like a mime artist, Carlyle stands either side of a transparency and, apparently bumping into it from both sides, suggests its visible presence. Professor Teufelsdröckh is on one side with his text, the editor is on another, presenting bits of that text together with bits of the Professor's life assembled out of six paper bags sent by Herr Heuschrecke, and the editor turns to the audience to confirm the presence of an imaginary line by their presumed reactions to that which is both and neither of these things. We as readers are not quite identical with this implied audience, who function like an imagined chorus between us and the imagined text. We can see how Carlyle works up these effects if we look at sections of his journal, written directly and very much in the manner of his description of Dickens, and then compare them with the equivalent passage in *Sartor Resartus*. It is clear that what Carlyle does is to dress up his original plainer prose. He does not dress it up so as to set it forth more memorably but so as to ensure that, in the act of our apprehension, the style will suggest but fail to reach its object.[24] We fall into that metaphor of 'dressing up' quite naturally. The genius of Carlyle in *Sartor Resartus* is properly seen in this dressing up which is it itself sign of the activity but not of the result of dressing. We should admire Carlyle's astonishingly sustained profusion of apparent surface where no surface is, which is signalled by a witty clamourousness either side of the space where a surface might be. As such it is a text of great brilliance but, in my view if not Carlyle's, it functions best as 'a poetic sport'. Carlyle claimed that he did not admire 'the naked formlessness of Puritanism' since 'the *formed* world is the only inhabitable one' yet he insisted that 'forms which are consciously *put* round a substance' are bad (*On Heroes*, p. 431). *Sartor Resartus*, which is, I think, his best formed work, is as good as it is, notwithstanding his contrary insistence, because Carlyle does 'consciously *put*' forms round the thereby intimated substance. It is a work of wit, that is, what Pope defined as '*Nature* to Advantage drest'.[25] Unfortunately, it is still often read, or more usually not read, as though there actually is a 'clothes-philosophy' in it. We will find such a philosophy, if we want it, in *Great Expectations*; for Dickens undoubtedly knew something about clothes.[26]

Notes

1. *Froude's Life of Carlyle*, abridged and ed. by John Clubbe (London: Murray, 1979), pp. 387–8.
2. Thomas Carlyle, *Sartor Resartus [and] On Heroes and Hero Worship* (London: Dent, 1908), p. 205. Further references are given in the text by page number in this edition.
3. Fred Kaplan, *Thomas Carlyle: A Biography* (Ithaca: Cornell University Press, 1983), p. 307.
4. Repr. in Kaplan, *Thomas Carlyle*, p. 411, and in *Froude's Life*, p. 539.
5. Thomas Carlyle, *Life of Schiller and Life of Sterling* (London: Chapman and Hall, 1892), pp. 168, 230.
6. Kaplan, *Thomas Carlyle*, p. 256.
7. *Ibid.*, p. 83.
8. Froude was not present at Carlyle's inauguration as Rector but wrote that 'I believe – for I was not present – that he threw off the heavy academical gown' (*Froude's Life*, p. 589).
9. In 1850, for instance, Froude tells us that 'In his steady thrift, he had his clothes made for him in Annerdale, the cloth bought at Dumfries and made up by an Ecclefechan tailor' (*Froude's Life*, p. 498). Eight years later, in order to go to Germany, 'an entire new wardrobe was provided, dressing-gown, coats, trousers' (*Froude's Life*, p. 545). Carlyle's one sartorial eccentricity seems to have been a taste for odd hats. A photograph taken in 1861 shows him on horseback wearing a low-crowned, wide-brimmed hat (reproduced in *Froude's Life*, p. 559). Perhaps he was wearing the same hat later on a bus with Froude where a passenger commented that the 'old fellow 'ad a queer 'at' (*Froude's Life*, p. 631).
10. Charles Dickens, *Great Expectations*, ed. Margaret Caldwell (Oxford: Clarendon, 1993), p. 139. Further references are given in the text by page number in this edition.

11. Carlyle, *Sartor Resartus*, p. 218.

12. Leonard Forster, *The Icy Fire: Five Studies in European Petrarchism* (Cambridge: Cambridge University Press, 1969).

13. The unperformed reading version of *Great Expectations* reverted to the original conception and excluded Eros (see Dickens, *Great Expectations*, pp. xlviii–xlix).

14. This preference for the second ending is not a universal one and, by some, may even be thought superfluous if we are normally to read computerized texts which can present variants without necessarily choosing between them (apart from brief local attention and at the behest of whim). If, however, Pip were to be as isolated (though wiser) at the end of the novel as at its beginning, the novel's morality would consist simply in this negative insight. Whereas if he ends up with an undefined, painful but possible relation then the title *Great Expectations* takes on an oddly positive as well as an ironic meaning which is in all respects (fictional and ethical) superior to the latter on its own. Similarly if the novel ends without a final visiting and exiting from the ruined garden, then the primacy of the decaying, imprisoning landscape of its opening chapters is not overthrown. In a different context (Hardy for instance) this could be a strength but Dickens, on any view, means to recommend the real power of certain kinds of loving in the novel. The second ending, therefore, is truer to the ethical and symbolical dynamics of *Great Expectations*. We do not know what arguments Bulwer-Lytton used to persuade Dickens to alter the ending but both Forster's *Life* and Dickens's letters stress that these reasons appeared 'good' ones to Dickens (see *Great Expectations*, pp. xli–xlii).

15. Carlyle, *Sartor Resartus*, p. 165. See also p. 163: 'his Canonicals, were they Pope's Tiaras, will one day be torn from him, to make bandages for the wounds of mankind; or even to burn into tinder, for general scientific or culinary purposes'. This is not, of course, to deny the powerful effect of the constant collocation and generation of images everywhere in Carlyle about which John Holloway wrote so perceptively in *The Victorian Sage: Studies in Argument* (Basingstoke: Macmillan, 1953). The section on Carlyle's language is reprinted in *Thomas Carlyle*, ed. Harold Bloom (New York: Chelsea House, 1986), pp. 17–31.

16. Carlyle, *On Heroes*, p. 243.

17. This applies most evidently to *Sartor Resartus* but even in his historical studies such as *The French Revolution* (1837) and *Frederick the Great* (1858–65) and despite the assiduousness of his historical researches, Carlyle wishes us to be somewhere in between a factual and a prophetic version of history. He never wishes to be simply an historian. His history is, as it were, promulgated rather than simply recorded.

18. Michael Goldberg, *Carlyle and Dickens* (Athens, GA: University of Georgia Press, 1972), p. 166.

19. H. M. Daleski, *Dickens and the Art of Analogy* (London: Faber, 1970), p. 265.

20. Alexander Pope, *Essay on Criticism* (1711), in *The Poems of Alexander Pope*, ed. John Butt (London: Methuen, 1963; repr. with corrections 1968), p. 153, l. 446.

21. Walter Benjamin, *Ursprung des deutschen Traverspiels* (Frankfurt: Suhrkamp, 1963), trans. by John Osborne as *The Origins of German Tragic Drama* (London: Verso, 1977), pp. 159–60.

22. Psalm 102, verses 25–7, Authorized Version. Carlyle paraphrases it thus: 'It is written, the Heavens and the Earth shall fade away like a Vesture; which indeed they are: the Time-vesture of the Eternal' (*Sartor Resartus*, p. 55), but he turns God instantly into 'the Eternal' and relativizes the actual historical process which has brought this insight to him in the nineteenth century. It becomes an instance of a floating universal truth.

23. George Levine, *The Boundaries of Fiction* (Princeton: Princeton University Press, 1968), p. 55.

24. Carlyle seems to have admired this in Jean Paul in whom he found a justification for his own 'heroic' or 'preaching' manner. See the useful discussion in G. B. Tennyson, *Sartor Called Resartus* (Princeton: Princeton University Press, 1965), pp. 107–25.

25. Pope, *Essay on Criticism*, p. 153, l. 297.

26. Among recent critical studies of topics raised in this essay, the following articles are of most interest: D. Franco Felluga, 'The Critic's New Clothes: *Sartor Resartus* as "Cold Carnival" ', *Criticism*, 37 (1995), 583–99; Anne M. Buck, 'Clothes in Fact and Fiction, 1825–65', *Costume*, 17 (1983), 89–104; Bernard Howell, 'Heroisme, dandyisme et la "Philosophie du Costume": Note sur Baudelaire et Carlyle', *Rivista di Letteratura Moderne e Comparale*, 41 (1988), 131–51; John Cunningham, 'The Christian Allusion, Comedic Structure and the Metaphor of Baptism in *Great Expectations*', *South Atlanta Review*, 59 (1994), 35–51; Michael Haig, 'The Allegory of *Great Expectations*', *Sydney Studies in English*, 10 (1984–5), 51–60. See also Alison Lurie, *The Language of Clothes* (London: Heinemann, 1981).

5

Rereading G. W. Reynolds's *The Mysteries of London*

Trefor Thomas

The Victorian sociologist Henry Mayhew, researching the culture of the London working classes in 1850, records an interview with an 'intelligent working-man' who offered him a graphic account of a reading practice common among the costermongers.

> Another intelligent costermonger, who had recently read some of the cheap periodicals to ten or twelve men, women, and boys, all costermongers, gave me an account of the comments made by his auditors. They had assembled after their day's work or their rounds for the purpose of hearing my informant read the last number of some of the penny publications.[1]

The group join boisterously in the performance, cheering radical sentiments, cursing the aristocracy and references to the police – 'the blessed crushers is everywhere', shouted one – and demanding interpretations of the wood engravings. This convincing account of a set of reading practices quite unlike those usually associated with the more private contexts of respectable fictional modes seems to offer clear evidence for placing Reynolds's novel-sequence firmly within literary categories of the popular or the radical. This essay, however, has been prepared using a uniform twelve-volume set of the novels, finely bound in decorated cloth, and bearing the bookplate and coat of arms of Almeric Hugh Paget, first Baron Queenborough. The literary and cultural paradoxes signalled here in the contrast between the ephemeral weekly pamphlets consumed with such raucous, collective enjoyment on the streets of London, and the twelve stately volumes of the library set, are emblematic of the difficulties of definition and interpretation which confront the student of cheap Victorian fiction.

G. W. M. Reynolds's novel-series *The Mysteries of London* (1844–6), with its sequel *The Mysteries of the Court of London* (1854–6) has some claim to be considered the most important piece of cheap fiction to have been produced in nineteenth-century England.[2] In the complete series, which commenced in October 1844 and concluded in October 1856, there are 624 weekly penny numbers, each illustrated with a dramatic wood engraving. The work, which was originally inspired by Eugène Sue's *Les Mystères de Paris*, was rapidly translated into most European languages, including Russian.[3] In its early and most distinctive form the text is constituted from a shifting kaleidoscope of literary modes – eighteenth-century gothic horror, the high-life romance, the radical press, documentary-style explorations of city life, journalism, melodrama, street broadside and ballad, and soft porn, all combined with the energetic wood engravings which led each penny number. Its commencement in 1844 marked a significant movement in the mass urban readership towards the transgressive pleasures of sensation rather than moral progress and education. Although some social and cultural historians have mined the series for its accumulation of unusual factual information about early Victorian low-life in London, and its importance in the formation and publicization of radical ideas is widely recognized (Reynolds was an active Chartist, and his political journal *Reynolds's Weekly Newspaper* was influential throughout the nineteenth century),[4] until recently there have been few attempts to theorize the tales from a more up-to-date critical perspective.[5]

The driving force of Reynolds's commercial success was the weekly penny number: it was the exploitation of this format above all which gave popular serial fiction its characteristic energy, variety and immediacy. The weekly publication mode created a dialectical tension between the long serial narratives set twenty or thirty years in the past, and the week-by-week reporting in footnotes and narrative interpolations of the flow of actual historical events occurring in England and elsewhere. Thus weekly penny fiction can be understood as an impure, almost hybrid mode, half weekly newspaper, half romance. The varied reading practices associated with the form also define its distinctive identity. Penny numbers were often enjoyed casually and collectively in workplaces, alehouses, street corners, coffee-houses and political meetings, or were, as Mayhew's informant indicates, the subject of informal dramatic performances by literate readers from the working class, complete with appropriate audience reaction in the manner of popular melodrama. Although the penny-number format was the dominant mode, the text could also be purchased as monthly parts, or in annual volume form. Thus readership cannot be simply identified by reference to categories such as 'working-class', 'radical', or 'popular'. Clearly, the transgressive pleasures of the text available in this novel-series attracted readerships in ways which cut an unexpected transect across Victorian society.

Modern readers using bound volumes can easily overlook the fact that the original penny numbers were issued over a twelve-year period which was marked by significant ideological change.[6] The raw radicalism and crude energy of the penny numbers published in the years up to 1850, with their passionate focus on the evils of poverty, their overt republicanism and their daring exploration of the boundaries of gender, are replaced in later series by a more contained, orderly and less obviously politicized mode. This evolution can be identified particularly clearly through a study of the wood engravings which were so typical of the format. Early engravings were often anonymous, produced collectively in print workshops, and utilized an energetic, demotic graphic style. In this literary mode text and image worked together in ways which were helpful and familiar to the semi-literate reader. Engravings of this kind often portray groups of working men and women engaged in active and collective leisure pursuits, rather than individualized portraits. The many illustrations of crowded and chaotic low drinking dens provide one example of this. Equally, many popular beliefs surface in this graphic genre. In one example, the murderer Bill Bolter is haunted in a dungeon by the avenging phantoms of his children and his dead wife.[7]

Illustrations after 1852, however, are no longer anonymous, but usually ascribed to particular artists and engravers.[8] They are highly decorative, and often portray domestic interiors or portrait-style representations of individualized characters in tableau-like static repose. The ornate, detailed illustration of domestic surface detail in these later engravings is a further feature of a graphic mode quite unlike the stylized conventions characteristic of the earlier numbers.[9]

The ideological changes which can be identified in this way can also be traced in the strategies adopted in the text at different periods. All the series which constitute the *Mysteries* are narrated by a third-person 'voice', offering an interpretation of the action as improving and exemplary. If the tales seem to dwell on the 'hideous deformity of vice', Reynolds remarks in his epilogue to the first series, it is only to reveal the beauty of virtue, and to dramatize the exemplary social influence of 'one good man'.[10] The recurrent favourable references within the text to an implied readership identified with what are here called the 'industrious classes' are also part of this moralizing process. This term, with its implicit puritan stress on defining categories of usefulness and productivity, included the economically active lower middle class and the skilled working man and woman. It is also associated with the concept of respectability, and reinforced by the many articles on aspects of etiquette, domestic manners and moral education which were a staple of the weekly magazines which Reynolds edited.[11] This

Figure 5.1 The murderer Bill Bolter is haunted by the phantoms of his children and dead wife

Figure 5.2   Eliza, Duchess of Marchmont

social grouping is represented as occupying a valorized centre ground between the idle, degenerate landed aristocracy on one hand, and the degraded criminal classes on the other. The ideal implied reader constructed within this rhetorical frame reads the tales for their moral lessons and their commitment to the traditional puritan values of hard work, family values, sexual self-control, and social advance through gradual moral and educational progress. In the later series of the *Mysteries*, those written after 1852, the hierarchical ordering of narration within the text is more manifest. Conventional closures are deployed to reward virtue and punish vice, while other voices within the text are subdued or repressed. Interpolated narratives by minor characters tend to support and reinforce the values promoted in the over-arching narration.

Thematically, the focus of the later series moves away from London itself into a more conventional mode of high-life romance, in which pastoral settings are common, and the mysteries involve missing wills and lost inheritances rather than the haunting social contrasts of the metropolis itself. In the final series of *The Mysteries of the Court of London* (issued from 1854 to 1856), for example, Reynolds again deploys the device he had used to structure the opening series of *The Mysteries of London* (issued from 1844 to 1846), in which two brothers follow different trajectories through life, and are rewarded or punished for their conduct: here, however, the brothers are undergraduates at Oxford University; one becomes dissolute and the other remains honourable. The honourable brother, Bertram, is banished to America after a financial misunderstanding, where he is reported to have died in a boating accident: however, he later returns to find that his betrothed, Eliza Lacey, has married a rogue, the Duke of Marchmont. In the closure, each receives due reward or punishment. In these later numbers narrative commentary functions as a more convincing and dominant language of truth within the text.

The early penny numbers, and in particular the two series of *The Mysteries of London* produced during an historical conjuncture of extreme political crisis in England and revolution in Europe, are, however, less easily contained within the broad realist conventions of closure and narrative control. Indeed, it seems at times that moralized closure and commentary in the earlier series is little more than a kind of textual play or game, offered to the reader with a knowing, mocking wink. The ideal implied reader from the respectable industrious classes, who seeks and finds in the tales enlightenment and moral lessons, is implicitly a figure of fun, almost consciously mocked within the sub-text. Despite the narrative claims made for the improving reading, the opening penny number of the whole series is led by an engraving of a young woman dressed as a youth, signalling unequivocally by her self-dramatizing pose that a potentially transgressive exploration of the boundaries of gender will be a significant theme. The third number in its original printing shows the same woman lying languorously on a couch, revealing part of her bosom. Significantly, this illustration was re-engraved in later mid-century reprints, in a more decorous style. It is difficult to believe that many early readers of *The Mysteries of London* purchased the numbers for enlightenment and improvement, rather than for the forbidden textual pleasures of violent sensation, political subversion, and sexual titillation. Although the artisans and clerks who purchased the penny numbers in Abel Heywood's Manchester shop may have appreciated its radical sentiments, they were also attracted by its sexual licentiousness. Heywood describes a typical purchaser as 'a spreeing sort' of young man, the kind who frequent taverns, and appear with cigars in their mouths in a 'flourishing way', and also remarks that numbers of women were customers.[12]

In these early penny numbers the inherited modes of the novel genre itself are tested to, and beyond, their conventional limits by the attempt to represent within them the social and cultural tensions of an almost revolutionary conjuncture in English life. Thus the penny numbers of the 1840s enact a striking movement away from holistic notions of the unity and coherence of the novel-form. The recurrent interpolated interventions in which low-life characters narrate the story of their own lives also challenge in their organization and language the moral reading asserted by the over-arching narration. Many of these interpolated autobiographies give a voice to groups usually excluded or repressed: the prostitute, the child-worker, the transported convict, the body-snatcher, the thief. The narratives explain the choice of a life of crime as the inevitable consequence of their experiences in a profoundly unjust society. Thus the autobiography of Anthony Tidkins, the Resurrection Man or body-snatcher who haunts the heroic and romanticized Richard Markham as his horrific other, explains how he became an incendiarist, and later took up his grisly trade:

> How could I remain honest, even if I had any longer been inclined to do so, when I could not get work and had no money – no bread – no lodging? […] I thought I might as well add *Incendiary* to my other titles of *Rogue* and *Vagabond*. Besides, I longed for mischief – the

world had persecuted me long enough, the hour of retaliation had arrived. I fired the barn and scampered away as fast as I could. [...] Oh! How happy did I feel at that moment! Happy! That is not the word! I was mad – intoxicated – delirious with joy! I literally danced as I saw the barn burning. I was avenged.[13]

Even the ultimately subversive act of incendiarism, so feared by the owners of property, is celebrated in verse, composed by a fugitive who has been imprisoned for stealing food:

> The Lucifer-match! The Lucifer-match!
> 'Tis the weapon for us to wield
> How bonnily burns up rick and thatch,
> And the crop just housed from the field!
> The proud may oppress and the rich distress,
> And drive us from their door: –
> But they cannot snatch the Lucifer match
> From the hand of the desperate poor![14]

These structural tensions can also be clearly traced in reactions to, for example, the early illustration of a London drinking-den, where the engraving produces at one level of response a moralized shock of horror at the degradation of the 'low', but at another a barely concealed carnivalesque or even Rabelaisian pleasure in the subversive, transgressive energies of the underworld.[15]

In this way the incorporation into the texts of linguistic features from non-fictional genres – the street ballad, the graphic conventions of popular woodcuts, interpolated low-life autobiographies, the immediacy of journalism – decentres the dominant codes of conventional fiction and disrupts the unifying power of the dominant discourse.

One of the most striking features of the penny numbers up to 1850 is their ability to represent contemporary political debate at a number of levels, and to respond on a week-by-week basis to events. The romanticized hero of the first series, Richard Markham, travels to the Italian state of Castelcicala, where he assists in a revolutionary overthrow of the despotic ruler. The state eventually becomes a model of an ideal republic, in which honest rulers, a conscientious legislature and a democratic system work together to eradicate poverty and recognize the rights of labour. Many precise details of the new social order are given. There is a universal state pension for the old or infirm, and a

Figure 5.3   The Kinchin-Ken

minimum wage. Employers are bound to keep operatives in work, even during periods of economic depression, and to pay a living wage:

> [...] in Castelcicala a fixed *minimum* for wages has been established – the lowest amount of payment ensuring a sum sufficient to enable a working-man to maintain himself and his family in respectability. [...] The results may be said to have been almost instantaneous. Crime diminished rapidly: [...] statistical returns soon proved that intemperance experienced a remarkable decrease. [...] Even employers speedily began to recognise the advantage of the new state of things. [...] Labour is recognised in Castelcicala and positively stated to be the working-man's *capital*, and bears constant interest, as well as money placed in the funds.[16]

This populist utopian vision should not be read simply as a mode of escapist romance, but rather as a fictional exploration of the boundaries of the actual and the potential. The exposure of the symbolic power of the monarchy as a hollow sham, and its ceremonies as outmoded primitive magic, as revealed in the repeated episodes in which a pot-boy breaks into Buckingham Palace and overhears conversation between the young Victoria and Albert, is another aspect of the process by which alternative definitions of Englishness and its history are explored.[17] In this way the utopian mode works directly against hierarchical versions of the social order as in some way fixed or immutable, and encourages active speculation about possible re-constitution. The overthrow of the feudal system in Castelcicala is, however, only accomplished after violent revolutionary struggle, and the confrontation of despotic power in battle. The account of the overthrow of the traditional monarchy in Castelcicala, and the establishment of a Model Republic, is presented episodically in penny numbers of *The Mysteries of London* during the whole of the crucial historical crisis which took place in England between 1844 and 1848.

The political discourse conducted in this way includes detailed reviews of important radical publications as they appear, and regular journalistic-style analysis of events as they occur, week-by-week. Thus the overthrow of Louis Philippe in France in 1848 is celebrated in the text in the weekly number following the event:

> [...] we cannot do otherwise, on reaching this point in our narrative, than avail ourselves of so fitting an opportunity to notice the grand and glorious struggle that has so lately taken place in the capital of France. Oh! the French are a fine people, and are destined to teach the world some signal lessons in the school of POLITICAL FREEDOM! [...] We are averse to the exercise of physical force, but France has shown that, when moral agitation fails, violence must be used:– and if freedom can be gained by the loss of a few drops of blood – why, those drops should be shed cheerfully.[18]

Footnotes regularly appended to the weekly numbers explicitly relate the events in Castelcicala to the current state of England: one striking example of this relates to the great protest meetings of 6 March 1848 (Trafalgar Square) and 13 March (Kennington Common) at which Reynolds himself was chosen by popular acclaim to take the Chair. The following penny numbers include extensive footnotes which give a detailed account of the speeches made by the author, and an approving report of the progress of the revolution in France.[19] Penny Number 82, a month after the Chartist meetings, outlines the social aims of the new Model State set up in Castelcicala.

> All men were originally equal; and in no country, therefore, should any privilege of birth give one family a right to monopolise the

executive power forever. [...] The following elements of a constitution become absolutely necessary:–

> Universal suffrage
> Vote by Ballot
> No Property Qualification
> Paid Representatives
> Annual Parliaments
> Equal Electoral Districts

[...] The French now stand at the head of the civilisation of Europe. They are on the same level as the fine people of the United States of America, and England occupies an inferior grade in the scale. Alas! that we should be compelled to speak thus of our native land! [20]

Other political causes advocated in footnotes or narrative interpolations at this time include the establishment of a National Pension Fund to support older workers of both sexes, the abolition of the death penalty, the emancipation of women, prison reform, and a national minimum wage.

In the representation of political debate it is thus possible to disentangle a number of voices or levels of discourse which co-exist in the text. There is a formal rhetoric carried by the narrative commentary, and reinforced by reference to the supposed concerns of the industrious classes, which relates to the need to retain social order, advocating restraint in pressing political demands, and in favour of slow progress towards limited reformist objectives. However, in both the imaginary state of Castelcicala, and in the intervening footnotes and narrative comments, there is at some key historical moments a barely concealed recognition that the possessors of political power will not relinquish it without a struggle. This sub-textual revolutionary discourse reaches its peak in penny numbers issued during the crisis leading up to the events of 1848, and surfaces in the fictional narration of battles for democracy in Castelcicala, and in the parallel interpolated account of revolutionary activity in France and England. Thus penny-number fiction was uniquely able to respond to the events of the day, and to incorporate an almost journalistic sense of immediacy into the imagined narrative.

A further striking example of the ability of this text to contain and orchestrate different discourses can be identified by an examination of the treatment of gender in the series. Throughout the twelve years of its history, women are represented at one level through what Gilbert and Gubar refer to as a 'stylised hagiography', in which the spiritualized heroines are denied life and activity in the text, and appears as little more than a set of static icons representing purity and chastity.[21] In the final series, written between 1854 and 1858, a central female protagonist, Eliza Lacey, is described in this familiar mode:

> A cloud of raven tresses fell around her oval countenance; her complexion was matchless in its transparent purity. [...] The delicately pencilled raven brows arched nobly above eyes which were large and dark, and which, though so bright, had an ineffable sweetness of expression. Her features were outlined with a perfect regularity, and her teeth were as white as pearls. [...] Her disposition was amiable and good – naturally trustful and confiding; incapable of guile herself, she suspected it not in others.[22]

These stylized angels haunt the text, in language, theme and, especially, the conventionalized imagery which recurs in the many woodcut illustrations. Denied activity within the plot, they exist only as empty icons whose purity is absolute: the binary opposition of virtue and vice is unquestioned. Thus the representations symbolize absence of agency within the moral order. The symbolic obverse of the angel in the house, the monster on the street, is also present in Reynolds's demonology, in the many degraded and brutalized women who become harlots or criminals. Familiar angel/monster, virtue/vice oppositions are reproduced as structuring features in these fantasies of divided identity.

However, there is also a recurrent narrative motif in which the cultural practices by which women are represented, often by men, are themselves questioned. Flawed mirrors, misleading portraits, statues which come alive, mistaken identities, imposters, pseudonyms, cross-dressing, are part of a thematic exploration, amounting at times to subversion, of the social demarcation of gender roles. In a chapter entitled *Mysteries of Old Paintings*, counterfeit portraits of women by old masters line the walls of a fashionable London gallery. The gallery claims that they are genuine. 'I shall soon discover whether they are originals or copies,' says a visitor. 'If you find any copies here, sir,' replies the keeper, 'I'll eat 'em!'[23]

It is, however, possible to identify a sub-textual discourse which actually works to undermine the dominant definitions of gender within the symbolic social order. The politics of gender are represented as more fragmented and contested than the recurrent static images of women might indicate. The first penny number of the whole series, for example, published in October 1844, includes on the title page an engraving which became famous. A young woman disguised in male clothing poses theatrically in a London street, with St Paul's in the background.[24]

The woman, who is concealing her gender for complex plot reasons to do with a disputed inheritance, is only the first example of a motif which recurs throughout the early series: women who choose to pass as male in order to explore the roles and social contexts normally reserved for men, and to walk the streets more freely.[25] The recurrence of other situations in which this process takes place is a textual sign of

G.STIFF DEL ET SCULP.

Figure 5.4   Young woman in male clothing from *The Mysteries of London*

Figure 5.5 'The Amazon', Letitia Fluke

the potentially disruptive social tensions surrounding gender. The particular interest of this text, therefore, can be identified not in its reproduction of the pervasive symbolic dichotomy familiar from the work of many more respectable male Victorian novelists, but in the fact that in *The Mysteries of London* there is another layer of discursive context, characteristic of popular culture defined more widely, which celebrates in narrative and in iconography the energy, activity and social engagement of some female lives. Rosenman notes that the novel is unusual or even unique in that 'female bodies are not simply appropriated for male pleasure', and that female characters 'depart dramatically from the nearly hegemonic Victorian treatment of female sexual experience'.[26] In the first series of the tales, for example, a seamstress, Ellen Monroe, faced with unemployment, enters the world of popular entertainment in London, and becomes a mesmerist's assistant, a model for a sculptor and a photographer, and finally a dancer and actress. Although the trajectory she follows in her escape from urban poverty is condemned within the moralized narrative, at another level, her energy, enterprise and sexuality are celebrated. Similarly, in the first series of *The Mysteries of the Court of London* (1849–50) a central female protagonist is Letitia Fluke, known as 'The Amazon' for her commanding appearance, extraordinary energy and intelligence, and propensity to wear male clothing at every opportunity.

Born in the emblematic 'miserable attic in the rookery of St Giles',[27] she was seduced as a young woman by the celebrated highwayman Jack Rann, known as 'Sixteen String Jack', the hero of several well-known penny bloods. She later marries a 'wealthy and amorous baronet' old enough to be her grandfather, for his money, and becomes part of the life of fashionable London, finding expression for her 'gay and joyous nature, and her warm and voluptuousness temperament'.[28] Finally, she is introduced to the Prince of Wales in her male garb; she reveals her true sex, and seduces him after a scene in which they share the royal bathchamber. She later successfully blackmails him after discovering that he is also attempting to seduce a beautiful orphan milliner, Camilla Morton. In many episodes of this kind, women appear as objects of a voyeuristic male gaze, often partially unclothed and secretly observed, but at the same time they are allowed to enjoy female pleasures of performance, agency and cultural activity.

There are also a number of interpolated first-person biographical accounts of women's lives, of a kind rarely found in respectable fiction, which explore the problems facing women in more realistic modes which derive from the emerging literary sub-genre of documentary reporting. 'The Rattlesnake's History', for example, gives a detailed account, authenticated by factual and statistical evidence taken from a government report, of the life of Meg Flathers, from her origins as a child-worker in a coal mine, to her time in London as the partner of a notorious thief and murderer.[30] Her later criminal activities are explained as the inevitable consequence of the cruelties she underwent as a child. In a further and unusual interpolation of this kind, 'The History of an Unfortunate Woman', Lydia Hutchinson gives a

Figure 5.6　The Amazon meets the Prince of Wales

first-person account of the processes by which she came to walk the
London streets as a prostitute.[31] The daughter of a poor curate, she is
sent to London to take up a post as a junior teacher in a girl's school.
She befriends a pupil, Adeline, and by chance they meet two aristo-
crats, Captain Cholmondeley and Lord Dunstable, in Hyde Park.
Lydia's friend becomes pregnant as the result of the liaison. When the
child is stillborn, Lydia conceals the corpse in her room to protect her
friend, but she is dismissed when the body is accidentally revealed. She
asks her acquaintance Lord Dunstable for assistance, but he plies her
with drink and seduces her while she is helpless. When her father discovers her shame, he dies of a broken heart. Her brother also dies in a
duel with Lord Dunstable. She collapses from hunger in the street, and
is taken in by a female brothel-keeper who puts her to work. There is a
detailed account of the ruses used to attract young women to the trade,
and of the blackmailing of respectable customers, but little moral con-
demnation of the women. Indeed, the purpose of the narrative is to
attract sympathy for the plight of the 'unfortunate'. 'Oh! let those who
are prone to turn away from the unfortunate woman with disgust and
abhorrence, rather exercise a feeling of sympathy in her behalf. She

does not drag her weary frame nightly along the pavement through choice but from necessity.'[32]

Thus there is in these penny numbers a conventionalized discourse idealizing women and treating them as decorative objects. It co-exists, however, with another discursive frame which represents some women as innocent victims of a social system which denies them justice, while others are active agents of change and transformation within the plot, move freely in the cultural life of the metropolis, become economically active, and are able to explore the boundaries of their own sexuality. At this discursive level, and unusually for Victorian fiction, the issue of gender is actually explicitly politicized: Penny Number 87, for example, includes a passionate plea for the emancipation of women, as part of the reforms associated with republicanism:

> The intellect of woman is naturally as strong as that of man; but it has less chances and less opportunities of developing its capacities. The masculine study of politics would aid the intellect of woman in putting forth its strength; and we hope that the day is gone by when the female sex are to be limited to the occupations of the drawing-room, the nursery or the kitchen.[...] We are anxious to behold them thinkers as well as readers – utilitarians as well domestic economists. [...] Is it not absurd, then – is it not unjust, to deny to woman the right of exercising her proper influence in that society of which she is the ornament and delight? [33]

Although the *Mysteries* are on the surface concerned to reproduce and reinforce the values of the 'respectable' classes discussed earlier, at a deeper level the text demonstrates a persistent, almost obsessive fascination with the manifold forms of transgression. In this carnivalesque ritual inversion the pleasures of disobedience and rebellion are secretly desired and enjoyed by the readers. This may be read as a coded attack on the authority of the ego, through the repeatedly deployed motifs of sexual excess, drunkenness, sadistic violence, dissolution of conventional demarcations of gender and class, and joy in destruction. Thus the sub-text becomes open to much that is denied or repressed in the dominant symbolic order. In a perverse litany of the grotesque, images of illegality, violence, revolution, disorder, lust, sadism, transvestism, incendiarism and body-snatching are presented as subjects of endless fascination to the readership. A further dimension of this fragmented literary carnival involves the subversive power of laughter and mockery.

In this way the text attracts a readership which cuts a transect across the symbolic social formation not determined by categories of class, gender, or even of broader concepts such as the popular, the industrious or the productive. The 'pleasures of the text' which attract these readers are related to the unconscious fascination of transgression. The Resurrection Man who dances with fierce joy as he burns the Squire's barn, the pot-boy who penetrates Buckingham Palace and seats himself on the throne of England, the heroines who walk the streets of London in male attire, the carousers in low drinking-dens, are all protagonists in this drama of disorder and rebellion. At one level this may be understood as a shrewd marketing by author and publisher of the rough and rebellious characteristics of much popular urban culture. The 'respectability' to which the text makes its surface narrative appeal appears as little more than a thin veneer or performance. Lip service is paid to the moralizing impulse of the respectable classes, but much of the sub-text is actually driven by a fascinated, voyeuristic gaze at a London underworld which combined libertinism and revolution. In a tradition going back to the eighteenth century, many of the Holywell Street pornographers were also revolutionary radicals. This combination of the anti-clerical, the seditious and the revolutionary, with a belief in the liberating power of bawdy and soft pornography is also present in *The Mysteries of London*.[34]

What is most striking, therefore, about *The Mysteries of London* is its resistance to easy labelling, and its openness to the interpretative processes of different groups. It offers a range of possible readings which different social groups could use actively in the construction of identity within the symbolic codes. These identities were not wholly governed by the dominant definitions of social order. Women from across the social spectrum could find models of female transgression, of economic and cultural activity, and of sexual expression, denied in more respectable fiction. Equally, other readers from across the class structure were attracted by the textual pleasures of licentiousness and rebellion.

At the centre of this debate is the city of London itself, and its fictional representations. Much middle-class fiction of the period represents the city through a moralized organizing frame as dangerous and diseased. Its slum districts are occupied by a swarming mass of the poor, crammed into the rookeries which became a lasting symbol of fear and disgust. Many novels of the period represent the paradoxical, inexplicable urban juxtaposition of extreme wealth and degrading poverty through the recurrent tropes of maze and mystery. The

London which emerges from these structuring metaphors is certainly reproduced in *The Mysteries of London*, though at a cruder, less sophisticated cultural level. However, other 'Londons' are also present. City life is shown to represent opportunity, variety, and a range of sexual, political and social choices to be found nowhere else.[35] Thus penny fiction of this kind is able to represent the city as above all a dynamic social context which can offer new styles of being, new social identities and social models, to its inhabitants. The self is represented as more varied and multiple, rather than defined by demarcating categories of class, region or gender. The association of the city with modes of individualism is celebrated in this fictional form, amounting almost to a symbolic empowerment of often excluded minorities. Models of an hierarchical stable state, with the monarch as its symbolic head, compete with exploration of a potential republican future, in which freedom of expression and the universal franchise are central.

In the celebrated engraving illustrating the first number of the whole series, a young woman dressed in male clothing poses dramatically before a background of vibrant street-life, with the cathedral of St Paul looming behind. In its dramatic representation of cultural and social oppositions this image neatly summarizes the conflicting and sometimes contradictory impulses which this essay has charted.

Notes

1. Henry Mayhew, *London Labour and the London Poor*, 4 vols (London, 1861–2; repr. London: Frank Cass, 1967), I, 25.
2. The relative lack of critical discussion of the text is due in part to the difficulty of obtaining access to it in its original form. Only a few specialist research libraries have a complete set, as the original penny numbers were fragile and ephemeral. The recent volume of selections from the first series of *The Mysteries of London*, ed. Trefor Thomas (Keele: Keele University Press, 1996), makes some of this material widely available for the first time.
3. Eugène Sue's *Les Mystères de Paris* first appeared as a weekly serial in a Paris newspaper, *Le Journal des Débats*, from June 1842 to October 1843. It was rapidly translated, and several cheap English-language editions were available by 1845.
4. The fullest account of Reynolds's political career can be found in *The Dictionary of Labour Biography*, eds Joyce M. Bellamy and John Saville, 9 vols (London: Macmillan, 1982), III, 146–51.
5. There is little contemporary criticism of Reynolds which discusses the literary aspects of his work rather than his significance in popular politics. See, however, A. Humphreys, 'G. W. M. Reynolds: Popular Literature and Popular

Politics', *Victorian Periodicals Review*, 16 (1983), 79–89; A. Humphreys, 'Generic Strands and Urban Twists: the Victorian Mysteries Novel', *Victorian Studies*, 34 (1991), 463–72; A. Humphreys, 'The Geometry of the Modern City: G. W. M. Reynolds and the Mysteries of London', *Browning Institute Studies*, 11 (1983), 69–80; and E. B. Rosenman, 'Spectacular Women: The Mysteries of London and the Female Body', *Victorian Studies*, 40 (1996), 31–64.

6. There were two series of *The Mysteries of London* (1844–6 and 1846–8), and four series of *The Mysteries of the Court of London* (1848–50, 1850–2, 1852–4, and 1854–6). Each series was published as two annual volumes, making a total of 12 in a complete set.

7. G. W. M. Reynolds, *The Mysteries of London*, Series I (London: George Vickers, 1844), I, 65.

8. Early illustrations were engraved in a workshop owned by George Stiff. Many are anonymous, rather than ascribed to a particular artist, although some are signed by Stiff himself. Later series distinguished the skills of designing and engraving, and used a variety of identified artists, including H. Anelay, E. Hooper, and W. H. Thwaite. Rodney K. Engen, *A Dictionary of Victorian Wood Engravers* (Cambridge: Chadwick-Healey, 1985) includes biographical background and a detailed bibliography. Geoffrey Wakeman, *Victorian Book Illustration* (Newton Abbot: David & Charles, 1973) includes much invaluable technical information about the processes of wood-engraving.

9. G. W. M. Reynolds, *Mysteries of the Court of London*, Series IV (London: John Dicks, 1855), I, 17.

10. Reynolds, *The Mysteries of London*, Series I, II, 424.

11. The best known and most popular of these penny weekly magazines was *Reynolds's Miscellany of Romance, General Literature, Science and Art*. The content included sensational fiction as well as improving and informative articles.

12. Abel Heywood was a major distributor of penny fiction in the important Lancashire market. The evidence he gave to a Parliamentary Select Committee on Newspaper Stamps (reprinted in *Nineteenth Century Parliamentary Papers*, (Dublin: Irish University Press), *Newspapers*, I, 371–89) is one of the few contemporary accounts of readership based on direct experience.

13. Reynolds, *The Mysteries of London*, Series I, I, 196.

14. *Ibid.* Also worth noting here is the ballad of the 'Thieves' Alphabet' ('A was an Area-sneak, leary and fly / B was a Buzgloak, with fingers so sly'): Reynolds, *The Mysteries of London*, Series I, I, 60. This celebration of the vitality of criminal slang became a popular hit.

15. Reynolds, *The Mysteries of the Court of London*, Series I, I, 33.

16. Reynolds, *The Mysteries of London*, Series II, II, 91. This penny number includes a lengthy and detailed account of the post-revolutionary social order established in Castelcicala. The death penalty has been abolished, and prisons attempt to reform offenders rather than punish them.

17. A recurring motif in penny fiction of this period is a rewriting of English history, with a pantheon of popular 'freeborn' heroes, from Robin Hood to Jack Cade and Wat Tyler. The twice-repeated episodes of *The Mysteries of London* in which a pot-boy breaks into Buckingham Palace and seats

himself on the throne of England are also part of an attempt to demythologize the monarchy, and to encourage speculation about alternative social orders.

18. Reynolds, *The Mysteries of London*, Series II, II, 199. The chapter from which this narrative interpolation is taken, 'Political Observations', contains the most violent and radical attack on the English system of government to be found in the whole series.

19. It is rarely easy to identify exact dates at which penny numbers first appeared, as they were regularly re-issued to meet demand, but the presence of detailed footnotes referring to specific historical events makes it possible here. Penny Number 78 (Reynolds, *The Mysteries of London*, Series II, II, 201–9) includes an account of the Trafalgar Square meeting of 6 March 1848, at which Reynolds himself took the Chair.

20. Reynolds, *The Mysteries of London*, Series II, II, 232–3.

21. Sandra M. Gilbert and Susan Gubar, *The Madwoman in the Attic* (New Haven: Yale University Press, 1979), p. 25.

22. Reynolds, *The Mysteries of the Court of London*, Series IV, I, 3.

23. Reynolds, *The Mysteries of the Court of London*, Series I, I, 186.

24. Reynolds, *The Mysteries of London*, Series I, I, 3.

25. The 'passing' motif is common in Victorian street literature. Charles Hindley, *Curiosities of Street Literature* (London: Reeves and Turner, 1871) includes several examples of popular broadside ballads of this kind, including 'The She–He Barman of Southwark' (p. 141). Henry Fielding's *The Female Husband* (1746) was reprinted in popular forms in the early Victorian period, and Reynolds himself wrote a popular penny novel entitled *Pope Joan, the Female Pontiff* which was serialized weekly from August 1850 in *Reynolds's Miscellany*.

26. E. B. Rosenman, 'Spectacular Women: *The Mysteries of London* and the Female Body', *Victorian Studies*, 40 (1996), 31–64.

27. Reynolds, *Mysteries of the Court of London*, Series I, I, 56.

28. *Ibid.*, 285.

29. Reynolds, *The Mysteries of the Court of London*, Series I, I, 89. This illustration is signed H. Anelay.

30. Reynolds, *The Mysteries of London*, Series I, I, 353.

31. Reynolds, *The Mysteries of London*, Series I, II, 115.

32. Reynolds, *The Mysteries of London*, Series I, II, 132.

33. Reynolds, *The Mysteries of London*, Series II, I, 115.

34. The cultural and literary boundaries between penny fiction, radicalism and the burgeoning trade in cheap pornography at this period are far from clearly defined. Some material was bawdy and populist, but not pornographic. The fullest account of this little studied aspect of early nineteenth-century culture is Iain McCalman, *Radical Underworld: Prophets, Revolutionaries and Pornographers in London, 1795–1840* (Cambridge: Cambridge University Press, 1988). McCalman remarks that the group of 'Holywell Street entrepreneurs' which included Reynolds's first publisher, George Vickers, had 'moved beyond the old restricted radical audience towards an emerging mass reading public which cut across middle and working-class boundaries', and sold the exotic culture of London's 'seamy underworld' to a wider, more respectable middle-class audience (p. 236).

Although some penny-blood publishers, and especially Reynolds's rival, Edward Lloyd, continued to meet a demand among the working-classes for escapist sensation and horror, Reynolds, Vickers and Dicks broke new ground in their targeting of a wider social grouping.

35. Richard D. Altick, *The Shows of London* (Cambridge, MA: Harvard University Press, 1978) documents the extraordinary variety of street entertainments available in London during this period. Reynolds's fiction records some of the attractions of this energetic urban culture. The first series of *The Mysteries of London*, for example, includes a very early and detailed description of a commercial photographic studio.

6
The State of *Dracula*: Bureaucracy and the Vampire

Gary Day

Criticism of Bram Stoker's *Dracula* (1897) falls into three broadly related categories: class, race and sexuality.[1] The first of these sees the novel as an example of bourgeois hatred of a parasitic aristocracy characterized as 'blood sucking vampires', while the second views the figure of the Count as the focus of fears concerning the decline and degeneration of the British race.[2] The third category, which accounts for the bulk of writing on *Dracula* and on which I want to dwell briefly, represents so many variations on David Pirie's claim that the novel portrays 'the great submerged force of Victorian libido breaking out to punish the repressive society which had imprisoned it'.[3] Hence the reader's attention is directed to the transgressive nature of female sexuality, as in Lucy's desire to marry three men; to the hints of bisexuality in the novel evident in Mina looking at Lucy through the eyes of Arthur, her gaze lingering on that 'sweet puckered look [...] which Arthur says he loves, and indeed, I don't wonder that he does' (p. 128); and to the homoeroticism that characterizes the relationship between the male characters in the book, the most intense expression of which is Dracula's fury when he sees the three vampire women about to feed on Harker. '[T]his man belongs to me' he hisses, pulling them back and, in answer to their taunt that he has never loved, he looks 'attentively' into Harker's face and says, 'in a soft whisper: – "Yes, I too can love" ' (p. 55).

Closely related to discussions of sexuality in the novel are considerations of gender. What the novel reveals, it is argued, is that gender categories are unstable.[4] One example of this is the episode mentioned above. The vampire women, with their hard, penetrating teeth, 'are masculinised seducers' while Harker 'is the coy maiden, peeping out from under his eyelashes'.[5] Other examples include Mina having 'a man's brain' while Van Helsing, in giving way to 'a fit of hysterics' behaves, in the words of Dr Seward, 'just as a woman does' (pp. 302, 225). By such means *Dracula*, it is claimed, calls into question the conventional expectations of gender, thereby accentuating anxieties that had already been aroused by the trial of Oscar Wilde and the emergence of the New Woman.

Such approaches to the novel are considered radical to the extent that they show that gender is not a function of biology but a social construct which can be dissolved to allow for the creation of a plurality of overlapping 'masculinities' and 'femininities'. The same can be said of discussions of sexuality in *Dracula*. Hence Lucy's transformation into a vampire articulates a more active sense of female desire than was allowed in the marital relationship, where it was tied to the duty of reproduction rather than the experience of pleasure. Nina Auerbach argues that one of the reasons for the enduring popularity of the vampire is that it offers 'an escape from patriarchy': it is, she asserts, 'women opening windows beyond the family and, in the guise of victims, surging into themselves'.[6]

In short, criticism of *Dracula* is progressive because it intervenes in constructions of gender and sexuality. It disrupts the conventional understandings of masculinity and femininity and, in revealing the play of desire in the novel, holds out the promise of more mobile, non-hierarchical sexualities. There is no doubting the appeal of such arguments, but they rest on the hypothesis that Victorian culture was repressive, a hypothesis that Foucault subjected to a searching critique in the first volume of his *The History of Sexuality*.[7] His claim was that far from being silenced or censored, sex, from the eighteenth century onwards, 'was driven out of hiding and constrained to lead a discursive existence'.[8] A whole array of discourses, but particularly those of biology, medicine and psychiatry, produced sexuality as an object of knowledge. It therefore fell under the control of qualified experts who alone could tell subjects the truth of their sexuality. In Foucault's words, these discourses serve

> to bring us almost entirely – our bodies, our minds, our individuality, our history – under the sway of a logic of concupiscence and desire. Whenever it is a question of knowing who we are, it is this logic that henceforth serves as our master key.[9]

Dracula criticism may be seen as yet another discourse on sex and, as such, it reinforces the idea that sex is the 'truth of ourselves' and the 'explanation of everything'.[10] In short, far from being radical, criticism of *Dracula* has the same disciplinary function as other discourses on sexuality; it seeks to delimit, define and control it. It is part of that 'wide dispersion of devices that were invented for speaking about [sex], for having it spoken about, for inducing it to speak for itself, for listening, recording, transcribing and redistributing what is said about it'. In this, it offers no resistance to those discursive formations of our society, from talk shows to advertisements, which strive to make sex the matrix of our body, our intelligibility and our very identity.[11]

The proliferation of discourses about sexuality was one instance of increasing state intervention which characterized the late nineteenth century. These incursions into civil society were prompted by a number of problems, chief of which was the condition of the poor, whose perceived immorality and appalling privations needed to be urgently addressed if Britain was to have a strong army to defend her colonies and an efficient workforce to compete with the new industrial powers such as Germany and the United States.[12] The size and scale of the problem of poverty was such that it could no longer be resolved by market forces but demanded the creation of a whole series of official bodies which would inquire into, report on, legislate for, implement and administer solutions to everything 'from illiteracy and crime to slum housing and industrial strikes'.[13] These agencies were one example of the growth of bureaucracy during this period.[14] Another was the administrative apparatus which arose as a result of the extensions of the franchise in 1867 and 1884. Democracy and bureaucracy, as R. C. K. Ensor noted, 'developed together'.[15] Similarly, the County Councils Act of 1888, whereby elected representatives replaced the old justices of the peace, meant an increase in the personnel and powers of the local government board. The addition to the electorate of a large number of people, many of whom were barely literate, was another factor in bureaucratic expansion, since it stimulated a series of Education Acts between 1870 and 1880, culminating in the creation of the Board of Education in 1899.

The growth of bureaucracy proceeded with the rise of the professions such as law and medicine.[16] The relation between the modern state and the law is, Gianfranco Poggi argues, 'particularly close'.[17] This is because the state no longer takes its legitimacy from God or Nature but from 'its appeal that its commands be recognised as binding because *legal*, that is, because issued in conformity with properly enacted general rules'. The state legitimizes itself by making laws and, in order to maintain this legitimacy, keeps making them. 'One can visualise the state', writes Poggi, 'as a legally arranged set of organs for the framing, application and enforcement of laws'.[18] In the same way that law was entering more and more into the fabric of life, so too was medicine. This was apparent in the continuing concern with public health, hygiene and sanitation, the growth of psychiatry and psychoanalysis and '[t]he medicine of perversions and the programs of eugenics' which, claims Foucault, 'were the two great innovations in the technology of sex in the second half of the nineteenth century'.[19] Law and medicine, indeed, cannot be considered apart since they were combined in numerous acts, for example the Food and Drugs Act 1875, the Public Health Act 1875 and the Contagious Diseases Acts of 1864, 1866 and 1868.

It was through the alliance of law and medicine that state intervention in civil society was most evident. *Dracula* bears witness to this in as much as two major discourses in the novel are those of law and medicine, represented by Harker and Seward respectively. Lawyers and doctors often appear as narrators in popular texts of the period, their distance from what they describe signalling their professional detachment: the lawyer Utterson is the controlling voice of *Doctor Jekyll and Mr Hyde* (1886), while Dr Watson faithfully chronicles the many adventures of Sherlock Holmes. This points to a hitherto neglected area of *Dracula* criticism: namely how the novel is implicated in the forms of discourse which characterized the rise of the professional class. The expanding influence of this class was an instance of the growing secularization of society. The development of science and technology, the geological discoveries of Charles Lyell and the biological ones of Charles Darwin, together with rigorous biblical scholarship, all combined to weaken the influence of religion. Consequently, remarks Bedarida, 'religion gradually lost its important role as a cohesive force in the community'.[20] The language of religion, organized around the opposition of good and evil, was being replaced by a language of expediency; the priest was giving way to the professional.

According to Harold Perkin, the professional class stood aloof from the old antagonisms of capital and labour that had structured Victorian society. It offered an expert, disinterested service and entrance to the professions was 'based on selection by merit'.[21] The language of the professions was structured around specialism, efficiency, efficacy and formal procedure and, as Perkin notes, it 'had a profound influence both on the demands made by other classes and the language in which they expressed them and on the way in which laws were framed and administered'.[22] It is the tension between this language, which 'repress[es] basic moral and existential components of human life' and that of religion, which addresses these issues, that informs much of *Dracula*, a point to which I shall return.[23]

First it is necessary to consider some of the other ways in which *Dracula* is complicit with the changes I have described. These are most evident in the *form* of the novel, which has received little attention in comparison to discussions of its treatment of sexuality and gender.

Its predominantly diary form, for example, says something about the nature of the professions themselves. As already mentioned, professional expertise is based on selection through merit. However, it is precisely the specialized nature of the professions which inhibits an understanding of society as a whole. The professional can see only details, not the wider pattern. This partial view of society is encoded in the very form of *Dracula* with its various journals, diaries, letters and so on. Of course there is no attempt to view society as a whole in *Dracula*, but there is an attempt to grasp the nature of the Count, who can be seen as a distorted image of society.

The vampire, for example, comes to prominence at the very moment the British economy becomes 'parasitic' rather than 'competitive'.[24] More importantly, the Count is associated with the law and therefore, remembering Poggi's argument, with the nature of the new state; Dracula, as Harker remarks, 'would have made a wonderful solicitor, for there was nothing that he did not think of or foresee' (p. 45). The vampire, indeed, lies at the root of the social bond. That bond, as characterized by the special relationship between Van Helsing and Seward, is patriarchal and professional, but it has its basis in an act that resembles vampirism, since the latter sucked poison from a wound once sustained by the former (p. 148).

One of the ways in which society is monstrous is that it deforms and violates human potential through the division of labour. Perhaps the best known example of this is Adam Smith's description of pin-making; the process can be divided into eighteen separate activities, each performed by a different person. This negates any sense of labour as creative activity and gives rise to what Marx called a condition of alienation. In this state the worker

> no longer feels himself to be freely active in any but his animal functions – eating, drinking, procreating [...] and in his human functions he no longer feels himself to be anything but an animal. What is animal becomes human and what is human becomes animal. Certainly, eating, drinking, procreating etc. are also genuinely human

functions. But in the abstraction which separates them from the sphere of all other human activity and turns them into sole and ultimate ends, they are animal.[25]

Although Dracula is an aristocrat, he is nevertheless associated in the novel with the working class. Both are defined in terms of their thirst: Dracula for blood, the working class for drink (pp. 292, 33). Furthermore, the Count is both human and animal, being able to transform himself into a bat, a dog and a wolf. He can also be seen as purely animal because of his appetite for human blood. As such he bears witness to the degraded condition of modern culture which deprives natural functions of a meaningful context.

Dracula seems to have no identity of his own and that is why he can be aristocrat, bourgeois, worker and animal simultaneously. This chameleon-like quality also says something about the nature of modern society. As Hall and Schwartz have pointed out, the various Representations of the People Acts provided a new political language based not on individual or group interests 'but on the more expansive category of citizenship'.[26] Citizenship emphasises what people have in common, not how they are different. Derek Sayer states the matter strongly when he writes 'the abstraction of individuality is the ground of citizenship'.[27] A particularly stark example of this is H. G. Wells's *The Time Machine* (1895), where the majority of characters are not named but are referred to by their professions: the psychologist, the editor, the medical man and so on. Dracula's ability to mirror the identity of others would suggest that he also can be seen in terms of abstract citizenship rather than concrete individuality.

But Dracula is not just a victim of this process; he is one its main perpetrators. The vampire is analogous to the state in his or her power to penetrate the private sphere. The state's social mission is to 'homogenise [...] a society conceived as inherently fragmented, atomised and centerless', and the vampire achieves a similar effect by recruitment to the ranks of the undead.[28] In both cases what is distinctly individual is absorbed into a generalized category: citizenship or vampirism.

The parallel between citizenship and the undead is underlined when we consider Thomas Bender's remark that, in an increasingly professional and bureaucratic society, '[v]alid knowledge, formerly concretised in individual relationships to nature and society, now seems to be defined in forms and processes one step removed from direct human experience'.[29] The transformation of life into discourse, in other words, is a form of death. Marx makes the point succinctly when he writes that, in a bureaucracy, 'real life appears dead'.[30] Vampires, in a very general way, illustrate this observation. Since they are associated with coffins they appear dead, but they also seem more alive than the non-vampire characters in the novel. As one of the undead, Lucy, writes Seward, was 'more radiantly beautiful than ever; and I could not believe that she was dead. The lips were red, nay redder than before; and on the cheeks was a delicate bloom' (p. 258). The vampire seems more alive than the other characters in the novel because he or she is identified with the body whereas they are identified with the written word.

However, this distinction cannot be maintained since Dracula is also identified with the written word. He himself remarks that 'the glories of the great races are as a tale that is told' (p. 43). The difference between him and the other characters is that they are the subjects of writing while he is its object. As a product of their various writings, from journals to solicitor's letters, Dracula serves to illustrate, in a very general way, how in this period subjectivity was increasingly an effect of that proliferation of discourses associated with state intervention. Identity was less a matter of unique selfhood than conformity to models of civic conduct; it was therefore open to public scrutiny, as indeed were the records of the Count's various business transactions, invoices, deeds of purchase, title deeds and so on. These underline how Dracula's identity is formal rather than substantial, a function of official documentation rather an expression of an individual essence. Moreover, this documentation is linked to death since the Count's pursuers rely on it to hunt him down.

The intensity of purpose that characterizes the pursuit of Dracula is reminiscent of the way that sex, in the nineteenth century, 'was tracked down by a discourse that aimed to allow it no obscurity, no respite'.[31] This cannot be read as a repression of sex but rather as an appropriation of it for use in the service of the state. Specifically, sex is a key element in the transformation of the individual into a citizen. The abstraction of individuality which this entails is accompanied by a sudden arousal. When Mina asks Jonathan who it is that he has recognized, '[h]is answer seemed to shock and thrill me for it was said as if he did not know that it was to me, Mina, to whom he was speaking' (p. 223). It is not surprising that the erotic charge of this moment is most apparent in the encounter with the vampire, since Dracula is, as I have argued, an analogy for how the state constructs citizenship by extracting individuality. The eroticizing of the loss of identity reconciles the subject to its anonymity as citizen. Criticism of *Dracula* which focuses on sexuality in the novel merely re-enacts this process; its rhapsodies on desire fix the subject ever more firmly in the social order.

The impersonal nature of this society is reflected in a number of ways in the novel. In the first place, the constant perusal by the characters of each others' writings shows that they only ever really encounter one another as texts. As Mina says to Seward, 'when you have read my own diary and my husband's also, you will know me better' (p. 284). Secondly, matters of personal significance are articulated in the phrases and formulae of the professions. Hence Mina surrenders the certainty of eternal rest in order to pursue Dracula. This 'sacrifice', she remarks, is what she can 'give into the hotch potch' which, as Seward reminds the reader, is a legal term (p. 424). More generally, the characters are so imbued with the professional approach to a problem that when they meet to discuss what to do about Dracula, 'they unconsciously form a sort of board or committee' and their decision to destroy him is 'taken in as businesslike a way as any other transaction in life' (pp. 304, 306).

As befits an impersonal society, the characters do not have an expressive relation to their writing. Harker and the journalist from the *Dailygraph*, for example, are compelled to write what others dictate (pp. 58, 108). The act of writing is here divorced from conscious intention and so is more mechanical than willed. This was also the case in the social sphere, where writing was becoming identified with clerks whose business was to copy, not to compose.[32] Not only is writing not expressive in *Dracula*, it is also a means of actively suppressing consciousness. This is apparent in the motives for keeping a diary or a journal. 'I turn to my diary for repose', says Harker, a view echoed by Seward, who finds that writing 'quiet[ens]' him. More strongly, Harker writes because he 'dare[s] not stop to think' (pp. 52, 136, 372). Writing, he asserts, should be concerned 'with facts – bare meagre facts verified by books and figures' not with 'experiences which will have to rest on my own observation or my memory of them' (p. 44). It is clear from this that writing is not just used to suppress consciousness but to eliminate the very notion of selfhood. The keeping of a journal sifts out individuality in the same way as do the discourses of the bureaucratic state.

The purpose of these discourses was the collection of data. This enabled problems to be broken down into their component parts for which specific solutions could then be devised. Hence the labouring poor were divided into separate categories, the unemployed man, the old-age pensioner, the idle loafer and so on, 'each corresponding to a specific practice of regulation by some apparatus of the state developed for that purpose'.[33] In a similar fashion, the aim of a journal is to keep a record. 'Let all be put down exactly', says Seward, while Lucy declares that her 'memorandum' – a revealing administrative term – 'is an exact record of what took place' (pp. 173, 183). The difference is that this record-keeping is not motivated by any particular objective. Van Helsing claims it is necessary to prove Dracula's existence, but at the end of the novel he declares, 'we want no proofs; we ask none to believe in us!' What matters, it seems, is the act of recording, not what is recorded. That is why Mina 'put[s] down everything [...] however trivial' (pp. 249, 486, 303).

Where recording has no purpose beyond itself, narrative begins to decompose. This is most evident in the death of Dracula, which seems out of all proportion to the narrative leading up to it. The way it is hurried over suggests an uncertainty about how to conclude which may be related to that divorce between means and ends so characteristic of bureaucratic society.[34] As its idiom is administrative rather than ethical, it is not equipped to evaluate goals, only to implement procedures. This incapacity to conceptualize ends, to dwell on the process instead of delivering the product, finds expression in *Dracula* in the disjunction between the planning of the Count's downfall, the procedures necessary to achieve this and the actual death itself. The narrative strategies of the novel, like bureaucratic procedures, delay an outcome whose significance resides more in the waiting than in the result. Consequently, Dracula's death seems unreal compared to the mass of records and documentation that precedes it. As Mina declares from her vantage point on the fatal attack, 'it was hard to believe' (p. 481). This chimes with Marx's observation that in bureaucratic society 'even the most potent reality appears illusory compared with the reality depicted in dossiers, which is official'.[35]

Although the form of *Dracula* corresponds in some measure to the protocols of bureaucracy, these exist in some tension with the religious rhetoric of the novel. This is concerned with the question of human ends but its power to comprehend these has been severely compromised by the discoveries of science. Nevertheless, there is in the novel an undoubted commitment to a religious view of the world. Van Helsing and the others continually conceive of the task of destroying Dracula in religious terms: 'we are ministers of God's own wish: that the world for men and whom his son die will not be given over to monsters' (p. 412). It is the age-old battle of good and evil.

However, the essential goodness of their cause is not matched by a corresponding sense of evil. In the first place, Dracula is mostly absent from the novel to which he gives his name and, in the second place, he does nothing to excite the reader's revulsion in the way that the male characters do by their ritual mutilation of Lucy. Arthur hammers the stake into her heart but, says Seward, 'I could have done it with savage delight' (p. 271). Both these give a specious quality to the religious rhetoric of the novel, as does the fact that it is not integrated into the detailed descriptions which characterize the rest of the text. Hence it forms a strong contrast to the emphasis on facts in the novel. Religion also exists in some tension with the professional ideology of *Dracula*. A religious view of the world, for example, entails notions of individual responsibility which are less pronounced in professional society. The religious rhetoric of *Dracula* evokes such notions of responsibility but is unable to realize them: the Count is not defeated by an heroic individual but, as mentioned earlier, by 'a sort of board or committee' with Van Helsing in 'the chair' (p. 303). There is an attempt to synthesize religion and professionalism in the person of Van Helsing who is a 'metaphysician and one of the most advanced scientists of his day' (p. 147). But, as his speech consistently shows – 'alas, that sentence is a puddle is it not?' (p. 403) – language fractures under the attempt.

That *Dracula* is a novel ultimately preoccupied with form is clear from the fact that it destroys its own content. The entire novel is devoted to hunting down and eliminating the character who gives it its name. This is a rather extreme expression of the point made above: there is a connection between discourse and death; immediate experience gives way to mediated knowledge, and the abstract citizen replaces the concrete individual. And, as an extreme expression, it is not entirely accurate. It would be better to say that the novel's form becomes its own content. *Dracula*, that is to say, is not only concerned with the formal act of recording but also with various mechanisms of transcription. Seward keeps his diary 'in phonograph' which Mina thinks beats the shorthand she practises so 'assiduously' (pp. 82, 74). Harker writes in longhand but is worried that the pen may lead to him becoming 'too diffuse', a fear shared by Mina who declares, 'I should have felt quite astray doing the work if I had to write with a pen.' Hence she is grateful to the man who invented the 'traveller's typewriter' (pp. 37, 450). The typewriter is the preferred method of transcription because it erases all trace of the personal. As Mina informs Seward, 'I have copied out the words on my typewriter and none other need now hear your heart beat.' Mina also types everyone else's diaries and documents with the result that, by the end of the book, 'there is hardly one authentic document, nothing but a mass of typewriting' (pp. 286, 488). The destruction of authentic documents proceeds *pari passu* with the pursuit and destruction of Dracula himself; his death coincides with the disappearance of literary writing; that is, with whatever is impressionistic, imaginative or expressive, in favour of fact-based writing. This illustrates, once again, how the novel is complicit in replacing structures of individuality with the forms of citizenship. The killing of Dracula is no less than the violent repression of the very possibilities of selfhood.

The identification of writing with a machine reinforces the point that the nature of writing is more mechanical than expressive. An interest in the means of transcription replaces an interest in what is transcribed, and this constitutes a type of fetishism which extends to signs themselves. These are removed from direct experience due to the growing codification of language in various knowledges and regulations governing ideas of citizenship and social interaction. One example of this distance between language and life are those signs used to repel the vampire: garlic, crucifixes and so on. These are fetishized to the extent that the contexts which originally gave them meaning, primitive and Christian religions, have declined and they thus appear anachronistic in a culture of scientific fact. What they illustrate most dramatically is that the sign is used to banish the possibilities of life encrypted in the vampire.

The mechanical nature of writing is also apparent in the way Mina collates the various journals that make up the novel. The chief criterion for organization is chronology: 'dates', she declares, 'are everything' (p. 288). It is important to remember here that Mina is 'the train fiend'; she makes a 'study' of railway timetables and learns them 'very carefully' (p. 435). Matthew Arnold observed that for the bourgeois of his day, 'it was the acme of civilisation that trains ran every quarter of an hour between Islington and Camberwell, and that there were twelve deliveries of post a day between the same districts'.[36] Arnold's point was that the bourgeoisie confused systems of communication with their substance. It is this mentality that Mina brings to the ordering of narrative, with the result that the model for a story becomes a railway timetable; events are placed in sequence rather than related in a developmental manner. No wonder many readers find that *Dracula* tends increasingly toward tedium after the first hundred pages.

It is tempting to see the preoccupation with the forms of recording and the organization of narrative as a prelude to the formal experiments of modernism. A more plausible argument would be that modernism continues to develop the culture of administration that informs *Dracula*, thereby implying a complicity between 'high' and 'popular' culture which is occluded in discussions of what is and is not 'literary'. Modernist writing and bureaucratic language have a number of elements in common. For example, bureaucratic documents often do not inform the reader of the context in which they need to be read, and the same could be said, indeed was said, of a number of modernist poems, notably *The Waste Land* (1922). Similarly, the impersonal tone of much modernist poetry finds an echo in the language of administration.

However *Dracula* may anticipate modernist concerns, the real significance of the collation of papers lies in the establishment of a discursive hierarchy. All writing in the novel is subordinated to the style of the professional middle class, which aims at the clear communication of facts. This is incompatible with a foreigner's use of English and that is why neither Dracula nor Van Helsing are allowed to write their own record of events. Foreignness is manifest in a somewhat fanciful use of language: 'old beliefs' which 'pretend to be young' are compared to 'the fine ladies at the opera' (p. 246). Such whimsical comparisons are out of place in a novel where writing is linked firmly to the actual. Out of place, too, is the slang spoken by Quincey Morris, the American. His vigorous idiom, like Van Helsing's similitudes, is subordinated to the proprieties of a standard style.

The marginalization of the foreign in *Dracula* can be seen as part of the attempt to develop a national language whose characteristics were, among other things, 'masculinity, concrete statement, self mastery and a concern with racial purity', all of which can be found in the novel.[37] Arthur's masculinity, for example, is defined in terms of self-mastery. 'He was in a torture of suspense regarding the woman he loved and it took all his manhood to keep him from breaking down' (p. 197). The demand for concrete statement is illustrated by the various characters' preference for facts, while the anxiety over racial purity is allayed by destroying Dracula. The death of Quincey Morris, incidentally, may also be seen as a symbolic way of coping with the economic threat posed by America.

The working class appear in the novel as they did in the political system after the franchise extension of 1884; they are represented but denied the right to express their own interests or determine their own destiny. The rambling speech of working-class characters is contrasted unfavourably with the concentration on fact, while their accents and idioms offend against the ideal of clarity (pp. 178–9, 89–92, 336). In short, working-class dialects only appear in *Dracula* to reinforce the authority of middle-class English. They, like the foreigners, are denied the privilege of writing; the privilege that is, of leaving a record, of writing their history.

Dracula's suppression of literary qualities and its marginalization of foreign and working-class speech make it the ally not only of administration but also the newly emerging popular culture apparent in George Newnes's *Tit-Bits* (founded 1880), Alfred Harmsworth's *Answers to Correspondents* (1888) and *The Daily Mail* (1896). These papers, written in 'plain' English, catered for the new class of readers created by the Forster Education Act (1870). They fed them a diet of facts and sensation which are, of course, important ingredients in *Dracula*. *Dracula*, in fact, appears at the moment when a mass cultural audience is being constituted for the first time and it conditions this audience to submit to a form of writing that permits them neither individual nor class expression. It carries the formulae of bureaucracy into the area of mass entertainment and itself becomes a formula for commercial success. *Dracula*, that is to say, is deeply implicated in a process of social control at the level of both bureaucracy and popular culture, and this has been extended in the twentieth century by the novel's use in administering ideas about sexuality and gender.

I have argued that criticism of *Dracula* has not been radical but has been part of that proliferation of discourses which seek to control sexuality and gender. The novel is better understood in terms of how it encodes the forms and logic of the professions and the developing administrative apparatus needed to ensure state intervention in an increasing number of areas. As state intervention has grown in the amount of information held on computers and the spread of surveillance cameras, so has Dracula penetrated ever further into our culture, and where he once threatened to feed on us now we feed on him; there are Dracula lollipops as well as a breakfast cereal named after him: Count Chocula. But this does not mean that the novel is only a way of making palatable the extension of the state's monitoring activities. The figure of Dracula is, as I have argued, a complex one, testifying to the deformations of an administrative culture even as it enacts them. In this way the novel transcends those forms of citizenship and their attendant bureaucracy which it otherwise so effectively activates.

Notes

1. Bram Stoker, *Dracula*, ed. Maurice Hindle (Harmondsworth: Penguin, 1993). Further references are given in the text by page number in this edition.
2. D. Read, *Press and People 1790–1850* (London: Hutchinson, 1961), p. 53; Alexander Warwick, 'Vampires and the Empire: Fears and Fictions of the 1890s', in Sally Ledger and Scott McCracken (eds), *Cultural Politics at the Fin de Siècle* (Cambridge: Cambridge University Press, 1995), pp. 202–20.
3. David Pirie, *A Heritage of Horror: The English Gothic Cinema, 1946–1972* (Cambridge, MA: Harvard University Press, 1973), p. 4.
4. Christopher Craft, ' " Kiss me with those red lips": Gender and Inversion in Bram Stoker's *Dracula*', in Elaine Showalter (ed.), *Speaking of Gender* (New York: Routledge, 1989), pp. 86–104.
5. Warwick, 'Vampires and the Empire: Fears and Fictions of the 1890s', p. 204.
6. Nina Auerbach, *Our Vampires, Ourselves* (Chicago: Chicago University Press, 1995), p. 110.
7. Michel Foucault, *The History of Sexuality*, trans. Robert Hurley, 3 vols (Harmondsworth: Penguin, 1990), I; Robert Mighall discusses the failure of critics of *Dracula* to engage with Foucault in 'Vampires and Victorians: Count Dracula and the Return of the Repressive Hypothesis', in Gary Day (ed.), *Varieties of Victorianism* (Basingstoke: Macmillan, 1998), pp. 198–214.
8. Foucault, *The History of Sexuality*, I, 33.
9. *Ibid.*, I, 36, 78.
10. *Ibid.*, I, 69, 78.
11. *Ibid.*, I, 34, 155–6.
12. The major studies on poverty were Charles Booth's *Life and Labour of the People of London* (1889), William Booth, *In Darkest England* (1890), and B. Seebohm Rowntree, *Poverty: A Study of Town Life* (1901). These and other works suggested that poverty was caused by the structure of capitalism and could not be attributed, as it had been throughout most of the nineteenth century, to individual weakness. For more detail, see Donald Read, *The Age of Urban Democracy: England, 1868–1914* (London: Longman, 1994) pp. 287–94.
13. Harold Perkin, *The Origins of Modern English Society 1780–1880* (London: Routledge & Kegan Paul, 1969), p. 326.
14. Stuart Hall and Bill Schwartz, 'State and Society, 1880–1930', in Mary Langan and Bill Schwartz (eds), *Crises in the British State, 1880–1930* (London: Hutchinson, 1985), pp. 7–32; p. 19.
15. R. C. K. Ensor, *England, 1870–1914* (Oxford: Clarendon Press, 1952), p. 124.
16. Robin Gilmour, *The Victorian Period: The Intellectual and Cultural Context of English Literature* (Harlow: Longman, 1987), p. 174.
17. Gianfranco Poggi, *The Development of the Modern State: A Sociological Introduction* (London: Hutchinson, 1978), p. 102.
18. *Ibid.*, pp. 132, 102.
19. Foucault, *The History of Sexuality*, I, 118.
20. François Bedarida, *A Social History of England*, trans. A. S. Forster (London: Routledge, 1991), p. 110.
21. Perkin, *The Origins of Modern English Society 1780–1880*, p. 268.

22. *Ibid.*, p. 272.
23. Anthony Giddens, *Modernity and Self Identity: Self and Society in the Late Modern Age* (Cambridge: Polity Press, 1991), p. 167.
24. E. J. Hobsbawm, *Industry and Empire* (Harmondsworth: Penguin, 1968; repr. and rev. 1990), p. 192.
25. Karl Marx, *Economic and Philosophical Manuscripts of 1844* (London: Lawrence & Wishart, 1959), pp. 72–3.
26. Hall and Schwartz, 'State and Society, 1880–1930', p. 28.
27. Derek Sayer, *Capitalism and Modernity* (London: Routledge, 1991), p. 77.
28. Poggi, *The Development of the Modern State: A Sociological Introduction*, p. 121.
29. Thomas Bender, 'The Cultures of Intellectual Life: The City and the Professions', in J. Higham and P. K. Conkins (eds), *New Directions in American Intellectual History* (Baltimore: Johns Hopkins University Press, 1979), pp. 181–95 (p. 190).
30. Karl Marx, *Early Writings* , ed. Lucio Colletti (New York: Routledge, 1975), p. 108.
31. Foucault, *The History of Sexuality*, I, 20.
32. Janet Roebuck, *The Making of Modern English Society from 1851* (London: Routledge, 1973), p. 40.
33. Hall and Schwartz, 'State and Society, 1880–1930', p. 19.
34. Frank Kermode has explored the question of endings in fiction in *The Sense of an Ending: Studies in the Theory of Fiction* (Oxford: Oxford University Press, 1977). What remains to be explored is the relation of fictional endings to a society whose administrative apparatus precludes the question of ends.
35. Marx, *Early Writings*, pp. 343–4.
36. Cited in Bedarida, *A Social History of England*, p. 108.
37. Brian Doyle, *English and Englishness* (London: Routledge, 1989), p. 22.

7
The Godhead Regendered in Victorian Children's Literature

Jacqueline M. Labbe

In a century fascinated with angel women, divine mothers, and other paragons on the 'virgin' side of the good/bad dichotomy, readers of Victorian children's literature suddenly found that, instead of God the Father, these texts were substituting the Wise Woman, the Fairy Godmother, as their sage of choice. Was children's literature being taken over by the adherents of the fairy tale, those who, like Coleridge and Hazlitt in earlier years, had decried the work of writers such as Maria Edgeworth and Anna Letitia Barbauld as moralistic, dogmatic and unimaginative? Or, instead, was children's literature presenting a new theology, one based on a literalization of the feminine New Testament virtues of sacrifice and self-abnegation? Was Christianity itself being feminized? As my title suggests, this essay argues for the latter case; its aim is to identify and account for the manifestations of the female Godhead in some of the most popular children's writing of the nineteenth century, a genre directed at, apparently, the most vulnerable of readers (as well as their parents).

Roderick McGillis, in his notes to George MacDonald's *The Princess and the Goblin*, remarks on one primary character's divine qualities: 'the great-great-grandmother reminds us of Christ [...] she implies she is nearly two thousand years old [...]. Like Christ, the great-great-grandmother comforts, cleanses, heals, forgives, and saves'.[1] McGillis describes a female character who is Christ-like in her actions and inspirational quality, but MacDonald, as I argue, goes further than McGillis allows: MacDonald writes, not a Christ-like female, but a female Christ, regendering the Son and representing her as a grandmother. This essay discusses the female Father, Son and Holy Spirit in her incarnations as the great-great-grandmother in MacDonald's *The Princess and the Goblin* (1872) and *The Princess and Curdie* (1881), Mother Carey in Charles

Kingsley's *The Water-Babies* (1863), Lizzie in Christina Rossetti's 'Goblin Market' (1862), and the Godmother in Dinah Craik's *The Little Lame Prince* (1875). When God is regendered in Victorian tales for children, his virtues relocated in the body of a woman, the reader is presented with a confirmation of feminine sanctity and a realization of the empedestalled woman, interwoven with a subversive suggestion that Christianity itself needs rewriting. Child readers – and their adult monitors – are thus confronted with a complex theology that subtly rewrites the established hierarchy, religious, social and sexual. To a culture struggling with division and rupture in its religious belief system, it is strangely significant that readers find perhaps the most challenging theology in a context that many would regard as unsuitable. Much as Charles Kingsley may try and defuse the force of *The Water-Babies* by concluding 'this is all a fairy tale, and only fun and pretence; and, therefore, you are not to believe a word of it, even if it is true', most readers then and now picked up on its social and cultural critique; that it is precisely *not* nonsense is what gives *The Water-Babies* its enduring power.[2]

Robin Gilmour speaks of the 'historicisation of God', and by this he refers to what some commentators have also called the secularization of God in the nineteenth century. For instance, even Matthew Arnold describes the word 'God' as 'a term *thrown out*, so to speak, at a not fully grasped object of the speaker's consciousness [...] and mankind mean different things by it as their consciousness differs'.[3] In this way, Gilmour notes, Arnold sees the word as merely 'literary', as signifier, a convenient hook by which we mean myriad things. Indeed, given the characterization of Jesus as a model of New Testament-style submission and self-sacrifice, to re-present Him as Her is no great leap – Florence Nightingale writes in *Cassandra* (1859; publ. 1928), for instance, that 'the next Christ will perhaps be a female Christ'.[4] Even as the popular conception of Nightingale as the Lady with the Lamp situates her as a living model of the Jesus portrayed in Holman Hunt's *The Light of the World* (1853) so too her words suggest a cultural awareness of the fitness of allying Christ and femaleness. Indeed, the idea of feminine self-sacrifice is engrained enough to be almost a cliché; as James Holt McGavran notes when speaking of Coleridge's Christabel, 'Given a "World of Sin," which is also a world of possible Christian redemption through suffering, Christabel could [...] as her name suggests, sacrifice her innocent self to save the depraved Geraldine.'[5] Innocence sacrificed to save the guilty: this is also a basic tenet of Christianity, for Christ's purity and innocence have been designed to be sacrificed for sinful

Figure 7.1   Lizzie with the Goblin-men: in this woodcut from 1893, Lizzie hangs on to a tree, her arms extended above her head (Christina Rossetti, *Goblin Market*).

humankind, to save it from damnation. The preponderance of trinities centred on female characters in the books under discussion here also serves to reinforce the appropriate nature of a regendered Godhead. The nineteenth century is often described as a paradoxical combination of sincere religious belief and profound religious doubt; at the very least 'the religious life of this period was intense and disputatious [...] the very pervasiveness and variety of religious experience in Victorian literature is a sign of its importance in the culture at large' (Gilmour, *The Victorian Period*, p. 63). In the varieties of experience offered in children's literature we can uncover another trinity: religion, children's literature and gender anxiety. Their attendant problematics, while not usually linked, reveal an intimate and tropic connection if examined in the light of each other. MacDonald, Kingsley and Rossetti felt religion to be key in their lives; MacDonald, Rossetti and Craik were concerned with the position of women in their society, although they expressed their concern in different ways; all were vital figures in the children's literature writing community. That doubt and revisionism as well as certainty and mature authority inhabit their literature speaks to the vibrancy of these issues. That their versions of female Gods often exist in familial relations to the text's protagonist suggests also the closeness and familiarity with which they viewed a religiously redemptive figure.

Nineteenth-century religious doubt affected not only a system of belief that had sustained centuries of social stability as well as increasing levels of unrest and dissatisfaction; it also pervaded the structure of that system. One way to combat the insecurity arising from doubt is to restructure the principles of a system. Because fantasy and children's literature are of, and yet subordinate to, established or 'high' culture, they can provide fertile ground for the questioning or retelling of the myths and stories underlying adult culture: as Susan A. Walsh says, 'the fantasy tale's symbolic vocabulary easily accommodates what the conscious mind will not'.[6] One solution to a troubling lack of faith would be to import into Christianity a sanctity that already existed, paradoxically enough, in secular life, and, with the freedom gained through a 'symbolic vocabulary', re-establish a stable belief system, albeit one now at odds with convention. In other words, re-presenting the Father as a Mother lends familiarity and safety to an image otherwise receding further into intellectual distance; re-naming the Son as a Daughter allows for a sense of authority and even command over a figure also to be worshipped. This is the divine 'spirit of nature in its succouring, maternal capacity' (Walsh, 'Darling Mothers, Devilish Queens', p. 32), in its submissive capacity – a Christianity as much

Figure 7.2   Lizzie after being assaulted by the Goblin-men, again from 1893: here Lizzie assumes a position distinctly reminiscent of the crucified Jesus (Christina Rossetti, *Goblin Market*).

under the control of the worshipper as demanding to be worshipped. It suggests to the child and to its parents that even as God is pure and holy 'he' is also familiar and approachable: the dynamics of gender allow readers to worship a character who simultaneously worships them, and who offers assistance and care instead of demanding fealty. So that, for instance, we read about the Little Lame Prince, whose dreary existence shut up in a tower is relieved by his godmother's gifts of love and understanding as well as a magic cloak, and who is transported beyond 'the rosy clouds that overhung the Beautiful Mountains' in her company at the end of a long and blameless life.[7] Or we find Lizzie's self-sacrifice in 'Goblin Market' empowering both to herself and her sister. Even as 'a feminine cast of characters is substituted for the masculine cast of the Biblical sin–redemption sequence', as Marian Shalkhauser noted in 1956, so too Lizzie's actions reveal her as a '*female* Christ [...] who offers much more than merely an aesthetic of renunciation and self-sacrifice. [... Her] sacrificial action [...] can more appropriately be viewed as a positive act of defiance and, on Rossetti's part, as revisionist myth-making'.[8] These versions of the Godhead encourage our love and worship through gentleness, generosity and availability as well as mysterious and impressive displays of power.

Loss of faith is regained, even forestalled, through transforming the worshipped figure into someone more easily controlled as well as venerated, or conversely into a figure more easily identified with. And that strand of children's literature which may be called religio-fantastic figures the trajectory that leads from the idealization of the mother to her worship, that redraws the angel in the house as a god, also leads to the reinstitution of religious faith by the second half of the nineteenth century. The 'slow shift from the Atonement to the Incarnation, from Christ's death to his humanity' (Gilmour, *The Victorian Period*, p. 95), and therefore from guilt to a kind of companionable comfort, mirrors this movement. Fertility, self-sacrifice, controllability, beauty, spirituality – the negative virtues that define femininity – advance into prominence as the positive, teachable virtues of a Christianity revitalized, situated around a female figure who is there when you need her but not obtrusively so; who facilitates, influences and assists, but never dictates; whose beauty, age and mystery gesture towards a closer relation but whose divinity constitutes the final barrier. The grandmother, the mother, the godmother, the 'nice, soft, fat, smooth, pussy, cuddly, delicious' nurse who educates but never punishes: these familiar figures indoctrinate their charges without seeming to do so.[9] In some ways, these literary female Gods exemplify a peculiarly internal, personal

Christianity: one result of the familial position is the implication that each child protagonist is personally saved – and yet, like the best mothers, Christ never plays favourites.

Like the best religious allegories, too, these texts follow similar lines. There is a child, usually male, who is somehow isolated, different or alienated from his surroundings (a major exception is 'Goblin Market', a minor one Irene in *The Princess and the Goblin*). He is befriended by a female figure who appears to him at first to be mundane, even common: the homely Irishwoman in *The Water-Babies*, for instance: 'the nicest old woman that ever was seen, in her red petticoat, and short dimity bedgown, and clean white cap, with a black silk handkerchief over it, tied under her chin' (p. 37). In the traditional fairy tale, this old woman would be a witch, a threatening figure and the embodiment of evil: she even sits with 'the grandfather of all the cats'. Here, though, she teaches children 'their Christ-cross-row'; then after blessing Tom's 'pretty heart' three times, and mysteriously entering his dream/delirium to confirm that 'Those that wish to be clean, clean they will be' (p. 40), she precedes him into the water, and undergoes what could be seen as an anti-Incarnation, moving as she does from human to other:

> she had stepped down into the cool clear water; and her shawl and her petticoat floated off her, and the green water-weeds floated around her sides, and the white water-lilies floated round her head, and the fairies of the stream came up from the bottom, and bore her away and down upon their arms; for she was the Queen of them all; and perhaps of more besides.
>
> Kingsley, *The Water-Babies*, p. 41

This last phrase is typical of the strategy of hints and suggestion relied on by all the writers I discuss here: obviously, the naming of a female Godhead is more problematic than the drawing of her. Although the nineteenth century is notoriously shy about naming God as God – terms such as 'providence' become rife – this hesitancy is more remarkable when put in the context of the female Godhead. But the gestures made are plain: Kingsley's Irishwoman/fairy, for instance, exists as one of three: her sisters Mrs Doasyouwouldbedoneby and Mrs Bedonebyasyoudid take over Tom's education and indoctrination after he enters the water to be clean: to wash off the blackness of his human sins and ignorance and emerge as a fresh, innocent water-baby, fit to wend his way to manhood. I am not being original when I point out the baptismal significance of this scene. Each woman in Tom's life as a water-baby is part of the trinity, and all of it; each contains godhead within her but displays it in different ways. Mrs Bedonebyasyoudid exemplifies the Old Testament ethos of 'an eye for an eye' or, as she puts it, 'As you did to them, so must I do to you' (p. 110). She knows everything and, like the clockwork God created and feared by eighteenth-century deists, she 'work[s] by machinery, just like an engine; and [is] full of wheels and springs inside; and [...] cannot help going' (p. 111). She is also 'as old as Eternity, and yet as young as Time', and is 'the ugliest fairy in the world' (p. 112). Her sister, Mrs Doasyouwouldbedoneby, epitomizes forgiveness; she is 'the loveliest fairy in the world', and 'begins where [Mrs Bedonebyasyoudid] end[s], and [Mrs Bedonebyasyoudid] begin[s] where she ends'; she fills Tom with 'pure love', and tells him the story 'which begins every Christmas Eve, and yet never ends at all for ever and ever' (pp. 116, 118).

As MacDonald has his North Wind do in *At the Back of the North Wind* (1871), when she tells Diamond that she has heard that a little baby governs all her actions, Kingsley here constructs an alternative trinity dependent on the interaction of its three parts balanced by a readerly identification of their association.[10] Even as he implies that Mrs Doasyouwouldbedoneby is subservient to an absent, conventional Christ, he is plotting a character who is three in one, who combines the trinity in her person: Mother Carey. She sits in the middle of Peacepool, in 'the form of the grandest old lady he had ever seen – a white marble lady, sitting on a white marble throne [...]. Her hair was as white as the snow – for she was very old – in fact, as old as anything you are likely to come across' (Kingsley, *The Water Babies*, p. 157). Mother Carey directs without interference: she makes things make themselves. She is divine, and personifies omniscience. Within her are united the two fairies and the Irishwoman, whose compassion first allowed Tom to see he must be clean. At the end of his adventure, Tom has learned enough to see that Mrs Doasyouwouldbedoneby *is* Mrs Bedonebyasyoudid 'grown quite beautiful'; that they are both '"Mother Carey," said Tom, in a very low, solemn voice; for he has found out something which made him very happy, and yet frightened him more than all he had ever seen'; that she is the Irishwoman; and that 'she was [none] of them, and yet all of them at once' (*The Water-Babies*, p. 191). In her eyes lies the secret of her name, but Tom and his companion Ellie – an angel-in-the-water figure if ever there was one – are not capable of seeing this yet: 'And her eyes flashed, for one moment, clear, white, blazing light: but the children could not read her name; for they were dazzled, and hid their faces in their hands'

WATER-BABIES — *Frontispiece.*

Figure 7.3 The Water-Babies and Mrs Doasyouwouldbedoneby: in this illustration by Noel Paton, Mrs Doasyouwouldbedoneby strikes a pose that mirror exactly Jesus's own when he talks of his heavenly father; she also has a halo. Her feminity is assured not only by her facial features and long hair, but by her breasts. *The Water-Babies*, vol. IX of *The Works of Charles Kingsley* (London: Macmillan, 1883).

(p. 191). Tom is now prepared to be 'a man', but not until the Apocalypse, it is implied, will he be able to read Mother Carey's name. Kingsley's strategy is to embed – drown? – Christianity so deeply in his story as to change its nature altogether; he makes it clear that only the female can refine and cleanse the male, and he subsequently creates a pantheon of female deities. For Kingsley, the maternal Christ is the only possible Christ for a water-baby; her virtues of love, compassion and inherent knowledge of right take precedence in the divine order over the manly qualities Tom acquires in his journey. In Kingsley's version of the female Christ, he realigns Christ's gender, or rather his sex; this female Christ poses no threat to established gender roles, but rather makes plain the femininity of Christ's character. Perhaps one reason, or corollary, for this is Tom himself: the male child, if presented with a female Christ, is also being presented with a Mother, just as the male author could be said to be creating a daughter.

And yet these stories do not follow along completely pat gender lines. Craik's Little Lame Prince, crippled when the state nursemaid, 'so occupied in arranging her train with one hand, while she held the baby with the other [...] stumbled and let him fall, just at the foot of the marble staircase', finds his mother/saviour in the form of a god-mother, whose 'friend in the palace is the King's wife' (pp. 7, 11). The recent collection of essays, *Muscular Christianity*, argues for the central place held in arguments of gender, class and national identity of the idealized, 'hyper-masculinized' male body; Donald Hall tells us in his Introduction that, for those writers who espoused the principles of muscular Christianity (including Kinsgley and MacDonald) – and for those outside this movement, I would add –

> 'manliness' was synonymous with strength, both physical and moral, and the term 'Muscular Christianity' highlights [the] consistent, even insistent, use of the ideologically charged and aggressively poised male body as a point of reference in and determiner of a masculinist economy of signification and (all too potent) degradation.[11]

This collection argues that the strong male body defines the solution to cultural insecurity and religious doubt. And yet, the Little Lame Prince – Prince Dolor, named after his mother Dolorez – is characterized by his *lack* of musculature and his need for the idealized female god-figure. Shadowing muscular Christianity's reliance on the strong male mind in the strong male body is that strand of children's literature that balances the necessarily weak male child's body with the strength and endurance of a mother-god. Indeed, this applies even to Kingsley, despite his belief in 'the doctrine of complementarity', which classified men and women according to a biologically based gender.[12] Mother Carey's three-in-one replaces the male God the father's trinity, and Tom the water-baby only achieves strength of body through the facili-tating care of the girl Ellie and the spiritual ministrations of Mother Carey's incarnations. Ellie conforms to, and Mother Carey exemplifies, established gender roles, but it is Mother Carey who is divine. In Craik's story, Prince Dolor's simultaneous loss of his mother and of the use of his limbs results in his virtual incarceration in a high round tower – a male Rapunzel – and the circulation of the story of his death, precisely because the people he rules at his father's death rely on the muscular Ideal and cannot see him as a King: 'somehow people soon ceased to call him his Majesty, which seemed such a ridiculous title for a poor little fellow, a helpless cripple – with only head and trunk, and no legs to speak of'. The people prefer the Regent and his 'very fine children', whose physiques match the common perception of royalty (p. 23). Craik inverts the precepts of muscular Christianity by trans-planting its ideals into a disabled body, and she undermines the reliance on a muscular, male saviour when she gives Prince Dolor a godmother, whose very title, if stripped of its fairy-tale connotations, reveals the truth: she is Dolor's God-Mother, inherited by him through the female line. As the godmother says, 'The King knows nothing of me, more's the pity' (p. 11).

Even as the Irishwoman blesses Tom three times, this childlike old woman dressed all in the softest grey gives the baby prince three kisses at his christening, and bestows his name, after his mother. The matri-lineal nature of this tale pushes aside kings and father in favour of queens and (god)mothers; but, while Prince Dolor's disability could be seen to feminize him – and he is described as possessing the beautiful face of his mother – his boyhood is never in question. What *is* rewrit-ten is the muscular definition of masculinity, and the masculine nature of Christianity. The godmother 'could not come to [Dolor] until [he] said [he] wanted [her]'; she 'ha[s] not got a name – or rather, [she has] so many names that [she doesn't] know which to choose'; she 'melt[s] away just like the rainbow out of the sky' (Craik, *The Little Lame Prince*, pp. 36, 37, 40). This godmother conforms to the standards of the Evangelical version of the Saviour, where 'divine grace becomes avail-able through a physical form'; through this godmother's taking on physical form and enhancing the spiritual side of his life, Dolor achieves the grace that allows him, eventually, to become 'an excellent King'.[13] 'Nobody ever does anything less well, not even the commonest duty of common daily life, for having such a godmother as the little old woman clothed in gray, whose name is – well, I leave you to guess', comments Craik's narrator enigmatically. It is surely significant that the original title of this story read *The Little Lame Prince and His Travelling Cloak, A Parable*. Like biblical parables, *The Little Lame Prince* disguises its moral as well as its innovation, yet even so transmits both. Such generic allusions underpin the proselytizing nature of the story, and enhance the divinity of the god-mother. Indeed, after his accept-ance of the godmother into his life, Prince Dolor even makes a stab at muscularity:

> Prince Dolor was now quite a big boy. Not tall – alas! he could never be that, with his poor little shrunken legs, which were of no use, only an encumbrance. But he was stout and strong, with great sturdy shoulders, and muscular arms, upon which he could swing himself about almost like a monkey. As if in compensation for his useless lower limbs, Nature had given to these extra strength and activity. His face, too, was very handsome. It was thinner, firmer,

more manly; but still the sweet face of his childhood – his mother's own face.

Craik, *The Little Lame Prince*, p. 86

Craik suggests that true strength comes from the feminine, and that true faith discovers a feminine god-mother; it is even feminine Nature who gives Prince Dolor his strong upper limbs.

So far, so revisionist. But now we come to a structural difficulty: as if to underscore the fantasy aspect of children's literature, Craik, like Kingsley, like MacDonald, but *not* like Rossetti, cannot project a belief in her female god beyond the text or even beyond the generation represented by the man protagonist. Tom may be saved by Mother Carey, but he never passes on his faith: he and Ellie spend 'Sundays and sometimes [...] weekdays' together, but don't marry, because 'no one ever marries in a fairy-tale, under the rank of a prince or a princess' (*The Water-Babies*, p. 192). MacDonald's Curdie and Irene marry, 'but they had no children, and when they died the people chose a king' whose greed for gold finally literally undermines their city (*The Princess and Curdie*, p. 341). And Prince Dolor

Figure 7.4 Prince Dolor welcomes back his God-mother: in this illustration from 1948, the God-mother hovers, enveloped in a ray of light. (Dinah Maria Craik, *The Little Lame Prince and the Adventures of a Brownie*).

never gave [his subjects] a queen. When they implored him to choose one, he replied that his country was his bride, and he desired no other. But perhaps the real reason was that he shrank from any change; and that no wife in all the world would have been found so perfect, so loveable, so tender to him in all his weaknesses as his beautiful old godmother.

Craik, *The Little Lame Prince*, p. 120[14]

The godmother, then, can lead the child to spiritual belief and faith, but cannot be allowed to propagate herself or her doctrine past the first generation. Instead, she takes her own to her own: and so Prince Dolor does not die, but climbs on his magic cloak – the first gift from his god-mother – and floats away with his godmother to his spiritual home, the Beautiful Mountains, his own mother's birthplace. Matriarchy is upheld to the end, but the point is that there *is* an end. Craik's Prince may refute muscularity's relation to faith, but Craik cannot quite bring herself to refute the lasting validity of the Father.

In a way, George MacDonald's great-great-grandmother is the least ambivalent, most clearly-drawn version of the female Godhead yet discussed. Her trinity is centred on herself, on the implications derived from her name and actions: Nancy Willard points out that

as Irene, [the great-great-grandmother] is one of the three goddesses of Greek mythology who control the seasons. Irene brings peace, Dike justice, and Eumenia order. Though MacDonald's goddess bears only the name of the peacemaker, she could just as well answer to the names of her sisters.[15]

Her nominal connection to the Prince of Peace is obvious. She baptizes both her granddaughter and namesake Irene, and Curdie the miner's son, in fire; and Irene must first lose herself to find the great-great-grandmother. McGillis quotes Matthew 10.39 in his notes: 'He that findeth his life shall lose it: and he that loseth his life for my sake shall find it' (MacDonald, *The Princess and the Goblin*, p. 346, n. 9). Even the great-great-grandmother's location in the house is revealing. She lives at the very top of the house, up three flights of stairs, behind the 'third door': 'when Irene came to the top [of the stairs], she found herself in a little square place, with three doors, two opposite each other, and one opposite the top of the stairs' (*The Princess and the Goblin*, p. 11). If rendered pictorially, the great-great-grandmother's door occupies the space filled, on Calvary, by Christ's cross: the highest of the three.

Irene proves her worthiness by her willingness to enter this doorway, and the great-great-grandmother echoes Christ's washing of his disciples' feet when she 'stop[s] her wheel, and [rises], and, going out of the room, returned with a little silver basin and a soft white towel, with which she washed and wiped the bright little face [of Irene]' (*The Princess and the Goblin*, p. 12). McGillis's excellent notes make clear the biblical allusiveness of the great-great-grandmother's actions throughout both *The Princess and the Goblin* and *The Princess and Curdie*: she is associated with and crowned by aureoles of lights, her symbol is the white pigeon (perhaps a secular dove), she ministers, heals, leads and inspires devotion. MacDonald's contemporaries recognized her essence, although they are as coy in their recognition as the writers are in their storytelling: a review in the *Academy* in 1872 notes 'that there is allegory in all this' and that adult readers will 'guess what the beneficent grandmother is meant more or less explicitly to stand for'.[16] As McGillis says, 'MacDonald's work, especially *The Princess and Curdie*, recognizes the need to examine and question the myths with which Victorian society orders itself [...]. [P]atriarchal authority, rule by law, is vanity' (MacDonald, *The Princess and the Goblin*, pp. xv, xxiii), whereas matriarchal leadership allows the fulfilment of one's spiritual destiny and the overcoming of the forces of darkness – here, the goblins in *The Princess and the Goblin*, and greed and lust for gold and power in *The Princess and Curdie*.

MacDonald allows this female god to reconcile in her person both father and mother: the great-great-grandmother is Irene's 'father's mother's father's mother' (*The Princess and the Goblin*, p. 13). He also destabilizes Kingsley's strict classist ideology by marrying Irene the princess to Curdie the miner's boy, once both have proved their inherent – that is, not class-based, but deed-based – nobility. The great-great-grandmother is also an accessible god: even as Craik's godmother ministered to Prince Dolor, the great-great-grandmother continues her attentions to Irene throughout *The Princess and the Goblin*, and switches to Curdie in *The Princess and Curdie* (although there she moves in more mysterious ways). On Irene's second visit to the great-great-grandmother's attic, the grandmother cements her position while ministering to Irene, kissing Irene three times ('on the forehead and the cheek and the mouth' (*The Princess and the Goblin*, p. 64) in a limited but nearly complete sign of the cross, sitting her on a chair and washing her feet, healing her hand, and finally telling Irene to return to her on a Friday. Later, she cures Curdie's wounded leg by 'wav[ing] her hand over him three times' (*The Princess and the Goblin*, p. 145). MacDonald loads on the symbolic trinities, but he keeps the great-great-grandmother in the background in *The Princess and the Goblin*; he waits until the apocalyptic climax of *The Princess and Curdie* to present her in her divine glory. And if the great-great-grandmother of *The Princess and the Goblin* is a sweet, forgiving Christ, that of *The Princess and Curdie* is an avenging god. McGillis contends that

> The control of events by the feminine spirit secures us in the first book, but she and her power are less evident in the second. This explains why the myths of Persephone and the Virgin Mary inform *The Princess and the Goblin*, and the myths of Odysseus and Christ inform *The Princess and Curdie*.
>
> MacDonald, *The Princess and the Goblin*, pp. xix–xx

But such a division insists on a gendering that MacDonald himself ignores in these books, as much as he might reinforce them in other writings; that which McGillis identifies as akin to the Virgin Mary in *The Princess and the Goblin* is more properly evocative of Christ, while his 'Christ' in *The Princess and Curdie* I would call 'God'. When the great-great-grandmother, in the shape of a humble kitchen-maid, leads her faithful followers against the debased followers of Mammon in the chapter entitled 'The Battle', she is still herself, as Curdie comes to recognize after the battle; there is no male figure who supersedes her in mystical power and force. Seated on a red horse, she

> wav[es] her arm towards the battle. And the time of the motion of her arm so fitted with the rushes of birds [the pigeons who assist in the battle], that it looked as if the birds obeyed her gesture, and she were casting living javelins by the thousand against the enemy. The moment a pigeon had rounded her head, it went straight off as bolt from bow, and with trebled velocity.
>
> MacDonald, *The Princess and Curdie*, p. 335

These pigeons, 'the white-winged army of heaven' (p. 336), rout the enemy, and the maid, revealed as the great-great-grandmother, wears royal purple in victory. 'The king rose and kneeled in one knee before her. All kneeled in like homage. Then the king would have yielded her his royal chair. But she made them all sit down [...]. Then in ruby crown and royal purple she served them all' (p. 339). Both father and mother, the great-great-grandmother is also both Old Testament and New Testament god; she 'is a face of God, welcoming, loving and motherly' even as she destroys her enemies.[17]

MacDonald's deployment of the great-great-grandmother as both peacemaker and warrior, and his union of Irene and Curdie as her representatives on earth, bring God direct to his child readers. John Pennington says that MacDonald

> 'feminizes' muscular Christianity to reflect his own less-than-muscular physical state; he balances his conceptions of the masculine, active body with the feminine, more spiritual body to create a composite hero in Curdie and Irene [...]. In MacDonald's universe, masculine and feminine can exist symbiotically, with no role privileged over another.[18]

And yet, the great-great-grandmother's gender determines her identity for Pennington and most other critics: she is a 'spiritually powerful entity', a 'feminized God(dess) figure' ('Muscular Spirituality', pp. 138, 147). Plainly, however, she embodies not a feminized, or feminine, but a female god; her power is derived as much from the cultural force attached to gods as to mothers. The unorthodox preacher who argued that dogs and cats were admitted to Heaven does not shy away from creating a female Godhead, and is the least coy of all the writers here under discussion when it comes to announcing the nature of her being in his text. Further, MacDonald enlarges on and subtly questions the tenets of muscular Christianity when he creates the great-great-grandmother and her two child soldiers; but again, he stops short of ensuring the futurity of his vision. As I have mentioned, Irene and Curdie have no children: combined, one in two, they are androgynous to the point of sterility, and the influence they wield over their people is lost with their deaths.

In fact, of the writers discussed here, only Christina Rossetti in 'Goblin Market' portrays a female Christ whose behaviour is a model of feminine virtues that not only lends strength but endures past the immediate event. Sylvia Bailey Shurbutt's article 'Revisionist Mythmaking in Christina Rossetti's "Goblin Market"' provides a salient and thorough reading of how Lizzie's Christ-like comportment points to her position as a female Christ, and she does not hesitate to name her as such. There is no need for me to rehash her argument; more and more readers now pick up on the distinctly religious tone of 'Goblin Market' anyway, and Mary Arseneau even notes that '*Laura*'s encounter with the goblin men is a parody of the Christ-like', a kind of dress-rehearsal for Lizzie's genuine enactment of the role ('Incarnation and Interpretation', p. 89; emphasis added). Lizzie 'purchases redemption for her sister, as Christ in his passion bought redemption for fallen humankind' (Shurbutt, 'Revisionist Mythmaking', p. 42). What really distinguishes Rossetti's use of this trope, however, is the triumph which underlies it, as well as the unalloyed femaleness of her extra-goblin world. There are no fathers to complicate things, no boy protagonists to grow too attached to their god-mothers. One of the distinguishing features of 'Goblin Market' is the division Rossetti builds in between the world of the goblin *men* and the safe haven inhabited by Laura and Lizzie. As much as Rossetti upholds conventional notions of the separate spheres, she adamantly features in her feminine space the more worldly qualities of fertility, religion and salvation, and of the authors here discussed, she is the only one to allow her female Christ an existence beyond the text. Laura and Lizzie marry, but the final image is of them and their children:

> Days, weeks, month, years
> Afterwards, when both were wives
> With children of their own
> [...]
> Laura would call the little ones
> And tell them of her early prime.[19]

Laura, in the apostle role, transmits the story of Lizzie/Christ to the next generation, and in this way the sister-god achieves what the god-mother, the grandmother, even Mother Carey, fail to: 'Goblin Market', like the Bible, tells the story of Lizzie's sacrifice and Laura's redemption, and of Lizzie's translation to the divine.

Commentators have frequently remarked on the endemic presence of Wise Women in Victorian children's literature. Undoubtedly Queen Victoria's pre-eminence in her culture had something to do with this, and so we have Red Queens and White Queens and Queens of the Fairies and also wicked Queens. They have, however, as frequently refused to account for the presence of the female Christ, preferring to see her as a pagan anachronism, a parody, an inconsistency, a bit of fairy-tale. Perhaps one reason for this is an unease with, or unwillingness to accept, what many would see as heresy, and the commonly held assumptions about a homogeneous Victorian culture might seem to militate against such an unconventional rewriting in what, for the sake of the children, 'should' be uncontentious, wholesome, right-thinking. But the placid surface of nineteenth-century cultural, gender and religious consensus only papers over ripples and shivers of debate and change, even in the world of children's fantasy. Seeing the mystical, spiritual woman who guides us through so much of the nineteenth-century's most popular and enduring children's literature as a female God opens many avenues of discussion. In her complexity and multiplicity of meanings, the female God as deployed by Kingsley, Craik, MacDonald, Rossetti and others invites her readers – the children for whom the text is written, the adult by whom the text is read, the thinker of any age at whom the text is aimed – both back into the fold of Christian belief and into the world of independent thought. The coy and elliptical nature of these authors' descriptions of their female Gods, however, reveals an uncertainty at the heart of their polemics: the female Godhead is the Yahweh, the named unnameable, of the child-oriented text. Conventions of culture and of gender in the nineteenth century clearly dissociate the feminine from power, authority or independence, unless it was of the domesticated, unspectacular sort, however, so the puzzle at the centre of these texts, is not why the Godhead was not overtly presented as female, or why the authors resorted to the assumed intimacy of a nudge and wink when it came to her identity. The enigma, rather, is that she exists at all.

Notes

1. George MacDonald, *The Princess and the Goblin/ The Princess and Curdie*, ed. Roderick McGillis (Oxford: Oxford University Press, 1990), p. 350. Further references are given in the text by page number in this edition.
2. Charles Kingsley, *The Water-Babies*, ed. Brian Anderson (Oxford: Oxford University Press, 1995), p. 184.
3. Robin Gilmour, *The Victorian Period: The Intellectual and Cultural Context of English Literature 1830–1890* (London: Longman, 1993), pp. 107, 99. Further references are given in the text. The quotation from Arnold can be found in *Complete Prose Works of Matthew Arnold*, ed. R. H. Super, 11 vols (Ann Arbor: University of Michigan Press, 1960–77), *Dissent and Dogma*, VI, 171.
4. In Sylvia Bailey Shurbutt, 'Revisionist Mythmaking in Christina Rossetti's "Goblin Market": Eve's Apple and Other Questions Revised and Reconsidered', *Victorian Newsletter*, 82 (1992), 40–4 (p. 43). Further references are given in the text.
5. James Holt McGavran, *Romanticism and Children's Literature in Nineteenth-Century England* (Athens, GA: University of Georgia Press, 1991), p. 2.
6. Susan A. Walsh, 'Darling Mothers, Devilish Queens: The Divided Woman in Victorian Fantasy', *Victorian Newsletter*, 72 (1987), 32–6 (p. 36). Further references are given in the text..
7. Dinah Maria Mulock Craik, *The Little Lame Prince and The Adventures of a Brownie* (New York: Grosset and Dunlap, 1948), p. 127. Further references are given in the text..

8. Marian Shalkhauser, 'The Feminine Christ', *Victorian Newsletter*, 10 (1956), 19–20 (p. 19); Shurbutt, 'Revisionist Mythmaking in Christina Rossetti's "Goblin Market"', p. 42.

9. Charles Kingsley, *The Water-Babies* (London: Puffin, 1984), p. 117. Further references are given in the text..

10. George MacDonald, *At the Back of the North Wind* (New York: Signet Classics, 1986), p. 49.

11. Donald E. Hall, 'Introduction', in *Muscular Christianity: Embodying the Victorian Age*, ed. Donald E. Hall (Cambridge: Cambridge University Press, 1994), pp. 1–16 (p. 9).

12. Laura Fasick, 'Charles Kingley's Scientific Treatment of Gender', in *Muscular Christianity*, ed. Donald E. Hall, pp. 91–113 (p. 92).

13. Mary Arseneau, 'Incarnation and Interpretation: Christina Rossetti, the Oxford Movement, and *Goblin Market*', *Victorian Poetry*, 31 (1993), 79–93 (p. 82). Further references will be given in the text.

14. This is the drawback to a female Christ: when the bridegroom becomes the bride, the male protagonist needs no other.

15. Nancy Willard, 'The Goddess in the Belfry: Grandmothers and Wise Women in George MacDonald's Books for Children', in *For the Childlike: George MacDonald's Fantasies for Children*, ed. Roderick McGillis (Metuchen, NJ: Scarecrow Press, 1992), pp. 67–74 (p. 68).

16. Sidney Colvin, review of *The Princess and the Goblin*, *Academy*, 15 January 1872, p. 24; quoted in McGillis, (ed.), *The Princess and the Goblin/ The Princess and Curdie*, p. x.

17. William Raeper, *George MacDonald* (Icknield Way: Tring, Lion, 1987), p. 262.

18. John Pennington, 'Muscular Spirituality in George MacDonald's Curdie Books', in *Muscular Christianity*, pp. 133–149 (pp. 136, 146). Further references will be given in the text.

19. Christina Rossetti, 'Goblin Market', in *The Complete Poems of Christina Rossetti*, ed. R. W. Crump, 3 vols (Baton Rouge: Louisiana State University Press, 1979-90), I, ll. 543–5, ll. 548–9.

8

Alice: Reflections and Relativities

Michael Irwin

The *Alice* books are centrally concerned with instability. In Wonderland the heroine suffers alarming shifts of size. In *Through the Looking-Glass* (1871) there is much straightforward physical disequilibrium. When the White Knight is sliding down the poker Alice notes that 'he balances very badly'.[1] He and the Red Knight repeatedly fall off their horses. Humpty-Dumpty is doomed to tumble from his wall and defy re-assemblage. In both stories there are strange translations and dissolutions. The Cheshire Cat vanishes and reappears. A baby becomes a pig. The White Queen turns into a sheep, the Red Queen into a kitten. Everyday assumptions about the workings of time, direction, language and personal identity are called into question.

The work itself – the two *Alice* books considered as a single entity – partakes of this precariousness and advertises the fact that it does so. It casts doubt on its own origins and status through a variety of self-descriptive paradoxes, ambiguities, dualities and circularities. Much of Carroll's subject matter has been assembled rather than invented and retains a residual autonomy. Alice Liddell and other real-life models lurk behind certain of the characters. In *Through the Looking-Glass* the essential rules of chess are observed. Nursery-rhyme protagonists bring their poetical destinies with them: Tweedledum and Tweedledee are fated to fight, as Humpty-Dumpty is to fall. The ghosts of the poems the author has parodied haunt his transcriptions. Carroll shows a constant awareness that his story is a construct, and that his control over his discrepant source-materials cannot be taken for granted. Altogether *Alice* can be seen as – indeed proclaims itself to be – an interesting test-case in relation to questions of originality, coherence and autonomy. Is this an integrated, self-standing work of art, child of its author, or does it fragment, on scrutiny, into a concatenation of sources and influences? And if it does so fragment, can it be 'put together again'?

A convenient starting-point for discussion is the famous squabble about the sleeping Red King:

> 'He's dreaming now,' said Tweedledee: 'and what do you think he's dreaming about?'
>
> Alice said 'Nobody can guess that.'
>
> 'Why, about *you*!' Tweedledee exclaimed, clapping his hands triumphantly. 'And if he left off dreaming about you, where do you suppose you'd be?'
>
> 'Where I am now, of course,' said Alice.
>
> 'Not you!' Tweedledee retorted contemptuously. 'You'd be nowhere. Why, you're only a sort of thing in his dream!'
>
> 'If that there King was to wake,' added Tweedledum, 'you'd go out – bang! – just like a candle!'
>
> 'I shouldn't!' Alice exclaimed indignantly. 'Besides, if *I'm* only a sort of thing in his dream, what are *you*, I should like to know?'
>
> 'Ditto,' said Tweedledum.
>
> 'Ditto, ditto!' cried Tweedledee.
>
> He shouted this so loud that Alice couldn't help saying
>
> 'Hush! You'll be waking him, I'm afraid, if you make so much noise.'
>
> 'Well, it's no use *your* talking about waking him,' said Tweedledum, 'when you're only one of the things in his dream. You know very well you're not real.'
>
> 'I *am* real!' said Alice, and began to cry.
>
> 'You won't make yourself a bit realler by crying,' Tweedledee remarked: 'there's nothing to cry about.'
>
> 'If I wasn't real,' Alice said – half-laughing through her tears, it all seemed so ridiculous – 'I shouldn't be able to cry.'
>
> 'I hope you don't suppose those are *real* tears?' Tweedledum interrupted in a tone of great contempt.
>
> (pp. 238–9)

Lewis Carroll clearly set some store by this passage. He recalls the problem it poses in Chapter 8, and again in his final chapter: 'Which Dreamed It?' Alice puts the problem to her kitten:

> 'You see, Kitty, it *must* have been either me or the Red King. He was part of my dream, of course – but then I was part of his dream, too! *Was* it the Red King, Kitty?'
>
> (p. 344)

The book closes by leaving the reader with the question: 'Which do *you* think it was?'

The crux is a famous one, much discussed, and earns a long and interesting commentary in *The Annotated Alice*. Who is the ultimate dreamer, Alice or the Red King? Could one decide? How would one even set about deciding? Martin Gardner's note on this problem of 'infinite regress' invokes 'that preposterous cartoon of Saul Steinberg's in which a fat lady paints a picture of a thin lady who is painting a picture of the fat lady who is painting a picture of the thin lady, and so on deeper into the two canvases'(*The Annotated Alice*, p. 239). Perhaps equally relevant is a picture independently rendered by both Steinberg and Escher which depicts a disembodied hand holding a pencil which is drawing a disembodied hand holding a pencil which is drawing the original hand – a circle rather than an infinite regression.

The simplest application of the dilemma is probably the theological one. 'Life, what is it but a dream?' (*Annotated Alice*, p. 345). It could be argued that the 'real' dreamer is God. We are His figments. The obvious counter-claim would be that, on the contrary, we 'dream' – that is, invent – the God we would like to think invented us. We are obliged to create this alleged Creator in our own image. Is not the very metaphor of dreaming, for example, derived, necessarily, from our own categories of experience? We can conceive only that which we have it in us, as human beings, to conceive. Hence the aphorism: 'If the triangles invented a God it would have three sides.'

But the paradox has also a literary dimension. In this context the presiding 'dreamer' would at first glance seem to be Carroll himself. Neither Alice nor the Red King has an existence outside his fictional creation. Again, however, the simple explanation proves inadequate. Carroll himself can hardly be said to exist. He is an alias, a version, of the real-life deacon and mathematician Charles Lutwidge Dodgson. Behind his fictional Alice is Alice Pleasance Liddell – who might be said to have brought Lewis Carroll to life by coaxing Dodgson into becoming a story-teller.

A version of this dilemma becomes a familiar theme in twentieth-century fiction. The theological analogy has been frequently and variously explored: as God is to Man so is the novelist to his or her characters. Nabokov, Isak Dinesen, Muriel Spark and Martin Amis are among those who have exploited the issue by hypothesizing attempts to break out of, or into, the narrative 'dream'. Characters rebel against the author in the name of free will, striving to elude the constrictions of the unfolding plot as a human being might attempt to escape a divinely imposed destiny. Conversely, the writer may make an appearance as a character within the world of his or her own novel, perhaps as a gesture towards the surrender of authorial power or as an acknowledgement of its limitations.[2] The epigram about the triangles suggests this further dimension of the topic. There is a sense in which characters can truly be said to portray their creator. They are, inescapably, aspects or refractions of the author's personality: for all their theoretical autonomy they derive directly from that source. The characters created by a given novelist, taken together, might be thought to offer the possiblility of a dot-to-dot picture of the creative psychology which brought them into such being as they have.

A third application of the episode, however, is perhaps of more topical academic interest than either of the other two. The question might be posed: is the 'dreamer' – the originating force, the controlling power – the author as conscious creator and manipulator, or that author's subconscious impulses and drives (an invisible and uncontrolled internal motor), or the social and historical context which shaped the author's tastes and opinions, and constitutes the current on which he or she, more or less helplessly, drifts? There would seem to be a relevant metaphor in the episode in which Alice steers the White King's pencil, writing for him against his will. The baffled King remarks, with unconscious Freudian humour: 'I really *must* get a thinner pencil. I can't manage this one a bit: it writes all manner of things that I don't intend' (*Annotated Alice*, p. 190).

Carroll himself invites this line of inquiry by making it clear that the *Alice* books indeed have to do with the subconscious – are in effect a fantastical rendering of the subconscious life of a seven-year-old. The worlds of the two stories are made up of elements derived from the experience of an upper-middle-class Victorian child: governesses, aunts, servants, pets, games, gardens, nursery-rhymes, improving texts. ' "It's something very like learning geography," thought Alice, as she stood on tiptoe in hopes of being able to see a little further' (p. 215). The final chapter of *Alice in Wonderland* offers a coda in which Alice's sister, half dreaming, deconstructs the story she has been told:

> So she sat on, with closed eyes, and half believed herself in Wonderland, though she knew she had but to open them again, and all would change to dull reality – [...] the rattling tea-cups would change to tinkling sheep-bells, and the Queen's shrill cries to the voice of the shepherd boy – and the sneeze of the baby, the shriek of the Gryphon, and all the other queer noises, would change

(she knew) to the confused clamour of the busy farm-yard – while the lowing of the cattle in the distance would take the place of the Mock Turtle's heavy sobs. (p. 164)

Jonathan Miller's *Alice*, made for BBC television in 1966, offered a reading of roughly this transcriptive kind. There are similar explanatory hints in the last chapter of *Through the Looking-Glass*.

But the interpretative reading that Carroll has solicited can hardly fail to register some odd absences from this subconscious world. There is no more than a hint of a reference to friends, and, still more surprisingly, none at all to parents. Could a child's dreams or imaginings plausibly encompass such vacancies? It is hardly surprising that many a critic has taken Carroll's hint but responded to it in a more radical spirit. Yes, the stories told are transliterations, but the notional originating impulses derived not from Alice's mind but from Carroll's, and were partly, or largely, outside his conscious control.

Such an approach might be thought to go some way towards explaining the peculiar intensity of the *Alice* books. These are emotional stories. There is much melancholy and wistfulness, much sighing and weeping, much anger and aggression:

The Queen turned crimson with fury (*Annotated Alice*, p. 109)

wringing her hands in despair (p. 250)

trembling with excitement (p. 202)

in a sudden transport of delight (p. 256)

in a helpless frightened sort of way (p. 245)

in a voice choking with passion (p. 240)

screaming herself into a fit (p. 187)

Alice is regularly cross-questioned, ordered about, patronized, rebuked, insulted. Violence abounds, actual or threatened. The Duchess's cook throws 'saucepans, plates and dishes', one such missile nearly carrying off a baby's nose. The baby itself is hurled at Alice, who fortunately catches it. Tweedledum and Tweedledee prepare to have a battle; the Lion and the Unicorn actually have one – as do the two knights. The Queen of Hearts repeatedly orders decapitations. Alice herself kicks a lizard out of a chimney. We are reminded 'that a red-hot poker will burn you if you hold it too long; and that, if you cut your finger *very* deeply with a knife, it usually bleeds' (p. 31). Both books deal in black humour, including jokes about death. The Jabberwock is duly slain; the oysters are eaten; the Bread-and-butter-fly is doomed to perish.

The shifts of mood, the anarchy, the aggression, the grief are certainly aspects of the power of the *Alice* books. It must be conceded that children in general have an uncomplicated appetite for comic violence and extremity. The majority of the incidents alluded to above are no more damaging than a snowball. But in a significant number of cases the snowball contains at least a small stone. I can still remember how, when I read *Alice* as a child, I felt I was traversing a lot of emotional ground, out of all proportion to the brevity of the action and the reassurance at its conclusion. Serious feelings were being obscurely invoked. It seems reasonable to suspect that these disconcerting energies derived from an aspect of Carroll's personality or imagination at the very verge of his conscious control.

A simple explanation, or part explanation, would relate them to something in the Dodgson family tradition. Here is Charles Dodgson senior, a notably serious and enterprising clergyman, writing to his eight-year-old son. The context is that young Charles has asked his father, who is travelling to Leeds, to buy him a file, a screwdriver and a ring:

> As soon as I get to Leeds I shall scream out in the middle of the street, *Ironmongers – Iron*-mongers [...]. I will have a file & a screwdriver, & a ring, & if they are not brought directly, in forty seconds I will leave nothing but one small cat alive in the whole town of Leeds, & I shall only leave that, because I am afraid I shall not have time to kill it. Then what a bawling & a tearing of hair there will be! Pigs & babies, camels & butterflies, rolling in the gutter together – old women rushing up the chimneys & cows after them – ducks hiding themselves in coffee-cups, & fat geese trying to squeeze themselves into pencil cases – at last the Mayor of Leeds will be found in a soup plate covered up with custard & stuck full of almonds to make him look like a sponge cake that he may escape the dreadful destruction of the Town.[3]

The passage is reminiscent of the 'Alice' books in a variety of ways: the surrealism, the energy, the extravagant verbs (screaming, bawling and tearing of hair), the cheerful murderousness. Even some particular details anticipate Carroll's work – notably 'pigs & babies' and the Mayor found in a soup plate. It would seem that there was a common strain of anarchic boisterousness in the imagination of both these apparently staid men of the cloth, something, perhaps, in the Dodgson genes. Certainly the younger man was representing himself as a divided being well before he wrote the *Alice* books: on the one hand the Deacon and mathematician, Charles Dodgson, on the other the occasional writer, Lewis Carroll or Edgar Cuthwellis (an anagram of 'Charles Lutwidge'). A case could conceivably be made that *Alice* represents the transmission of a family tradition of humour, and is hence a good deal less original than it seems at first glance.

But the recent tendency has been to tackle the topic much lower than this – to look for darker forces behind the complexities and intensities of *Alice*. Much is made of Carroll's notorious, amply documented – indeed self-documented – devotion to young girls (pre-pubertal girls, as commentators tend to say nowadays). On this theme there is the powerful testimony not merely of Carroll's diaries, but of his extraordinary photographs, with their haunting mixture of idealization and eroticism. The passions, the wistfulness, could be transcriptions of the author's own feelings.

On one reading of the books, Carroll's conscious theme is the impossibility of fulfilment. Allegories abound. *Alice*, like *Lolita* (1955), dramatizes the elusiveness of beauty. The 'large bright thing' in the shop is always just out of eye-shot (*Annotated Alice*, p. 253). The scented rushes fade when picked (p. 257). The fawn can walk 'lovingly' with Alice only so long as their identities are forgotten; at the edge of the wood 'A sudden look of alarm came into its beautiful brown eyes, and in another moment it had darted away at full speed' (p. 227). Above all there is the paradox of 'the loveliest garden you ever saw', which first becomes visible beyond a door at the end of a 'small passage' (p. 30). When Alice herself is small enough to get through that door she is too short to reach the key which would open it. When she is tall enough to reach the key she is too big to get out into the garden. Might not this be Carroll's way of insinuating the idea that the girl to whom he has given his heart *cannot* enter the garden of adult love?

Arguably – the point has often been made – Carroll includes himself in *Through the Looking-Glass* in the character of the White Knight, the amiable, kindly but absurd figure whose 'very, *very* beautiful song' Alice hears unmoved, before waving goodbye to him and going on her way.[4] Her response is perfectly reasonable. Taken at face value the White Knight's lay is a nonsense-work, an irreverent burlesque of Wordsworth's 'Resolution and Independence' (1802, publ. 1807). Since Carroll had published a version of his parody years previously, it can hardly be thought to relate closely to the context. On the other hand the scene is described with a seriousness most unusual in the *Alice* books:

> Of all the strange things that Alice saw in her journey Through The Looking-Glass, this was the one that she always remembered most clearly. Years afterwards she could bring the whole scene back again, as if it had been only yesterday – the mild blue eyes and kindly smile of the Knight – the setting sun gleaming through his hair, and shining on his armour in a blaze of light that quite dazzled her – the horse quietly moving about, with the reins hanging loose on his neck, cropping the grass at her feet – and the black shadows of the forest behind – all this she took in like a picture, as, with one hand shading her eyes, she leant against a tree, watching the strange pair, and listening, in a half-dream, to the melancholy music of the song.
> (p. 307)

Much could be made of the gentleness of tone, the sympathetic presentation of the Knight, the imagery of the blazing armour, the setting sun, the dark forest and the docile beast. Alice identifies the tune of the song as that of 'I give thee all, I can no more'. Martin Gardner quotes the poem in full, remarking: 'It is quite possible that Carroll regarded Moore's love lyric as the song that he, the White Knight, would have liked to sing to Alice but dared not' (*Annotated Alice*, p. 311). In this spirit one might see *Alice* itself as a similarly hopeless love-song to 'the child of my dreams' – the love-song of Edgar Cuthwellis. Beyond the deliberately absurd characterization, after all, stands another foolish knight who vainly served an impossible mistress: Don Quixote. It might well be that Carroll is writing about himself in the protection afforded by double inverted commas.

But an aggressive late-twentieth-century reading would deny Carroll this degree of control over his private story. There has been a relentless poring over diaries and letters, a terrier-like pursuit of unconscious symbolism. The claim is that Carroll is saying far more than he is consciously aware of saying about his 'condition'. The *Alice* books, of course, are a gift to the Freudian, proliferating as they do in holes, tunnels, doors, locks, keys, fluids and size-changes. That game is all too easy. It is disappointing to see how commentary a good deal more controlled can drift in the same direction. Morton Cohen asserts 'It is mean-spirited to attribute the *Alice* books [...] entirely to a suppression of natural drives, to a flight from [Carroll's] real troubled self'. Yet fifty pages earlier he himself has ventured: 'If Charles Dodgson's suppressed and diverted sexual energies caused him unspeakable torments, and they did, they were in all probability the source of those exceptional flashes of genius that gave the world his remarkable creative works.'[5] The former comment is the more persuasive. 'Mean-spirited' seems an apt term for an attempt to explain a work of art in terms of the mud from which it might conceivably be said to grow.

This kind of approach, whatever view one takes of it, locates the creative 'source' firmly within Carroll's psychology. Another kind of twentieth-century reading would locate it without – would see the *Alice* books as deriving from a variety of external influences and pressures. Two such influences might be the fairy-tale tradition, often cruel, often metaphorically suggestive, or nursery-rhymes, both surrealistic and violent:

There was an old woman who lived in a shoe

Hey diddle diddle, the cat and the fiddle,
The cow jumped over the moon

When the wind blows the cradle will rock;
When the bough breaks the cradle will fall

Down came a blackbird and pecked off her nose

She cut off their tails with a carving knife

I took him by the left leg
And threw him down the stairs.

Generations of children have spent hours in this strange world and taken the extravagance and ferocity for granted. Is not Lewis Carroll – was not his father? – drawing on common stock, manifesting certain widespread fancies and urges? Are they not belated practitioners in an old folk mode?

One might produce a rather different 'explanation' by pulling the string tighter. In a much narrower chronological sense, Carroll's idiosyncrasies were far from singular. He was representative of an *age* which idealized children with a passion psychologically maiming. The trend may perhaps be seen to find its culmination shortly after the turn of the century with the appearance of Barrie's *Peter Pan* (1904). Derek Hudson points out that Kilvert, the diarist, a clergyman contemporary with Carroll, responded very similarly to young girls.[6] The psychological and even legal restraints on such relationships were much weaker than they are today. Morton Cohen usefully reminds us that in the middle years of the nineteenth century girls could marry at twelve. He points out that Carroll's own brother, Wilfred, at the age of twenty-seven, fell in love with a fourteen-year-old, and indeed married her some years later.[7]

Clearly Carroll eventually had misgivings of some sort about his nude photographs of children; why else should he have had almost all of them destroyed? On the other hand he seems to have been orig-inally frank and unembarrassed about such activity, clearing it with his own conscience. He was scrupulous in obtaining parental permission for the pictures to be taken – which he could hardly have done without winning the total confidence of those concerned. It must have been a relevant factor that, despite the pruderies of the age, unclothed *children* were somehow deemed acceptable in painting and illustration, particu-larly in fairy-tale or vaguely pastoral contexts. This category of nudity was sanitized or even sanctified.

More particularly Carroll was very much an admirer of Dickens, who had regularly idealized and eroticized small girls. Florence Dombey and Little Em'ly are specifically presented, in their infancy, as potential sweethearts respectively for Walter Gay and David Copperfield. Above all Nell Trent may have provided Carroll with a precedent: a young girl who is seen in the shadow of the sexual threat represented by Quilp. The *Alice* books echo *The Old Curiosity Shop* (1840–1) – particularly the Mrs Jarley episode – in a number of particular ways. More generally Dickens structures his novel on an allegorical plan which Carroll pro-ceeds to borrow. His heroine, like Nell, is Innocence moving among monsters.

It would seem, then, that there is a case – a case merely sketched in the preceding paragraphs – for claiming that *Alice* was very much a product of its time. Carroll was arguably not an anomalous but in some sense a representative figure, formed by the tastes and the pres-sures of his age. Was it not 'Victorianism' that steered his pencil?

Interestingly such a question would not have seemed strange to Carroll himself, a proto-modernist with post-modernist premonitions. In *Sylvie and Bruno* (1889) he envisages a future era of linguistic exhaus-tion or repletion: ' "Instead of saying 'what book shall I write?' an author will ask himself 'which book shall I write?' " '[8] In the Preface to the first part of that same work, he claims that some of the ideas for it seemed to spring from nothing: 'specimens of that hopelessly illogical phenomenon, "an effect without a cause" '. But others he could 'trace to their source' – for example 'as being suggested by the book one was reading' (*Sylvie and Bruno*, p. 255). Later he adds that 'Perhaps the hardest thing in all literature [...] is to write anything *original*'. He does not know whether he can claim originality for *Alice in Wonderland*: 'I was, at least, no *conscious* imitator in writing it' (*Sylvie and Bruno*, p. 257). It would seem, however, that in some areas at least he was content to work generically: he acknowledges, for example, that the Red Queen is 'the concentrated essence of all governesses'.[9] More interestingly he says of the White Queen: 'There is a character strangely like her in Wilkie Collins' novel *No Name*: by two different converging paths we have somehow reached the same ideal, and Mrs Wragg and the White Queen might have been twin-sisters.'[10] The inference is that Carroll and Collins, with no thought of portraying an accepted 'type', have distilled social observations sufficiently akin to sponsor similar results. Within the confines of a given social or historical environment such coincidence need not seem far-fetched. Conceivably a writer might be reduced to wondering 'which *character* shall I create?' The notion of 'originality' would resolve itself back into a complex of possible social 'origins', generic antecedents: we are returned to the dilemma of the Red King's dream.

Many other images in the *Alice* books imply a similar reflexivity: 'once she remembered trying to box her own ears for having cheated herself in a game of croquet she was playing against herself'. Tweedledee tries to fold up an umbrella with himself inside it (*Annotated Alice*, p. 241). The Unicorn tells Alice: 'if you'll believe in me, I'll believe in you' (p. 287). An especially intriguing example is the sheep in *Through the Looking-Glass* knitting with fourteen pairs of needles at once – a vision of rampant auto-cannibalism not remote from the self-consuming toils of the Artist (*Annotated Alice*, pp. 253–4).

It seems likely, then, that Carroll's preliminary answer to the question 'Did you write these books or were you written *through*?' would be 'Both' – but that if pressed he would concede to the inescapability of derivativeness. Even the odd 'effect without a cause' would be seen as ultimately explicable.

Indeed this is a conclusion which can hardly be confuted. As Artists or anything else we can only dispense what by one means or another has been fed into us. That much is axiomatic. But since this truism, too crudely insisted upon, can be demeaning in its implications, especially with regard to the autonomy of the artist, it should not be accorded undue respect. I would like to conclude by tying some tin cans to its tail.

It must first be asked whether the proposed deconstruction of a literary work into its component elements has any status beyond the merely conceptual. A cake could be considered as a cultural construct or as an assemblage of separable ingredients. But it is not so considered. We eat it. That is what it is *for*.

The claim that originality is in *absolute* terms unfeasible may in any case come to seem uninteresting in the light of the complex relative position. The Gryphon, for example, could not be described as an original creation: he has antecedents, albeit of a mythical kind. The Cheshire Cat is less obviously derivative: Carroll has lent substantiality to what was previously a mere form of words. The Mock Turtle, which has no ancestry, comes yet closer to being a conception plucked out of the air. It is brought into some sort of theoretical existence, from nothing, by the shift of a notional hyphen – 'mock turtle-soup' becomes 'mock-turtle soup'. As an invention it very much recalls Carroll's reference to a thought 'struck out from the "flint" of one's own mind by the "steel" of a friend's chance remark' (*Sylvie and Bruno*, p. 255). Here the thought is solid enough for Tenniel to draw a picture of it. Carroll's transactional image defines the case rather neatly. Even if it is accepted that the 'chance remark' and 'one's own mind' are socially (or otherwise) determined, the unpredictability of the encounter allows for a randomness so extreme as to be effectively indistinguishable from 'originality'.

Attempted dismemberment of *Alice* may be inviting in terms of the self-proclaimed fissility of the work, but it is likely to prove in practice a curiously self-defeating enterprise, itself trapped in reflexivity. Here is a children's book which children (or so it is repeatedly claimed) no longer read. Has it not therefore largely lost its intrinsic life? Why not leave it alone and forget it? What is sought from it? Why the manifest eagerness to 'explain' it? Might it be explained away? If this happened, would we miss it? What is 'it'?

It should not be surprising that Carroll's artful circularities have the capacity to entangle those who seek to unravel them. But there is a specialized sense in which this particular work is calculated to deconstruct the deconstructers. The contemporary obsession with some of the issues concerned has its dubious aspect. An unhealthy flush tends to suffuse the face of late twentieth-century criticism when it gets a whiff of the possible sexual tensions of a bygone age. It must be doubted whether we can see such issues straight. How coolly can we assess the psycho-sexual stresses of the Victorian period from the vantage-point of an age of obesity, anorexia, body-building, body-piercing, silicone implants, AIDS and *The Sunday Sport*? Can we lodge our analytical scales and micro-scopes on firm ground? Might not Carroll be at least as likely to expose our prurience, our assumptions about the relationship between desire and art, as we to expose his?

The medium of the *Alice* books is peculiarly difficult to penetrate. In *The White Knight*, Alexander L. Taylor makes the brilliant comment that they recall the assumed madness of Hamlet or Edgar.[11] Of the two, Edgar offers the apter comparison, incidentally as recalling Edgar Cuthwellis, chiefly because his brand of 'madness' seems less explic-able, more in excess of its apparent function, than does Hamlet's. His extravagant verbal arias in the third act of *King Lear* could be inter-preted as verbal camouflage, an aspect of his disguise. But they *might* be uncontrolled, a kind of delirium, obliquely self-revelatory. The text offers no explanation. Who can confidently say what Edgar 'means' or where he is coming from? Much of his speech is, or might be, aleatory. So with Carroll's surrealistic creation.

Two essential kinds of material in *Alice* are particularly resistant to reductive analysis, since they involve plural and even self-contradic-tory effects. One is parody, an odd species of inter-textuality in that around what is written there hovers, by intention, the ghost of what has been altered. 'The Aged, Aged Man', for example, is coloured, however absurdly, by 'Resolution and Independence'. Only the reader who misses the point can escape the associations. The effect is rather like that of whistling two tunes simultaneously.

Then there is the use of sound. Repeatedly, verses which are ostens-ibly absurd are given a curious charge of dignity or pathos by their musical quality. In some cases – as with 'The Aged, Aged Man' – a known melody may be invoked; more often what is in question is a sustained pattern of euphony. Thus 'Jabberwocky' conveys hints of genuine portentousness, and 'The Walrus and the Carpenter' has an undertow of true melancholy. Should the prospective deconstructor seek, in such cases, separate sources for the discrepant effects, or rather an explanation for the capacity to combine them?

It must finally be observed that the main constituents of *Alice* – includ-ing idealized children, nonsense, pathos, pedantry, paradox, puzzles, comic verse, emotional intensity, violence, sentimentality – are all present in the large-scale work *Sylvie and Bruno*, which Carroll produced in the 1890s. It might have been assumed that a work sufficiently similar in general intention, and subject to the same 'influences', internal and external, would be roughly comparable in overall effect. In fact *Sylvie and Bruno*, by common consent, is a laborious work, often embarrassing and even painful to read. The various ingredients separate out. From the same defining circumstances Carroll has produced a very different result. The book doesn't 'work'. An attempt to analyse why it fails to cohere, and why the *Alice* books do cohere, would by definition have to proceed from a tacit reinstatement of the autonomy of all three works. It would call for an analytical study in the traditional modes of the discipline of English Literature.

Notes

1. Lewis Carroll, *Through the Looking-Glass*, in *The Annotated Alice*, introduction and notes by Martin Gardner (Harmondsworth: Penguin, 1965), p. 190. Further references are given in the text by page number in this edition. For those who wish to pursue issues developed in this essay, *Annotated Alice* probably offers the best starting point. For more recent perspectives see Donald Rackin, *Alice's Adventures in Wonderland and Through the Looking Glass: Nonsense, Sense, and Meaning* (New York: Twayne, 1991). It includes a full and helpful selected critical bibliography.

2. For example: Amis appears as (more or less) himself in his novel *Money: A Suicide Note* (1984), while Nabokov's Cincinnatus in *Invitation to a Beheading* (1960 in English) at one point physically takes himself to pieces, from the head downwards. In Muriel Spark's *The Comforters* (1957), the heroine, Caroline Rose, a writer and critic, comes to realize that she is herself a character in a novel – from which she struggles to break free. For further comment on Nabokov and related observations on Isak Dinesen see the final section of my 'Facts and Fictions' in *Exploring Reality*, ed. Dan Cohn-Sherbok and Michael Irwin (London: Allen & Unwin, 1987).

3. Quoted in Derek Hudson, *Lewis Carroll: An Illustrated Biography* (London: Constable, 1976; repr. 1982), p. 35.

4. See *Annotated Alice*, pp. 296–7, n. 4.

5. Morton N. Cohen, *Lewis Carroll: A Biography* (London: Macmillan, 1995), pp. 280, 231.

6. Hudson, *Lewis Carroll: An Illustrated Biography*, p. 212.

7. Cohen, *Lewis Carroll: A Biography*, pp. 101–2.

8. Lewis Carroll, *Sylvie and Bruno*, in *The Complete Works of Lewis Carroll* (London: Nonesuch Library, 1939), pp. 251–674 (p. 537). Further references are given in the text by page number in this edition.

9. See *Annotated Alice*, p. 206.

10. See *Annotated Alice*, p. 245.

11. Alexander L. Taylor, *The White Knight: A Study of C. L. Dodgson (Lewis Carroll)* (London: Oliver & Boyd, 1952), p. 144.

9
Place, Identity and *Born in Exile*

Ralph Pite

Gissing's *Born in Exile* was drafted in the first six months of 1891 and published in 1892; Gissing had recently remarried, achieved some success with *New Grub Street* and moved from London to Exeter.[1] The novel has been discussed most frequently either as autobiographical or in relation to the conflict between science and religion prompted, in the period, by evolution and geology.[2] These debates are certainly raised in the book, but they do not lie at its centre. Rather, in their substance and in the way people conduct them, the debates are seen as aspects of social exclusion. The book, in other words, is generated by an interest in exile, in particular the exile that occurs within a divided society.

This interest has been noted before – by Adrian Poole, John Goode and others – usually in the context of class relations and the psychology they engender.[3] One of the remarkable features of the novel, however, is its inclusion of so many unusually specific geographical reference points. Social exclusion on the basis of class is repeatedly juxtaposed with exclusion on the basis of place. This may suggest that the two forms of exclusion confirm each other. One's place of birth appears as debilitating as one's class origins: a northern boy is regarded by southerners as a working-class boy; a person from London's East End is, apparently by definition, less cultivated than someone from, say, Mayfair or Park Lane. While *Born in Exile* recognizes the currency of these assumptions and their consequent power, the novel also contrasts physical mobility with class mobility. A Cockney both can and cannot walk along Park Lane. He or she may visit the place and, by doing so, feel closer to the higher social plane which it represents. Yet physical nearness also frustrates social aspiration: it may confirm the elusiveness of upper-class society and its various techniques for closing itself against intruders.

Place in *Born in Exile* is associated with class and reveals itself to be, as it were, a front for class. One can be socially excluded on the grounds of not coming from the right place yet moving to the right place does not guarantee inclusion. Moreover, while place in the novel helps suggest that class is a system of exclusion (rather than a system of values or a code of conduct), place also reveals the especially intense desire for home that is created by class exclusion. This last aspect of place is Gissing's central concern when writing the book. It emerges as a destructive result of his protagonist's provincial expectations.

Born in Exile moves from the North of England to London and Devon. Godwin Peak, the novel's central character, visits Exeter, Budleigh Salterton and Ottery St Mary; he lives in Rotherhithe and Peckham Rye; at the end of the novel, he moves to St Helen's in Lancashire. However, at the start, he is found attending school in a generic northern town, 'Kingsmill'. The novel moves from fictional to actual places; its specificity about place sets up a contrast between real and mental geographies. In the process, the book alters a tradition of provincial fiction, present in, for instance, Elizabeth Gaskell's *North and South* (1854–5), set in 'Milton-Northern, the manufacturing town in Darkshire'. Gaskell contrasts Milton-Northern with real places – specifically with London, Oxford and Corfu – as well as with the fictional Helstone, in the South of England.[4] But the contrasts have a different effect from those in Gissing's novel. The real places Gaskell mentions are emblems of wealth, culture and romance; of all the things her heroine has been denied. Her locations confirm two conflicting perspectives – the northern and the southern – which the plot finally reconciles. *Born in Exile*'s real places are more specific and less glamorous than Gaskell's. They reveal the insufficiency of the binary oppositions provincialism employs. The book shows how 'country and city' or 'north and south' cannot encompass all the differences that exist in the world beyond 'Kingsmill'.

Similarly, the book's movement from one fictional place to a succession of different actual places epitomizes the assault on Godwin Peak's self-image that occurs during its narrative. Godwin thinks of himself as a provincial boy on his way to the big city; in the course of his journey, he discovers a more heterogeneous world than he expected to find and one that defeats his habits of thought. He remains excluded, nevertheless, from metropolitan culture: what divides him from the world he aims to enter cannot be located in the difference between country and city or between north and south, yet the division remains. Peak's way of understanding his own position is shown to be inadequate while his need to find a satisfactory position remains unanswered. That very need, however, is established by a provincial upbringing.

'Kingsmill', we are told at the novel's opening, is narrow, conservative and self-respecting – it is quintessentially provincial. Its characteristics are generated by its secondary status, the status granted by a metropolitan culture and confirmed by that culture's fictions. Godwin's reading of the other places he visits is continually distorted by the opposition between province and metropolis that was accepted by the citizens of Kingsmill. He cannot escape this opposition, although one of the book's minor characters shows how it might be avoided and disarmed.

Earwaker, Godwin's closest friend, becomes a successful man of letters; Bruno Chilvers, Godwin's arch-rival at school, is married to a titled heiress. Godwin never enters middle-class or upper-middle-class society. In Earwaker, in his unspectacular yet definite success and in his unashamed loyalty to his 'provincial' roots, Gissing suggests a life that opposes both Godwin's failure and Bruno Chilvers's extravagant success. Earwaker reaches a regional perspective in which he accepts his dual loyalty – to London and to his northern family – seeing the different places as of equal value and refusing to sacrifice one to the other.

The book, then, is concerned with an internal exile's distorted perception of place – his fetishizing of the place that offers 'homeliness' – and the distortions governing such a perception are seen as driving and controlling the narrative as well. If Godwin could for once be at home, the writing would stop. More fundamentally: if he could escape from the desire to be at home once more, his endless self-interrogation would come to an end.

In draft, the novel was entitled 'Godwin Peak', after its central character whose life story (and those of his school-fellows) the book narrates. Godwin Peak is a gifted, intellectual child, and modelled to some extent on his author: 'Peak is myself – one phase of myself', Gissing conceded in a letter to his German friend Eduard Bertz.[6] He resembles his creator in his provincial background, thwarted academic career and impecunious London life; probably, too, in his touchiness and irascibility. Early on in the novel, Godwin argues with his younger brother, Oliver:

[']I hate low, uneducated people! I hate them worse than the filthiest vermin! – don't you?'

Oliver, aged but thirteen, assented, as he habitually did to any question which seemed to await an affirmative.

'They ought to be swept off the face of the earth!' pursued Godwin [...]. 'All the grown-up creatures, who can't speak proper English and don't know how to behave themselves, I'd transport them to the Falkland Islands,' – this geographic precision was a note of the boy's mind, – 'and let them die off as soon as possible.[']

Born in Exile, pp. 29–30

Gissing's nearness to his protagonist can seem to infect him with the same hysterical snobbery.[7] However, 'you will not find' Gissing reassured Bertz, that 'Peak's tone is to be henceforth mine. [...] I described him with gusto, but surely I did not [...] take *his* point of view?' (*Letters*, V, 36). 'Gusto' implies some degree of affiliation, some willingness on Gissing's part to let loose this 'phase of himself' and see what it will do.

The book, though not its author, is aligned with Godwin because it follows his dizzying swerves from 'nervous cramp' (*Born in Exile*, p. 213) to outbursts of hatred; from the geographic precision of the Falkland Islands back to 'filthiest vermin'. Until its final sections, the book is structured by these swings from accuracy to harangue and back again. Godwin, accordingly, is at one moment a methodical industrial chemist and, at the next, a sceptical essayist, composing polemical articles 'at a few vehement sittings' (p. 114); similarly, too, Godwin is unable to live 'steadily' – and *steady* is a keyword in the book (for instance, pp. 128, 232, 415). The style of the narrative imitates the hero's volatility. It punctuates Godwin's furious outbursts with shrewd observations ('this geographic precision was a note of the boy's mind'); and elsewhere, it allows years of disciplined scholarly application or scientific work to go by with barely a word. It proceeds at the jerky pace of Godwin's experience, in an erratic rhythm of hurry and arrest.

Moreover, this is done without comment or hesitation. The narrative never stands outside Godwin's mind, judging his behaviour; but neither is it a story told from his point of view. Godwin seems to lack the resources from which to establish a point of view and so the narrative's ease in describing him feels like imprisonment.[8] Godwin's outbursts are attempts to throw off the shackles of being completely known by the narrative – and known in so objective a manner that his personality is both denied and anatomized. Because the book does not have an identifiable narrator or narrative voice, Godwin's hostility to being known overlaps with hatred of his self-perception. The emotional violence arises from his warring against his view of himself as socially identifiable, as nothing beyond his class definition. It is an account of himself that he is not equipped to dispute or overturn, so he becomes trapped in a continual rejection of something he cannot deny.

The book's closeness to Godwin – its imitation of his mind and yet its inability to grasp him, perhaps because there is nothing to grasp – creates uncanny effects of claustrophobia and vertigo. Such qualities in the narrative can be seen as aspects of its main character: his social confinement joined to his grand imaginings; his pettiness combined with his will to power. Style corresponds to character, then, and also to theme, since the novel's subject is these elements in Godwin: their origin, their co-existence, and how they might be better harmonized.

Godwin leads a life of 'paroxysms' which the unusual style of *Born in Exile* is created to record and analyse.[9] At the crisis of the story, Godwin is in Exeter 'straying about the Cathedral Close'; he 'moved idly within sight of the carriages' and 'mooned about the street under his umbrella' (pp. 119–20). His 'mere half-purpose, a vague wavering intention' is interrupted by his meeting an old school-friend and within a page the two of them are walking at high speed to his house.

'Peak soon found himself conversing rather too breathlessly for comfort.

"What is your latest record for the mile?" he inquired' (p. 121). His friend, Buckland Warricombe, has the decency to slow down but he never stops asking a string of incisive questions about Godwin's past, his present, his religious beliefs and his future plans. It is through being forced a little later to answer a similar question that Godwin begins lying. He is asked to assess the sermon that all the family has listened to at morning service: 'under the marvelling regard of his conscious self, he poured forth an admirable rendering of the Canon's views, fuller than the original – more eloquent, more subtle' (p. 128). This, Gissing tells us, is a crucial moment: 'the fatal hour of [Peak's] life has struck'. It has come upon him without prior warning or the build-up of any suspense, only seven pages after Godwin was wandering about in a daze. Peak, moreover, attains utter composure through telling lies: 'Peak met [his friend's eye], and encountered its steady searching gaze with a perfectly calm smile' (p. 128). Later on, he describes the whole day to himself as 'a mad dream, of ludicrous coherence' (p. 146). The narrative imitates exactly the instability and baffling, undeniable connectedness of such a dream. At the heart of it is a lurch from dream (mooning by the Cathedral) to sudden energy (in the hectic walk and the nervousness of introductions) and then back to a second dream (the deceptive speech), in which Peak is calm again, his troubling self-awareness removed.

The pattern recurs in the novel; when, for instance, Godwin meets his Cockney uncle in Chapter 1 (p. 19). Again, later, when living the lie, Godwin pulls himself from the dream of fiction: 'there came upon him an uncomfortable dreaminess [...] a tormenting metaphysical doubt of his own identity strangely beset him. With involuntary attempt to recover the familiar self he grasped his own wrist' (p. 206). While portraying Godwin's contradictions, Gissing is also asking whether novel-writing – that phase of himself – may have its source in a desire to escape the burden of self-consciousness; and whether, given that originating impulse, it may be impossible to write steadily or well.

T. S. Eliot wrote that 'Every country is home to one man / And exile to another'. Concluding one of the sections of 'Ash Wednesday' (1930), he quoted the Roman Catholic prayer, *Salve Regina*: 'and after this our exile'.[10] The phrase in its original context is appositional: 'after this which is our exile'; Eliot allows it to be read as also meaning 'and after this, then our exile'. Exile appears as present and future, as experience and destiny. Eliot's ambiguity suggests that exile is best understood as a condition which collapses such distinctions, robbing us of the possibility of change, as it constantly disappoints our hope of having found a home. Gissing's title, *Born in Exile*, similarly denies advancement or alteration.[11]

Peak grows up where he does because his parents inherit a house in the Midlands and move up to it from London where Peak's father, Nicholas, had been born – 'in a London alley, the son of a labourer'. Relatives and uncles 'disappeared in the abyss' (p. 21) and when they later showed themselves, in the form of Andrew Peak, the coffee-shop proprietor, they attract a 'dislike [that] amounted to loathing' (p. 29) in Godwin and his mother. Social mobility in the previous generation means Godwin is in exile from his family's sordid origins while he views himself as a banished 'aristocrat *de jure*' (p. 30). Godwin should associate with the upper class, an aristocrat being 'what he really was', yet he needs to be 'rescued from the promiscuity of the vulgar!' (p. 103). He thinks of himself as 'an aristocrat of nature's own making' (p. 30) precisely because the skeleton in the cupboard is his father's background, a past his mother had despised and obscured as best she could.

This family history brings out the various senses of the novel's title. Peak is 'born in exile' because he grows up in the provinces, banished from the cultural centre. Secondly, though, he grows up in exile from his actual roots in working-class London. He links himself with the aristocracy of nature in order to deny those shameful origins. Being '*born* in exile' continues this by expressing his sense of himself as disinherited; the title invokes Bonny Prince Charlie, Oedipus and all the banished princes of fairytale. Godwin's real, family background troubles his relation to Kingsmill, continually threatening to embarrass him; at the same time, it encourages him to create out of Kingsmill the scene of his exile. The place is perceived by Godwin as a starting-point for his re-entry into a better world.

As the book disappoints Godwin's belief in 'the country and the city', it undermines his idea of exile, showing it to be another symptom of his exclusion. The person exiled – like Ovid or Dante – can look back, with nostalgia and yearning, towards the home from which they have been exiled. The person 'born in exile' has never been at home; the longing to return has no foundation in experience and the place of origin has to be imagined. It is imagined as a reflection of exile, confirming the self's essential integrity by providing a place of complete integration.[12]

This is borne out by the book's emphasis on the connectedness of one generation with another which appears in Gissing's use of names. Godwin is named after William Godwin, author of *An Enquiry Concerning Political Justice* (1793), whom his father, Nicholas Peak, admired. Obedient to this naming, Godwin grows up an anti-clerical anarchist. Godwin's friend, Buckland Warricombe, is called Buckland by his geologist father in memory of 'William Buckland, the geologist' (p. 117). Buckland, accordingly, is an early enthusiast for geology, letting it go when it leads him into doctrinal conflict with his father. From then on, as he remarks to Godwin, they 'agree to differ, and get on capitally' (p. 122).[13] Similarly, Bruno Chilvers becomes a clergyman, following in his father's footsteps: 'It became the son of a popular clergyman, and gave promise of notable aptitude for the sacred career to which Bruno [...] already had designed himself' (p. 9). *Aptitude* is, once again, Chilvers's prominent advantage when he reappears later in the novel as a Broad Churchmen whose liberal theology verges, blithely, on unbelief. 'He trod in the footsteps of his father,' Peak reflects, 'and with inherited aptitude moulded antique traditions into harmony with the taste of the times' (p. 213).[14] Godwin's peers have, if not a genius, at least an aptitude for compromise. Those who have inherited are able to pass on an inheritance. Godwin, whose father is dead, cannot mould the antique into harmony with the present; he is wedded to the antique, believing it to be his birthright and his sacred duty to do so.

By naming his son after an intellectual hero, Nicholas Peak recalls Coleridge who named his children in the same way: Hartley Coleridge and Berkeley Coleridge honour the philosophers David Hartley and George Berkeley. In the novel, Peak and his friends walk to Coleridge's birthplace, discussing him on the way, and Andrew Peak has his child, Jowey, recite six stanzas of 'The Ancient Mariner' (1798), much to Godwin's disgust (pp. 252, 62). The reminders contribute to one's sense of Godwin's displacement: Coleridge felt himself to have been 'transplanted', as a child, from his family home in Devon; his greatest poems seek to recover a lost identity between self and place. In 'Frost at Midnight' (1798), it is his son, Hartley, who will attain it – he will 'wander like a breeze / By lakes and sandy shores' whereas Coleridge was 'pent 'mid cloisters dim'.[15] Hartley will be indistinguishably amid his world yet, ironically, as he *wanders* like a breeze, Hartley will still have no place of rest.

Gissing remembered Coleridge often when he was writing *Born in Exile*. The book acts, in some respects, as a sardonic commentary on Coleridge's hopes for his son.[16] Names expressing one's own intellectual loyalties seek to create a new family, distinct from the previous generation. They make a declaration of freedom comparable to the joyous wandering Coleridge imagines for Hartley. Such freedom, in *Born in Exile*, remains shadowed, however, by the fear of dislocation; to imagine oneself so free may prove only that one has no place. It is a freedom that feels contempt for and yet envies those whose names bring with them a restrictive but malleable connectedness to the past.

In Godwin Peak, such freedom also threatens continually to dissolve into mere fluency. Bruno Chilvers is a parody of the Broad Churchmen of his day, and Peak can imitate him perfectly. The ease with which he does so shows, perhaps, that Chilvers's 'moulding of antique traditions into harmony with' contemporary taste is altogether superficial (p. 213). But the effortlessness on Godwin's part, his intuitive ventriloquism, reveals something about him as well. When Peak impersonates despised attitudes so eloquently, he reveals that he is, truly, a *parson*. Early on, his mother had suggested the Church to him as a possible career and been rebuffed.

> 'I don't want to be a parson,' came at length, bluntly.
> 'Don't use that word, Godwin.'
> 'Why not? It's quite a proper word. It comes from the Latin *persona*.'
> (p. 24)[17]

As a fiery youth, Godwin had bluntly rejected the idea of playing a part. In adult life, not only is he doing this continually, he seems unable to avoid doing so: at his first re-encounter with Chilvers he starts to mimic his liberal theology, one very different from the strict orthodoxy Godwin has been learning to parrot for the Warricombes. Moreover, a real parson is enviable because his lack of sincerity is accepted as part of the role. He is called 'parson' in recognition that he speaks for the Church; his profession requires him to adopt a *persona* and to speak continually on the record. There is a kind of honesty about this acknowledged deceptiveness which Godwin finds amusing, because it shows up the hypocrisy of society. He also finds it uniquely desirable. The institution shows, above all, that your honesty or dishonesty depends upon the degree of your social acceptance. Godwin is a shady liar while Bruno is a parson. There is no essential difference between them and, at the same time, all the difference in the world.

In consequence, Godwin experiences adaptability as another kind of exclusion. His ability to play, at a moment's notice, any part that may be demanded of him is the product of his having – and knowing himself to have – no particular, assigned role. The range of possibilities open to him only enforces his sense of being separated from those to whom an adopted position is natural or inherited. This produces, in turn, an extreme abreaction. He celebrates Bruno's dubious accomplishments and then, immediately, he condemns himself: '[Bruno] with inherited aptitude moulded antique traditions into harmony with the taste of the times. Compared with such a man, Peak felt himself a bungler. The wonder was that his clumsy lying had escaped detection' (p. 213). The reader understands this envy while thinking it misplaced: Bruno is far more transparent than Godwin. He can afford to be. Similarly, though it is extraordinary that Godwin is not seen through earlier and has to be exposed, we do not think him a 'clumsy' liar – quite the opposite. His success is disturbing – and often funny – because it shows how much 'escapes detection' in social interaction and how little there is of mutual understanding or genuine exchange. This outburst of self-hatred then sounds naïve: Godwin's over-valuing of people like Bruno lies at the root of his social ambitions and brings with it a paranoid and yet strangely idealistic belief in the perceptiveness and the candour of the world which he wants to enter.

Godwin persistently 'feels himself a bungler'; he cannot rid himself of the self-abasement that follows from seeing the middle classes as superhuman – extreme in their insight, their social graces and their intolerance. His savaging of middle-class society, of Bruno as the representative of its hypocrisy, and of the Church as generalized mumbo-jumbo – all Godwin's violence stems from the failure of these groups to live up to the impossible standards of perfection he sets for them. That perfectionism derives from his status as an outsider, in a manner that corresponds to one part of post-colonial experience: to the ideals of the 'home-country' that are held by those it has colonized.[18] His rage is provoked by the way in which a corrupted ideal belittles his aspiration, showing him up as a fantasist.

If one part of Godwin's experience is that of the colonized, another is that of the colonist: the solution he finds for homelessness is emigration. 'On a long voyage, such as he had all but resolved to take, one might perchance form acquaintances. He had heard of such things; not impossibly, a social circle might open to him at Buenos Ayres' (p. 120). The elaborate caution here has a comic edge to it. Godwin's painful modesty (which continues the solitude it bemoans) sounds excessive as well as understandable and not only because we read it from within (arguably) a more fluid society. Godwin's reverence towards social forms, his belief in their rigidity and their truth buoy up his self-esteem while, simultaneously, they prevent him from forcing his way in. His deference reveals the romanticism which his scientific training has both suppressed and exaggerated. His need for place becomes a need for heroism and that is possible only in the colonies, where the *arriviste* can be lost in the ambassador of culture.

When he is most agonized about his deception of Sidwell and the rest of the Warricombe family, Godwin dreams of travelling abroad again:

> He must resume his purpose of seeking some distant country, where new conditions of life would allow him to try his fortune at least as an honest adventurer. In many parts of colonial England his technical knowledge would have a value, and were there not women to be won beneath other skies [...]? Reminiscences of scenes and figures in novels he had read nourished the illusion. He pictured some thriving little town at the ends of the earth [...] he saw the ideal colonist [...] with two or three lovely daughters about him [...] living amid romantic dreams of the old world, and of the lover who would some day carry them off (with a substantial share of papa's wealth) to Europe and the scenes of their imagination.
>
> (pp. 212–13)[19]

It is characteristic of the novel's knottiness, the involutions of its ironies, that this passing fancy (Godwin soon abandons the idea) is recalled repeatedly by the sub-plot concerning Malkin. Malkin is one of Peak's London friends who secretly pursues Bella Jacox, the barely pubescent daughter of the vulgar Mrs Jacox. When rebuffed, Malkin retreats to New Zealand and returns towards the end of the book, claiming to be attached to the daughter of an ideal colonist, only to rediscover his passion for Bella, who is now of marriageable age. Malkin's ideal wife would be a perfect *tabula rasa* to whom he could teach his advanced views. While he is away in New Zealand, he arranges for a highly qualified governess to educate his prospective mate. The imperial dream is realized by colonizing the lower class. Once that is achieved, one can reclaim one's right to take part in the 'old, hidebound civilisation' by visiting 'the scenes of [...] imagination' (pp. 212–13). Malkin and his young wife go on honeymoon to the sights of Europe: Switzerland, Rome and Naples. There, to confirm the irony, they come across Godwin Peak.

The Malkin plot reflects one impulse behind Godwin's hopes and, through its comic absurdity, suggests that Godwin may outgrow his earlier errors. Gissing, however, disappoints this hope. At the end of the book, Peak's poverty is relieved by his inheriting money from Marcella Moxey, the sister of Christian Moxey, another of Godwin's schoolfriends and herself as radical and emancipated as any of them. Marcella had been in love with Godwin, and he had never recipro-cated; in an act of disinterested generosity that he can scarcely credit, she bequeaths him £800 so that he will be free to marry Sidwell. He accepts the money but, after a struggle, Sidwell turns him down. So 'with a substantial share of [...] wealth' (p. 213) Godwin goes on a tour of the Continent, to all the scenes of his imagination and imagining that money will make him free to join society.

> On the Continent I shall make no fixed abode, but live in the places where cosmopolitan people are to be met. I shall make friends; with money at command, one may hope to succeed in that. [...] Nothing to hide, no shams, no pretences. Let who will inquire about me. I am an independent Englishman, with so and so much a year.
>
> (p. 396)

All this is spoken to Earwaker, Godwin's schoolfriend. The contrast between them is distressing and it is heightened by the cautious reser-vations Earwaker expresses about this latest 'romantic dream of the old world' (p. 213). While the other characters are gradually being settled by the plot, Godwin, the most gifted of them, has no route into com-promise. His obtuse persistence in dreaming of a hypostasized 'society'

and in hoping to enter it while remaining 'independent' is at once disagreeable, poignant and chilling. The bequest has left him where he
was, only more arrogant – where earlier 'one might perchance make
acquaintances', now he 'shall make friends'. Furthermore, his greater
arrogance destroys his irony. Possessing wealth blinds him to the coincidence between money and culture that he dryly observed when,
earlier, he dreamed of carrying off the girl, plus 'a substantial share of
papa's wealth' (p. 213).

The harshest of these judgements on Godwin comes in his last letter
to Earwaker, written after he has been very ill in Naples. Malarial fever,
he writes, 'came of some monstrous follies there's no need to mention.
A new and valuable experience. I know what it is to look steadily into
the eyes of Death' (p. 415). The clipped, fragmented sentences pigeon-
hole the experience as valuable without valuing it; Godwin's tone
keeps him an aristocrat to the very end. He remains 'what he was',
'pinnacled above mankind' (p. 30), even when 'mankind' is himself
alone. A pinnacle is a infinitesimal point, where it is hard to keep your
balance and where balance is everything. The word implies the
cramped condition of a displaced person and the inhuman equanimity
Godwin aspires to when he says he has looked 'steadily into the eyes of
Death'. One would normally say the *face* of Death: looking into
another person's eyes is always difficult and to do so steadily is an act
of commitment.[20] Godwin has turned into the English gentleman he
aimed at becoming: well-dressed, discreet, formal. He is the 'English
Gordon' of Geoffrey Hill's *The Mystery of the Charity of Charles Péguy*
(1983), 'stepping down sedately into the spears'.[21] Godwin's 'steadily',
though, is more absolute and unbelievable than the velvety sedateness
of General Gordon, regal and aloof. It is felt as a contrast with the true
steadiness of Earwaker, patiently listening to his friends and 'steadily
making his way in the world' (p. 232).

Godwin, one might say, continually mistakes *calm* for *steadiness*, so
that (at the crucial moment of his first lie) he 'encounters [Buckland's]
steady searching gaze with a perfectly calm smile' (p. 128). In the same
way, in his last conversation with Earwaker, he underestimates the cost
and the limits of success. 'You look back on life,' he suggests, 'no doubt,
with calm and satisfaction.' 'Rather, with resignation,' Earwaker replies.
Godwin sees his friend as contentedly submissive, in the same way that
he sees Sidwell as uncomplicatedly devout. Earwaker rejects this image of
himself and questions Godwin's belief in freedom. 'But what form,'
Earwaker asks his friend, 'will your happiness take?' (pp. 395–6).
Earwaker's resignation does not bring with it the ease Godwin imagines

nor an untroubled harmony between self and world. Instead, Earwaker accepts that happiness implies limitation.

Earwaker is resigned because he accepts the limitedness of his power and freedom. While we admire him for this, we remember that he is lucky enough to be limited. In the opening chapter, where the various school-fellows receive prizes, Bruno Chilvers is first in almost everything and Godwin Peak an inglorious second (except in Logic where he excels). Earwaker, however, 'hitherto undistinguished', wins both prizes in English and nothing else (p. 10). Steadiness, the quality that the book yearns for most intensely, seems to be made possible by self-knowledge and self-knowledge is brought about by knowledge of one's limitations. The contrast between Earwaker's sobriety and Godwin's wild, rebellious ambitions does not mark the latter out as just 'another deluded superman' (which is John Carey's judgement of him).[22] Peak is deluded because he is unlucky enough to have no limitations – intellectual, familial or social. His cravings 'to be a man' and 'to be what he was', similarly, do not betray unquenchable hubris. Rather, they are the result of a natural desire for place being distorted by exile into an abstract idea of identity. He pursues Sidwell in the hope of finding relief from the need to attain such an identity. Through her, he may 'knit [himself] into the social fabric' (p. 396) – this fabric he takes her both to represent and, innocently, to inhabit. The completeness of her social integration allows her, in his eyes, to be what she is. It is an idealization of her which the book shows to be false – her life is more complex and compromised than Godwin can perceive it to be. Yet, it is an idealization that Godwin cannot avoid. Sympathy for him is coupled, moreover, with a sense that his aim is, in some ways, admirable. Without realizing it and without knowing how, Godwin is trying to recover the 'normal' situation – the one, that is, where he would be both independent and part of a tradition, like all his fellows, who are admitted into social life either by their filial inheritance or through a particular, professional talent.

For this reason, Godwin is particularly susceptible to Devon, a place chosen with geographical precision by Gissing as well as autobiographical pleasure. 'Devonshire means' (to Henry James) 'the perfection of England', and Godwin talks of it as epitomizing all that is good in the nation.[23] At the same time, it is remote enough from the centre to give him a chance of independence. It can be, imaginably, a part of 'colonial England' – a place already English to the core yet offering Godwin a small, unusual chance of becoming 'an honest adventurer'.[24]

Notes

1. For details of composition, see Michael Collie, *The Alien Art: A Critical Study of George Gissing's Novels* (Folkestone: Dawson, 1979), pp. 135–44.

2. See Pierre Coustillas: 'It is a novel firmly rooted in the substance of [Gissing's] life and, as such, a fruitful, if dangerous quarry for the biographer' (George Gissing, *Born in Exile*, ed. Pierre Coustillas (Brighton: Harvester Press, 1978), p. ix), and Jacob Korg: '*Born in Exile* dramatizes the limitations of the scientific materialist philosophy as a spiritual guide' (Jacob Korg, *George Gissing: A Critical Biography* (Seattle: University of Washington Press, 1963), pp. 175–6).

3. See Adrian Poole, *Gissing in Context* (Basingstoke: Macmillan, 1975), p. 173: 'This reading of the novel sees it primarily as an anatomy of the psychology of exile'; and John Goode, *George Gissing: Ideology and Fiction* (London: Vision Press, 1978), p. 61: 'what dominates Peak's mind is a concept of class, and although this is ideologically modified, it is not in such a way that the class structure is challenged.' I am very grateful to Adrian Poole for his comments on an early draft of this essay.

4. Elizabeth Gaskell, *North and South* (London: Dent, 1993), p. 33.

5. Gissing wrote of Dickens: 'Among his supreme merits is that of having presented in abiding form one of the best of our national ideals – rural homeliness' (quoted in Goode, *George Gissing: Ideology and Fiction*, p. 20).

6. *The Collected Letters of George Gissing*, ed. Paul F. Matthieson, Arthur C. Young and Pierre Coustillas (Ohio: Ohio University Press, 1990–), V, 36. Further references to this edition are given in the text by volume and page number.

7. Goode, *Ideology and Fiction*, p. 56: 'Gissing is one of the most reactionary writers I know'. See also John Carey, *The Intellectuals and the Masses* (Oxford: Oxford University Press, 1992), p. 113: 'But much of what Godwin believes in, Gissing himself never outgrew'.

8. On this aspect of the book, see Charles Swann, 'Sincerity and Authenticity: the Problem of Identity in *Born in Exile*', *Literature and History*, 10 (1984), 165–86.

9. 'Paroxysms' is frequently used – see George Gissing, *Born in Exile*, ed. David Grylls (London: Dent, 1993), pp. 253, 319. Further references to *Born in Exile* are given in the text by page number from this edition. Similarly, Godwin is convulsive: 'sudden confusion beset his mind – a sense of having been guilty of monstrous presumption – a panic which threw darkness about him and made him grasp the chair convulsively' (*Born in Exile*, p. 223).

10. T. S. Eliot, 'To the Indians who Died in Africa', ll. 12–13 and 'Ash Wednesday', IV. 29, in *Collected Poems 1909–1962* (London: Faber and Faber, 1963), pp. 231, 101. See Derek Traversi, *T. S. Eliot: The Longer Poems* (London: Bodley Head, 1976), p. 77 for discussion of the quotation from the *Salve Regina*.

11. See *Letters*, IV, 282 and V, 11 for Gissing's comments on the novel's title.

12. The persistent desire for home, despite rejection by it and exile from it, is discussed in relation to the exiles from Nazi Germany in David Morley and Kevin Robins, 'No Place like *Heimat*: Images of Home(land) in European

Culture', *Space and Place: Theories of Identity and Location*, eds Erica Carter, James Donald and Judith Squires (London: Lawrence & Wishart, 1993), pp. 3–31, and Dan Stone, 'Homes without *Heimats*? Jean Améry at the Limits', *Angelaki*, 2 (1995), 91–100.

13. Buckland's name connects him to Devon, in particular, to Axminster, William Buckland's hometown. Similarly, Sidwell is named after a local saint. Wherever, therefore, Godwin finds a possible home, he finds somewhere that has already been colonized by earlier occupants.

14. Bruno's 'aptitude' is contrasted with Godwin's brain: 'a brain inferior to that of few men' (*Born in Exile*, pp. 112–13). Godwin, Buckland, Earwaker, Marcella Moxey and Sylvia Moorhouse, all the young freethinkers in the book, possess unmediated intelligence. Such braininess is another aspect of the ambiguous freedom which they enjoy and/or escape in the course of the novel.

15. Samuel Taylor Coleridge, 'To the Rev. George Coleridge' (1797), ll. 17–18: 'Me from the spot where first I sprang to light / Too soon transplanted'; and 'Frost at Midnight', ll. 54–5, and l. 52, *Poetical Works*, ed. Ernest Hartley Coleridge (Oxford: Oxford University Press, 1912), pp. 174, 242.

16. 'Yesterday I went to Budleigh Salterton [...]. Coleridge's country lies in the valley of the Otter, which flows into the sea just beyond Budleigh' (*Letters*, IV, 270). Later, in Somerset, Gissing enjoys the 'Exquisite rural scenery [...] because of old stories connected with it', in particular those concerning Wordsworth and Coleridge (*Letters*, V, 111).

17. Mrs Peak's piety would have been offended by the word 'parson', which was 'usually more or less depreciatory' according to the *OED*, which quotes Hannah More: 'The clergy are spoken of under the contemptuous appellation of The Parsons'.

18. Godwin resembles the colonized person, who impersonates the manners and beliefs of the colonizing power, and does so excessively, with an idealistic naïvety which proves his or her failure to assimilate – a failure implicit in the need to attempt assimilation at all. See Rosemary Marangoly George's discussion of immigrant narratives in *The Politics of Home: Postcolonial Relocations and Twentieth-Century Fiction* (Cambridge: Cambridge University Press, 1996), pp. 171–97.

19. Most of the action of *Born in Exile* takes place between 1884 and 1886. H. Rider Haggard's *King Solomon's Mines* was a bestseller in 1885 and *She* was serialized the following year. These may be the novels Gissing alludes to. Certainly, Haggard wrote of the colonies that their land '*makes a man*' and that, out there, 'it was possible for a man of moderate means to start his children in some respectable career [...] and to have a fair chance of getting on in the world' (quoted in Gail Ching-Liang Low, 'His Stories?: Narratives and Images of Imperialism', *Space and Place*, eds Carter, Donald and Squires, pp. 187–219 (p. 194)).

20. Earlier, Godwin had perceived Marcella Moxey's love for him 'when he unsuspectingly looked into her troubled face'; he cannot return it because 'he was himself incapable of pure devotedness' (*Born in Exile*, pp. 258–9).

21. Geoffrey Hill, *The Mystery of the Charity of Charles Péguy* (London: Agenda Editions and André Deutsch, 1983), p. 18.

22. Carey, *Intellectuals and the Masses*, p. 113.

23. Henry James, 'North Devon', *The Nation* (1872), repr. in *Transatlantic Sketches* (1875) and *English Hours* (1905); text from *Transatlantic Sketches*, Essay Index Reprint Series (Freeport, NY: Books for Libraries, 1972), pp. 33–43 (p. 33). On Devon's general significance, see Sam Smiles and Michael Pidgley, *The Perfection of England: Artist Visitors to Devon c.1750–1870*, (Plymouth: University of Plymouth, 1995). Godwin finds in Exeter 'natural delight in a form of beauty especially English' and in its surroundings 'A spot of exquisite retirement: happy who lived here in security from the struggle of life' (*Born in Exile*, pp. 117, 119). Gissing enjoyed the Devonshire countryside but remained more ambivalent about it: 'Somerset always seems to me much more genuinely rustic than Devon' (*Letters*, V, 111).

24. In this respect, it differs from Gissing's portrayal of Teignmouth in *In the Year of Jubilee* (1894), where the Devonshire countryside is charged with an innocent, though dangerous sexuality rather than representing a social idyll.

10
Stages of Sand and Blood: the Performance of Gendered Subjectivity in Olive Schreiner's Colonial Allegories

Scott McCracken

The appearance of the New Woman, typically characterized as riding a bicycle, smoking a cigarette and wearing bangs and bloomers, was nothing if not a performance, but this was more a matter of necessity than choice.[1] In the 1880s and 1890s, working- and middle-class women demanded a more independent public role in the spheres of work, politics and culture; but the pervasive image of the public woman was the actress, and the actress was herself closely tied in the public mind with the prostitute.[2] The New Woman's quest for a public role was hindered by the image of woman as spectacle rather than spectator and as commodity rather than agent. Feminists' aestheticization of the political was therefore part of an inevitable battle over representation. To paraphrase Walter Benjamin, while the reactionary press rendered suffragist politics aesthetic through cartoons, parody and public ridicule, feminists responded by politicizing art.[3] In poetry, plays, novels, short stories and allegories, in processions, fashion, placards, slogans and flags, the woman movement (as it then proclaimed itself) fought over the sign of woman as it attempted to transform women's public role.[4] Questions of performativity were central to these struggles.

Performance played an important role in the fiction of one of the most original writers of the late-Victorian period, Olive Schreiner. Born and brought up in colonial South Africa, Schreiner's first novel, *The Story of an African Farm* (1883), created a sensation when it was published in London. A pioneer of what came to be called 'New Woman fiction', her novels, allegories and political writings engage and counter masculinist narratives of modernity, but her own accounts, like virtually all writings on gender in the period, were indebted to social Darwinism. Like many New Woman writers, Schreiner had a complicated relationship with the novel form. Despite the success of *The Story of an African Farm*, she never completed another novel and seemed happier writing allegories, which she found to be a more effective way of representing feminist ideas. The New Woman is represented as a performance in two of the short allegories published in her collection, *Dreams* (1891). In 'Three Dreams in a Desert', scenes are staged in front of an ungendered dreamer/narrator, who elicits meaning from them in dialogue with a male interpreter. In 'The Sunlight Lay Across My Bed', the New Woman's experience of the city is related to a history composed of tableaux of exploitation. Both allegories are remarkable in their recognition of the importance of colonialism for the formation of modern, European, gendered subjects. All New Women writers were working within the constraints already laid down by social Darwinism where the discourse of gender was enmeshed in the discourse of Empire; but Schreiner's allegories are unique in the way they take the available categories of 'race' and gender and show them to be performative rather than essential terms.

The concepts of performativity and performance have moved to the centre of recent debates in cultural studies.[5] The most influential recent work on performativity and cultural politics has been provoked by Judith Butler. The debate was begun in Butler's *Gender Trouble*, but as Emily Apter has acknowledged, at that time Butler used the term sparingly, preferring 'parody' to performativity. The concept emerged more fully in Butler's later work, *Bodies that Matter*, which was partly a response to *Gender Trouble*'s critics. Here she argued forcibly against any impression that the performative statement – 'what I say is what I do' – indicates a free choice by a humanist subject. In Butler's terms, Schreiner's understanding of colonialism as one of the constraints that limits the performance of a New Woman subjectivity can be understood in terms of what Butler calls the 'paradox of subjectivation':

> the subject who would resist such norms is itself enabled, if not produced, by such norms. Although this constitutive restraint does not foreclose the possibility of agency, it does locate agency as a reiterative or rearticulatory practice, immanent to power, and not a relation of external opposition to power.[6]

This recognizably Foucauldian formulation is useful in that it complicates any simple idea of resistance: the subject's ability to act is structured by already existing constraints (norms). As a paradox it describes well the position of the New Woman, for whom the script had already been written. However, Butler's philosophical account of the formation of the subject pays too little attention to the insight of an earlier theorist of performativity, Bertolt Brecht. Brecht argued that, in the performance, the actor inevitably draws attention to the conditions that limit the production.[7] In 'Three Dreams in a Desert' and 'The Sunlight Lay Across My Bed', Schreiner draws attention to the limits of the stage on which the New Woman performed.

Allegory was of key importance to her project. In 1888 she wrote to Ernest Rhys, 'Sometimes I find by throwing the thing into the form of an allegory I can condense five or six pages into one, with no loss, but gain to clearness'.[8] Whereas in her novels and non-fictional writings she tended to oscillate between the explanatory power of social Darwinist discourse and her developing anti-racist, anti-colonial politics, allegory allowed her to explore a more flexible materialism than that offered by nineteenth-century science.[9] She first employed the form in *The Story of an African Farm* (1883), where the invasion of the farm by the impostor Bonaparte Blenkins represents the violence of colonialism. Bonaparte inflicts a reign of terror on the farm's children as he attempts to gain possession of the land. As Anne McClintock has pointed out, the African population is pushed to the margins of the text, marking the border points, the edges of the stage upon which the action happens.[10] The allegory erases and then re-presents history, complicating a linear narrative and distancing familiar co-ordinates.[11] In *The Story of an African Farm*, the experience of Africans is denied only to return in that of the white settlers. In the figure of Lyndall, the New Woman heroine, feminist consciousness and the experience of colonialism are brought together.

The Story of an African Farm was written when Schreiner's anti-imperialism was still underdeveloped. By 1896 she was writing to J. X. Merriman, 'There are two and only two questions in South Africa, the native question and the question – Shall the whole land fall into the hands of a knot of Capitalists. The Dutch and English question [...] is nothing – in fifty years it shall not be'.[12] In a letter a few months later she expresses a 'peculiar antipathy towards novels' to the same correspondent; and already in a collection of allegories published in 1891, *Dreams*, she had begun to explore further the relationship between New Woman subjectivity and the history of colonialism.[13] In 'Three Dreams in a Desert' and 'The Sunlight Lay Across My Bed', the performance of a New Woman subjectivity is staged through two powerful images, sand and blood respectively, each of which represents both a history of gendered difference and of colonial dispossession. While Schreiner never provides a full critique of colonialism, her allegories are sufficiently self-reflexive to site the New Woman as both enabled and limited by Empire. In 'Three Dreams in a Desert', the African desert is the stage and the New Woman the performer. The image of the desert figures in almost all Schreiner's fiction. Both *The Story of an African Farm* and *From Man to Man* (her third, last and unfinished novel, published posthumously in 1926) open with the South African karoo. In both texts the New Woman heroine is brought into relief by an unforgiving terrain. The asocial, deterritorialized land-scape signifies the violent erasure described by Judith Butler as neces-sary for the performance of a new subjectivity. For Butler, the attainment of subjecthood is 'reiterative and citational'; it follows a prior cultural script but 'exclusions haunt signification as its abject borders or as that which is strictly foreclosed'.[14] Butler, however, pays remarkably little attention to questions of audience. By contrast, in Brecht's writings, the term *'Gestus'* also describes a performative act that is 'reiterative and citational', but the *Gestus* deliberately draws attention to the stage, denaturalizing the conditions of the act and showing it to be socially constructed: 'The epic theatre [...] works out scenes where people adopt attitudes of such a sort that the social laws under which they are acting spring into sight.'[15] Combining both insights, we can see that Schreiner's desert is a *tabula rasa* and a knowing literary device: a stage that is foregrounded to demonstrate the limiting conditions of colonialism. In this sense she employs a *Verfremdungseffekt* ('distancing' or sometimes 'alienation' effect) that draws the audience's attention to the edges of her stage. Thus, the performance is seen to be enacted within a delimited time and space.

The literary genealogy of the desert is too long to trace fully here, but at least two strong influences are clearly present. The first is the Bible. The Christian imagery is so strong in Schreiner's texts that it is difficult to believe that she had rejected the Protestant faith of her missionary parents. In fact, Schreiner adapts the role of the prophet in the wilder-ness, taking the force of its imposition of truth and turning it into a dialogue so that truth is not given, but negotiated. The role of Christianity in the process of colonization is foregrounded as one of the norms that constrains her text. The second powerful influence is Romanticism. For the Romantics, the desert figured the limit of ra-tional civilization: nature to its culture. In Shelley's 'Ozymandias' (and *Dreams* is clearly indebted to Shelley), the traveller is confronted by ruins in 'the lone and level sands' and instructed to 'Look on my Works, ye Mighty, and despair!'[16] The metaphor of the border is one of the central images of 'Three Dreams'. Light and shade, wake and sleep, dream and reality are the alternate states between which the allegory moves. In the opening passage, we are told, 'all along the horizon the air throbbed'.[17] The dreamer/narrator is 'on the border', while in the desert itself the allegorical figure, woman, emerges from beneath the sand, from which she is at first almost indistinguishable, to rise and act.

The articulation of a New Woman subjectivity is thus a definition of borders. It marks a division between the conditions of action and action itself (stage and performance), and between actor and society (stage and audience). In this process of separation, Africa, in the shape of the desert, is cast off. It is, to use the psychoanalytic term employed by Butler, abjected. The subject, here literally, throws away that which would deprive it of a meaningful autonomy.[18] The period before this separation is signified by the interpenetration of body and desert: 'the ground was wet with her tears and her nostrils blew up the sand' ('Three Dreams in a Desert', p. 70). Selfhood, in so far as it is defined at all at this early stage, is defined by the limits of her body. The moment of action or agency occurs with the onset of modernity, the 'Age-of-nervous-force', and this requires a more sustainable boundary between subject and the abject, which, nonetheless remains the ground on which it the subject stands. Like a desert or the apparently depopulated space of the colony, the 'abject designates', in Butler's words, 'precisely those "unlivable" and "uninhabitable" zones of social life which are [despite appearances] nevertheless densely populated by those who do not enjoy the status of the subject, but whose living under the sign of the "unlivable" is required to circumscribe the domain of the subject.'[19]

Schreiner's ambivalence about the actual (rather than abstract) inhabitants of the karoo was demonstrated in a letter to Mary Sauer, where she felt able only to make a weak case against the 'inevitable' extermination of the 'Bushmen': 'I don't why the Bushmen must die: they have kept alive a variety of the original wild cattle of Europe in a certain Park in England.'[20] In 'Three Dreams', that ambivalence is signalled by the traces left in the desert of a sedimented history of the excluded. This history can be read in the similarity of the mounds to archaeological, perhaps Egyptian, ruins, in the 'Rocks of language' and in the 'hard-baked clay of Ancient Customs'. These are references to nineteenth-century philology and anthropology, those potentially enabling – but so often disenabling discourses – which drew heavily on what colonialism had thrown away to define modern gendered subjectivity.[21] Thus the desert signifies both erasure and historical precedent: deterritorialization and reterritorialization. In effect, it functions as

Bertolt Brecht's provisional but functional stage for a transformative performance, where it is the limits of the performance that are foregrounded. This is where the woman's gaze is fixed: 'And she seemed to look for something on the far-off border of the desert that never came' ('Three Dreams in a Desert', p. 72).

Schreiner's attention to the limits of the stage on which a New Woman subjectivity could be performed acknowledges the narrow space available to her, caught as she was between social Darwinist definitions of woman as less evolved and a rigidly masculinist version of intellectual thought.[22] 'Three Dreams' attempts to explore that space, but Schreiner's own use of social-Darwinist categories in her non-fiction raises the question of how far she means the prostrate figure in the desert to be interpreted as an African woman, still bound by the Age-of-Muscular-Force ('Three Dreams', p. 70). In an unpublished fragment (that was to have been an introduction to a new edition of Mary Wollstonecroft's 1792 *A Vindication of the Rights of Woman*), Schreiner reproduces a self-description by an African woman, which she saw as stemming from 'the perception that it is her *duty to submit*': 'It is a woman; sell it – let us get many oxen for it; let it now bear child and work. See! she has the child – give it milk; she works in the field, she builds the house, she is the servant; let her work.'[23] Nonetheless, while here Schreiner felt compelled to represent an unforgiving state of being, her allegories permit a more complex account of the relationship between subjectivity and 'nature'. Thus, in 'Three Dreams', the emergent subject of the New Woman is both cut off from and yet dependent on that which she leaves behind as a stage for future action. Her performance dramatizes the contradiction between the material body and subjectivity: 'veins stood out'; 'her sides heaved'; 'drops stood out on her' ('Three Dreams', p. 73).

Self-sufficiency is urged by the masculine interpreter: '*she must help herself*' is an imperative that seems to insist that autonomy requires a violent exclusion of the past and society; but while the allegorical woman appears to act on her own, the meaning of her actions (and to some extent her actions themselves) are produced intersubjectively in a dialogic relationship with the two who watch. The contrast between the two actors and the watchers suggests a dialectic between necessity and freedom, where the watchers represent a less absolute, discursively constructed version of gender. That the narrator's gender is not identified contrasts the undecided nature of identity in culture with the overdetermined conditions that weigh down woman as actor.

This suggests that Schreiner's sense of performativity is closer to Brecht's than to that of Butler, who seems unwilling to countenance the dialogical element in performativity. Both Brecht and Schreiner deliberately draw attention to the dialectic between performance as bounded act and that which the performance disavows. This has the effect of foregrounding the historical dimension of the drama – the way in which to act (in both senses) can never be just 'a reiterative or rearticulatory practice', because the new context (or stage) separates and makes it different from what has gone before.[24] In the theatre that difference is figured by the division between stage and audience. Whereas naturalist theatre erects a 'fourth wall' to create the illusion of a timeless world or perfect identity, Brecht's theatre situated each gesture in a historical and dialogical context. Schreiner's allegories attempt a similar feat. New Woman subjectivity emerges in the context of a history of colonialism, but the colonial stage also provides a fresh context for action – the dramatic dialogues that would define a new feminist politics.

The other important limit for New Woman subjectivity is defined by the dominant perception of masculinity or, what we might call more broadly, masculinism in Victorian thought. Here Schreiner's approach is ingenious. If we understand the law of the father as a centrifugal force which organizes meaning around a powerful masculine signifier, then Schreiner both stages and disperses the unilateral logic of that power through a succession of male figures who interpret the vision in each of the three Dreams. The figures might be seen to represent the systems of knowledge produced by Victorian culture with which any emergent subjectivity must grapple. In the case of Schreiner this engagement was from a marginal position in the Empire, deprived of the educational opportunities available to the male intellectuals with whom she debated. The narrator asks questions of the interpreters (questions which perhaps they are incapable of asking themselves), but whose answers she/he has to relate to her/his own observations and experience. This process re-stages Schreiner's own feelings of powerlessness in her discussions with openly imperialist and social-Darwinist academics in London, men such as Karl Pearson and Havelock Ellis. On the one hand, the constraints placed on the woman in the desert embody the narrator's lack of educational capital. On the other, the staging of that exclusion provides the opportunity for a dialogue that makes the question one of social rather than natural laws.

In this sense, the allegories are a form of *écriture feminine*, engaging with and attempting to put into question systems of thought that exclude women's experience. The plurality of male figures and the undecidability of the narrator's gender mark a refusal to essentialize gender positions. In the second Dream (which continues the metaphors of limits and borders), the old man is not himself reason, but carries reason, which he then hands to the woman. Later in the same dream, masculinity appears as a burden on women, reversing the imagery of the first dream, so that it is not women's reproductive role that holds humanity back, but men's inability to overcome their dependent and sexualized nature. Here man is what Edward Carpenter called 'the ungrown', unable to make the leap into subjecthood, while it is woman who envisions a more equal relationship: 'He has lisped one word only to me in the desert – "Passion!" I have dreamed he might learn to say "Friendship" in that land' ('Three Dreams', p. 80).[25]

If the first dream deals with the stage built by history, the second dream confronts the future. Once again the allegorical woman is positioned at a border. Once again a process of divestment is required to free her from her past. She has to achieve a clear outline, a firmer definition of the body: 'one white garment that clung close to her' ('Three Dreams', p. 78). In other words, a hardening of identity (again against an African landscape) is necessary if she is to realize the vision that appears on the horizon, at the edge of possibility.

> 'I see nothing, but sometimes, when I shade my eyes with my hand, I think I see on the further bank trees and hills, and the sun shining on them!'
> He said, 'That is the Land of Freedom.'
>
> 'Three Dreams', p. 76

The transformative passage across the river, which again is full of Christian imagery, also involves a dialectic between individualist and collectivist visions.

> 'Have you seen the locusts how they cross a stream? First one comes down to the water-edge, and it is swept away, and then another comes and then another, and then another, and at last with their bodies piled up a bridge is built and the rest pass over.'
>
> 'Three Dreams', p. 82

The analogy of the locusts recalls the red ants which appear before the dream 'in the red sand' and after it in their 'thousands'. If the ants are inhabitants of the 'uninhabitable' desert and suggest a collective form of society, the locusts suggest both the mass politics of the late nineteenth century and modernity's capacity for mass destruction: the waste of 'a thousand times ten thousand and thousands of thousands'. The costs of attaining subjecthood are enormous. Crossing the river is a kind of sacrifice, and the individuality the woman invokes is as likely to be destroyed as sustained by the forces that created it.[26] So it is significant that the third dream is a vision of collectivity, in which heterosexual and same-sex couples exist in the kind of free association envisioned by nineteenth-century utopian socialists. Here the religious connotations of heaven are firmly materialized: it is 'On earth' ('Three Dreams', p. 84). However, at this point, Schreiner deploys one final *Verfremdungseffekt*. The third vision is abruptly distanced in the last line, which brings back to consciousness the dream-state's reliance on wish-fulfilment. The sun, which has been ever-present (and is, perhaps, the progenitor of the dreams) is unexpectedly gendered: 'Then the sun passed down behind the hills; but I knew that the next day *he* would rise again' ('Three Dreams', p. 85; my emphasis). The shock effect of the masculine pronoun is to render starkly present the current state of things in Africa, where colonial and gender relations remain unchanged, if not unchangeable.

The second allegory, 'The Sunlight Lay Across my Bed', seems to start where 'Three Dreams' leaves off, but the title directs the African sun into the heart of the metropolis. The bedroom constructs a feminine position by context rather than through an identifying pronoun, evoking what Schreiner in *Woman and Labour* called 'sex-parasitism': middle-class women's dependence on men for support and their reduction to a purely sexual function.[27] The narrator is placed in relation to the discipline of the city: 'the policeman's beat on the pavement'; structures of class and gender, 'the wheels of carriages roll home from houses of entertainment'; and, with the 'woman's laugh below my window', against the other women who work in those houses ('Sunlight', p. 133). The open window was often used in nineteenth-century texts to construct the bourgeois subject as above and distinguished from the proletarian mass. The disorder of outside was figured by the crowd and the noise of the street and that disorder was often explicitly gendered in the voices of prostitutes.[28] Here the woman's laugh complicates the construction of femininity and announces a dream that will explore further the relationships between the bedroom, the imperial city and Empire.

The dream itself proceeds directly from the preoccupations of the earlier allegory. This time the dialogue is with 'God' and in the tradition of religious allegorists like Dante or Bunyan, visions of heaven and hell figure alternative realities, each of which relates to histories of colonialism. Hell for example is 'fair', an epithet that signifies at once beauty, equality and whiteness; the women there are 'tall and graceful and have yellow hair' ('Sunlight', p. 134); but apparent fairness disguises competitive individualism. In the first of several images that combine religious myth with an evocation of vampirism, the narrator observes the inhabitants of hell poisoning fruit.

> God said, 'They touch it with their lips; when they have made a tiny wound in it with their fore-teeth they set in it that which is under their tongues: they close it with their lip – that no man may see the place and pass on.'
> I said to God, 'Why do they do it?'
> God said, 'That another may not eat.'
> I said to God, 'But if they poison all then none dare eat; what do they gain?'
> God said, 'Nothing.'
>
> 'Sunlight', pp. 135–6

The narrator is then led to where 'Hell opened out onto a plain', but this time, the ruling metaphor is not the landscape. The narrator observes a Bacchanalian feast where not wine but blood is consumed. While this has been interpreted as a socialist critique of class exploitation, the image goes well beyond this.[29] In the context of nineteenth-century colonial discourse, blood signifies not just the extraction of surplus labour, but 'race', a double monstrosity that was to be exploited later in the decade by Bram Stoker.[30] The drama works through a number of intersecting levels of meaning. Firstly, there is the Christian Eucharist (of which the vampire myth is a form of perversion, just as the stake through the heart repeats the crucifixion), but here the blood drunk is not Christ's but the blood of the exploited. The hypocrisy of a sacrament in the context of exploitation is mocked in the figure of a priest whose sleeves and beard are soaked. Secondly, there is the powerful image of mixing. The orgy involves both consumption and a bizarre form of miscegenation with those it excludes. The wine/blood is extracted then exchanged and shared between men, women and children so that it binds together the 'fair' family:

> And mothers poured out wine and fed their little children with it, and men held up the cup to women's lips and cried, 'Beloved! drink,' and women held their lovers' flagons and held them up: and yet the feast went on.
>
> 'Sunlight', p. 143

This drama underlines the integral relationship between the Victorian middle-class family and concepts of 'race', where a racial other is needed to sustain a pristine sense of civilized society. Again it is reproduced through the reactions and observations of the narrator in her dialogue with God; and it is she who draws attention to the edge of the stage, the curtain that moves with Shelley's revolutionary (West) wind.[31] Instead of envisaging the collapse of this Empire, however, the narrator is taken back in time past a series of ruined banquet houses, each of which represents a former imperialism that collapsed under the weight of its own contradictions. The image in 'Three Dreams' of the desert as blank canvas gives way to images of the land as sedimented layers of imperial exploitation, each soaked in blood. By way of Rome, 'on seven hills', the 'marble blossoms' of Greece, Jerusalem and the scene of the crucifixion, the narrator travels to Egypt and back to the African landscape of 'Three Dreams': 'as I looked across the desert, I saw the sand gathered into heaps as though it covered something' ('Sunlight', p. 157). The allegory thus delves into an archaeology of colonial discourse leading from and to Africa and it is no accident that the image of co-operative labour in the utopian vision of the last dream involves digging. On one level the image evokes diamond mining and the transformation of South Africa from a pastoral to a capitalist–industrial economy, a transition that Schreiner herself witnessed when she went to live in the diamond fields as a young woman. On another level, the digging metaphor reverses the image of burial, which appears in both allegories. It suggests that, instead of denying it, a future collectivity will need to return to an abjected colonial history to achieve its identity.

Recent work on performativity has argued that identity is always a performance, but Schreiner's allegories suggest that we need to look carefully at the stage on which the performance takes place. In *Bodies that Matter*, Judith Butler argues against an invocation of matter as a ground of feminist enquiry. Instead matter should be seen as 'a sedimented history of sexual hierarchy and sexual erasures which should surely be an *object* of feminist inquiry, but which would be quite problematic as a *ground*'.[32] In this she adheres to the impetus of much post–structuralist theory which encourages us to abolish foundations. By contrast, Schreiner's solution was closer to Brecht's modernist impulse: the answer to the New Woman's dilemma was to dig deeper into the material conditions that limit agency. In Schreiner's allegories, the New Woman was not just a product of metropolitan centres. New Woman identities were performances played out betwixt and between colony and metropole. In 'Three Dreams in a Desert' the colony is the stage on which the New Woman performs, but where the limits of that stage limit the possibilities of the performance. In 'The Sunlight Lay Across My Bed', the dream shows that the metropolitan femininity must be understood in terms of a history of imperialism that has not yet ended. If the history of the colonized was still an absent voice – Schreiner did not directly acknowledge the subjectivity of the colonial subject – she was almost unique amongst her contemporaries in making an understanding of colonialism a necessary precondition for an understanding of freedom. Thus, at the end of the final dream in 'The Sunlight Lay Across My Bed', the narrator wakes to see the teeming masses of the city streets:

> In the streets below, men and women streamed past by hundreds; I heard the beat of their feet on the pavement. Men on their way to business; servants on errands; boys hurrying to school; weary professors pacing slowly the old street; prostitutes, men and women, dragging their feet wearily after last night's debauch; artists with quick impatient footsteps; tradesmen for orders; children to seek for bread [...].
> And suddenly I heard them cry loud as they beat, 'We are seeking! – we are seeking!'
>
> 'Sunlight', pp. 180–1

Notes

This essay was first published in *Women's Writing*, 3, no. 3 (1996).

1. See Patricia Marks, *Bicycles, Bangs and Bloomers* (Lexington, KT: Kentucky University Press, 1990).
2. See for example Jill Liddington, *One Hand Tied Behind Us: The Rise of the Women's Suffrage Movement* (London: Virago, 1979); Martha Vicinus, *Independent Women: Work and Community for Single Women 1850–1920* (London: Virago, 1985). There is an ongoing debate about the extent to which middle-class women were able to occupy public space in the late-nineteenth-century city. Janet Wolff argues that women were excluded from the public sphere: 'The Invisible Flâneuse: Women and the Literature of Modernity', *Theory, Culture and Society*, 2 (1985), 37–46. Elizabeth Wilson, on the other hand, cites evidence of women's increasing participation in the public life of the city and argues that the male flâneur was a fiction constructed in the face of the threat of the city's erosion of traditional gender roles: 'The Invisible *Flâneur*', *New Left Review*, no. 191 (1992), 90–110. For an essay arguing the close association of actresses with the New Woman

through a 'racialized' discourse see Bridge Elliot, 'New and Not so "New Women" on the London Stage: Aubrey Beardsley's Yellow Book Images of Patrick Campbell and Réjane', *Victorian Studies*, 31 (1987), 33–57.

3. See Sally Ledger, 'The New Woman and the Crisis of Victorianism', in *Cultural Politics at the Fin de Siècle*, eds Sally Ledger and Scott McCracken (Cambridge: Cambridge University Press, 1995), pp. 22–44.

4. See Lisa Tickner, *The Spectacle of Women* (Chicago: University of Chicago Press, 1988).

5. For recent work on performance and performativity see Judith Butler, *Gender Trouble* (New York: Routledge, 1990) and *Bodies that Matter: On the Discursive Limits of 'Sex'* (New York: Routledge, 1993); *Performativity and Performance*, eds Andrew Parker and Eve Kosofsky Sedgewick (New York: Routledge, 1995); *Performance and Cultural Politics*, ed. Elin Diamond (New York: Routledge, 1996).

6. Butler, *Bodies that Matter*, p. 15. See Emily Apter, 'Acting out Orientalism: Sapphic Theatricality in Turn-of-the-Century Paris', in Diamond (ed.), *Performance and Cultural Politics*, p. 15.

7. *Brecht on Theatre*, ed. John Willett (New York: Hill and Wang, 1966), p. 86.

8. *Olive Schreiner: Letters 1871–1899*, ed. Richard Rive (Oxford: Oxford University Press, 1988), p. 198.

9. See, for example, Schreiner's 1911 *Woman and Labour* (London: Virago, 1978), where Schreiner describes the breaking of the supposedly 'organic connection' between 'potatoes, pigs, mud-cabins and Irishman' in the colonies, where the Irish become judges within two generations (p. 165), but argues against intermarriage between 'races and classes which are in totally distinct stages of evolution' (p. 248).

10. Anne McClintock, *Imperial Leather: Race, Gender and Sexuality in the Colonial Contest* (New York: Routledge, 1995), p. 268.

11. The best account of Schreiner's allegorical method is given in Laura Chrisman, 'Allegory, Feminist Thought and the Dreams of Olive Schreiner' in *Edward Carpenter and Late Victorian Radicalism*, ed. Tony Brown (London: Frank Cass, 1990), pp. 126–50.

12. *Olive Schreiner: Letters 1871–1899*, p. 278 (25 May 1896).

13. *Ibid.*, p. 286 (29 June 1896).

14. Butler, *Bodies that Matter*, p. 188.

15. That the act is a social product then demonstrates that an alternative society is possible: 'Human behaviour is shown as alterable; man himself as dependent on certain political and economic factors and at the same time as capable of altering them' (*Brecht on Theatre*, p. 86).

16. Percy Bysshe Shelley, *The Poetical Works of Percy Bysshe Shelley* (London: George Newnes, 1902), p. 782.

17. Schreiner, 'Three Dreams in a Desert', in *Dreams* (London: T. Fisher Unwin, 1891), p. 67. Further references are given in the text by page number in this edition.

18. 'The abject has only one quality of the object – that of being opposed to the I. If the object, however, through its opposition, settles me within the fragile texture of a desire for meaning, which, as a matter of fact, makes me ceaselessly and infinitely homologous to it, what is abject, on the contrary is radically excluded and draws me towards the place where meaning collapses'

(Julia Kristeva, *Powers of Horror: An Essay on Abjection* (New York: Columbia University Press, 1982), pp. 1–2). I am indebted here to Anne McClintock's argument that European colonial identity was founded on the abjection of African women (see, for example, McClintock, *Imperial Leather*, p. 270). However, I disagree with McClintock when she suggests that in reading Schreiner, it is 'easy to forget she was walking on plundered land' (p. 266). Schreiner's use of the karoo as an image of lack shows that colonial dispossession is central to her concerns.

19. Butler, *Bodies that Matter*, p. 3.
20. *Olive Schreiner: Letters 1871–1899*, p. 285 (letter postmarked 25 May 1896).
21. For a full discussion of nineteenth-century anthropological theories in relation to ideas of gender difference, see Rosalind Coward, *Patriarchal Precedents: Sexuality and Social Relations* (London: Routledge & Kegan Paul, 1983).
22. See for instance Havelock Ellis, *Men and Women* (London: Scott, 1894).
23. Quoted in Chrisman, 'Allegory, Feminist Thought and the Dreams of Olive Schreiner', p. 138. Of course, this is not the only interpretation of the speech. For further discussion of its meaning for Schreiner see Chrisman's article, which also argues that Schreiner's allegories are directly connected to the theoretical problems with which she was grappling in the introduction.
24. Butler, *Bodies that Matter*, p. 15.
25. Edward Carpenter, 'Love's Coming of Age', in *Selected Writings* (London: Gay Men's Press, 1984), pp. 108–13.
26. Julia Kristeva argues that the law is what curtails sacrifice. Here sacrifice is needed to perform a new subjectivity in relation to the law (Kristeva, *Powers of Horror*, p. 112).
27. Schreiner, *Woman and Labour*, pp. 69–150.
28. See Peter Stallybrass and Allon White, *The Politics and Poetics of Transgression* (London: Methuen, 1986), pp. 136–9.
29. Joyce Avrech Berkman, *The Healing Imagination of Olive Schreiner: Beyond South African Colonialism* (Amherst, MA.: Massachusetts University Press, 1989), pp. 164–6.
30. Bram Stoker's *Dracula* was published in 1897. On the development of vampire fiction in the nineteenth century see Alex Warwick , 'Vampires and the Empires: Fears and Fictions of the 1890s'; for a reading of Stoker see Judith Halberstam, 'Technologies of Monstrosity'; both essays in *Cultural Politics at the Fin de Siècle*, pp. 202–20 and pp. 248–66. For an account of the 'symbolics of blood' in relation to 'race' and Empire see Ann Laura Stoler, *Race and the Education of Desire: Foucault's History of Sexuality and the Colonial Order of Things* (Durham, NC.: Duke University Press, 1995), especially pp. 19–54.
31. In Shelley's poem 'Ode to the West Wind' (1819), the wind is a revolutionary force, sweeping away the old order. The poem invokes images of drunkenness and the ruins of Mediterranean civilizations which Schreiner draws upon.
32. Butler, *Bodies that Matter*, p. 49.

11
Sexual Ethics in Fiction by Thomas Hardy and the New Woman Writers

Jil Larson

In the fiction published in the 1880s and 1890s that focuses on the 'New Woman' or late-Victorian feminist, the break from traditional assumptions about women and ethics is sharp but not definitive. Likewise the rejection of conventional aesthetic choices often leads these writers not to narrative methods that are wholly innovative and successful but to strange experiments. In this transitional literature, written during a period of cultural upheaval, the exaggerated and the extravagant invade realism, as if to startle readers out of their complacency. Formal innovations enable the exploration of a new sexual ethics. In keeping with Victorian novelistic tradition, the New Woman writers tell stories about love and marriage. But marriage is no longer the goal toward which everything inevitably tends; it is, instead, an object of the text's ethical scrutiny.

The characters in this fiction are self-conscious about the awkwardness of rejecting old beliefs and values when the new ones are so inchoate. In the words of Waldo's Stranger in Olive Schreiner's *The Story of an African Farm* (1883), 'To all who have been born in the old faith there comes a time of danger, when the old slips from us, and we have not yet planted our feet on the new.'[1] Evadne, in Sarah Grand's *The Heavenly Twins* (1893), notes something similar when she observes to her husband that he is not to blame for ruining her life: 'It is not our fault that we form the junction of the old abuses and the new modes of thought. Some two people must have met as we have for the benefit of others.'[2] The painful struggle of the characters reflects the challenge these authors faced when striving to write honestly about women's experience and to benefit those who would continue this endeavour in the future; such an endeavour, as Patricia Stubbs points out, entailed 'a political as well as an aesthetic struggle [...]. The inoffensive heroine who could shock no one was a highly political creature, and only the most determined of writers were prepared to modify, let alone transform her.'[3] If the transitional groping of the New Woman writing mars it aesthetically and dooms its heroines to frustration, thus weakening its political impact, the fiction nevertheless merits our attention for what it reveals about the ethical concerns of late-Victorian feminism.

It is an emotional literature that afforded its audience a new way of thinking about emotion. As Lyn Pykett emphasizes in her study of the sensation novel and New Woman fiction, 'to some of its earliest readers and critics the New Woman writing simply was feeling; it was an hysterical literature, written (and read) on the nerves'.[4] In addition to being emotionally charged, however, this fiction often takes emotion as its subject, investigating the interplay of feeling and reason in women's choices. As Pykett argues, many of these writers 'simultaneously celebrate the feminine and/as feeling, and problematise the conventional association of woman with feeling'.[5] In that sense, these writers anticipate the concerns of twentieth-century feminists.

Reading Thomas Hardy's late novels, especially *Tess of the d'Urbervilles* (1891) and *Jude the Obscure* (1895) in the context of the fiction of the New Woman has been an ongoing project of Victorianists at least since Penny Boumelha's study of sexual ideology in Hardy's novels, published in 1982. One of the most intriguing of the recent efforts to contextualize Hardy's fiction in this fashion occurs in John Kucich's book on Victorian ethics, *The Power of Lies.* Unlike Kucich and other literary critics who attribute the ethical contradictions of Hardy's novels to his gender and describe him as significantly less feminist than his female contemporaries, I argue that preconceptions about women, emotions and ethics have kept too many critics from recognizing what Hardy has in common with such late-century women writers as Olive Schreiner and Sarah Grand.[6]

Kucich considers Hardy to be a detached aesthete who scapegoats women and who distances himself from emotion, sexual desire and subjectivity. This reading betrays an assumption not shared by the narrators and implied authors of Hardy's novels – the belief that emotion and desire interfere with responsible ethical choice. As I interpret Hardy's fiction, one of its central ideas is that reason and emotion are not truly 'separate spheres'. Hardy rejects the totalizing, absolute nature of the Victorian doctrine of separate spheres, constructing instead a contextual ethics of particularity. Like Grand and Schreiner, he seeks to forge new definitions of what can constitute gender identity and sexual morality. In contrast to earlier Victorian novelists, these writers critique a sexual ideology that punishes women for acting on their emotions and desires. Admittedly, however, several features of New Woman writing tend to obscure this critique or even to render it ambivalent. First, this fiction often resists the separate-spheres belief that women are naturally associated with feeling and men with reason. These writers question such a stereotype. But they also seek to redeem the ethical and cognitive potential of emotion. They associate emotion with women but no longer diminish women's power by doing so. Second, because a woman's emotions can make her vulnerable, this fiction often contrasts women whose intellect and education arm them with direct methods of self-defence with women who rely more exclusively on emotions and desires that lead them to indirect forms of influence and manipulation. What this contrast obscures, however, is the role played by emotion in the intellectual development of these New Women, the degree to which feeling and reason are interrelated. The fiction dramatizes a new kind of flirtation; unlike the traditional coquette, the late-Victorian feminist flirts not only to attract attention and indulge her desires but also to experiment and learn. Finally, the heroines rarely escape punishment or emotionally crushing defeat of some sort, though this could be said to be a mark of the honesty of the fiction, a clear-eyed acknowledgement of all that thwarted even the most progressive of late-century women.

I argue, then, that in its treatment of emotions and sexual relationships, Hardy's *Jude the Obscure* shares both the feminist concerns of the New Woman writing and its ethically complex treatment of emotion, reason and gender. To test the validity of this argument, I shall read Hardy's novel in the context of Olive Schreiner's 'The Buddhist Priest's Wife' (written in 1890; published posthumously in 1923) and *The Story of an African Farm* and Sarah Grand's *The Heavenly Twins*.

'The Buddhist Priest's Wife' tells the story of a New Woman leaving for India who must say goodbye to the man she loves without letting him know that she loves him. Like *Jude the Obscure*, this story critiques the ideology of separate spheres and the double standard, even as it demonstrates that in their relationships with men, women may appear powerful when they are actually at the mercy of inflexible patriarchal rules and ingrained assumptions about gender. The intellect seems more educable than the emotions and drives; hence, according to Schreiner's heroine, men and women are most alike intellectually. In keeping with separate-spheres imagery, the story's New Woman imagines circular disks representing the sexes. When it comes to their power to reason, men and women are equal, and that half of each disk is identical, a bright red. But the red shades into different colours, blue in one and green in the other, when it is a matter of the personal and sexual, areas in which men and women, according to the heroine, are most starkly different in their emotions and behaviour. Adopting a view characteristic of the New Woman, Schreiner's heroine attributes the difference to 'nature': 'it's not the man's fault,' says the heroine, 'it's nature's'.[7] But if the story accepts this as a reality, it also makes it seem cruel and unfair, for this difference empowers the man and strips the woman of agency. The fiction suggests that in sexual relationships a measure of power and influence is granted to the woman who ethically compromises herself through passive manipulation. Schreiner's heroine refuses to play this game:

> If a man loves a woman, he has a right to try to make her love him because he can do it openly, directly, without bending. There need be no subtlety, no indirectness. With a woman it's not so; she can take no love that is not laid openly, simply, at her feet. Nature ordains that she should never show what she feels; the woman who had told a man she loved him would have put between them a barrier once and for ever that could not be crossed; and if she subtly drew him towards her, using the woman's means – silence, finesse, the dropped handkerchief, the surprise visit, the gentle assertion she had not thought to see him when she had come a long way to meet him, then she would be damned; she would hold the love, but she would have desecrated it by subtlety; it would have no value.
>
> 'The Buddhist Priest's Wife', p. 92

Schreiner reveals here how the New Woman differs from the traditional woman: she is ethically more scrupulous, but her capacity for love is at once her strength and her tragedy, for the depth of her thwarted emotional longing combined with her intelligence means that 'in one way she was alone all her life' (p. 84). Like other New Women, this heroine finds that she is unable to address both her intellectual and her emotional needs. Complexly interrelated as these needs are, Victorian culture nevertheless structures them as antithetical and mutually exclusive.

Schreiner's heroine is too intelligent to blunder into the trap of simply acting like a man, directly expressing what she feels and wants and thereby alienating herself from the more conventional man she loves, but she is also too emotional, too deeply in love, to rest content with being this man's friend. The story is dominated by its heroine's efforts to intellectualize and rationalize her pain, to control it through an ability to understand it. Clearly, her emotions and her attachment to a particular person have led her to her ideas about gender, sexuality and ethics, though as she sees it, the intellectual life is apart from emotions; it allows a woman to 'drop her shackles a little' ('The Buddhist Priest's Wife', p. 93). In that, it is like death. The story begins and ends with reference to the heroine's beauty in death. 'Death means so much more to a woman than a man,' she says; 'when you knew you were dying, to look round on the world and feel the bond of sex that has broken and crushed you all your life gone, nothing but the human left, no woman any more' (p. 93). Escaping the shackles of sex, whether through cogitation or through death, is but one aspiration of this New Woman; an equally strong aspiration arises from her desire to be loved by the man who hurts her when he denies her sexuality, when he says, 'You're the only woman with whom I never realise that she is a woman' (p. 93). Given the norms of late-Victorian society, once gender difference is overcome and a man recognizes the humanity of a woman, she no long represents romantic or sexual possibilities for him. The protagonist of 'The Buddhist Priest's Wife' is thus caught in a double-bind: wanting this man's love but refusing the assumptions about gender differences that seem to make it possible.

Like Schreiner's story, *Jude the Obscure* takes as its subject 'the inseparability of emotional and intellectual aspiration', and again the characters muse on the possibility of friendship across gender lines: 'If he could only get over the sense of her sex,' Jude Fawley thinks about Sue Bridehead, ' what a comrade she would make.'[8] But like the woman in Schreiner's story, he finds that his desire makes this impossible. In contrast to his uncomplicated physical attraction to Arabella, his feelings for Sue include both intellectual and emotional affinity. In part the connection he feels with Sue arises from their shared sensitivity, their emotional response to life, of which Hardy thoroughly approves despite the pain that accompanies their capacity for love, fellow-feeling and empathy. Kucich claims that in Hardy's fiction desire and emotionalism, especially as they are associated with women, interfere with honesty.[9] The trouble with this argument is that it obscures Hardy's critique of the assumption that rationality, with its often inflexible regard for principle, is superior to emotion and awareness of multiple perspectives, including those shaped by the feelings that arise from particular attachments.

The chapter of *Jude the Obscure* that is key to an understanding of this dimension of the novel's ethics is the one that focuses on Richard

Phillotson's deliberations about Sue's request for a separation from him. This chapter clearly illustrates Hardy's belief in the importance of emotion in ethical decision-making. In conversation with Gillingham, Phillotson explains his decision to release his wife from her marriage vows so that she can live with her lover. His friend attempts to reason with him, to talk him out of this unconventional decision, but Phillotson responds, 'I am only a feeler, not a reasoner' (*Jude*, p. 243). As the chapter makes clear, however, Phillotson is indeed reasoning, but his thinking is guided by emotion: by his love for Sue, by his empathy with her pain – which he metaphorically alludes to as her 'cries for help' – and by his intuitive recognition that she and Jude share an 'extraordinary sympathy or similarity' (p. 241).[10] 'I simply am going to act by instinct, and let principles take care of themselves,' Phillotson declares. The implied author leaves us in no doubt that this is a responsible, compassionate decision.

Kucich argues that 'Hardy's women are regularly aligned with emotionalism, as opposed to the customary rationality of his men', but he begs the question by assuming that emotion is emotionalism and therefore suspect, and also by opposing feeling and reason, which, as in this chapter of the novel, are only apparent opposites (*Power of Lies*, p. 228). Moreover, Hardy's novel subverts the separate-spheres ideology by creating men, such as Jude and Phillotson, who are as tender-hearted and emotional as the female characters, and women who are intellectuals. Kucich is right that Sue loses her capacity for moral reasoning by the end of the novel, as Tess does by the end of *Tess of the d'Urbervilles* (1891), while the male characters gain philosophical wisdom (*Power of Lies*, p. 230), but it is too often overlooked that Sue, the novel's New Woman, educates both Jude and Phillotson through her intellectual superiority. Jude describes her as 'a woman whose intellect was to mine like a star to a benzoline lamp' (*Jude*, p. 422). Phillotson admits that 'her intellect sparkles like diamonds, while [his] smoulders like brown paper' (p. 241). And when he comes up with the radical idea that a woman and her children could very well be a family without a man, he realizes that he has 'out-Sued Sue' in his thinking (p. 243).

A traditional role for women is to influence men, and in that sense Sue is not unlike other Victorian heroines. Where she differs from them, however, is that her moral influence is not only as intellectual as it is emotional – it is thoroughly unconventional. Her collapse at the end of the novel into guilt-ridden hysteria is a symptom of her emotional susceptibility. Ironically, though, it is this very susceptibility that has made her such a sensitive teacher of radical ideas. After this breakdown, she unsuccessfully attempts to reverse the ethical education she has provided for Phillotson and Jude. Only as a force of conventional influence is Sue ineffectual. Through his heroine, Hardy subverts the paradigm of traditional feminine influence, but influence remains important to the ethics of this novel. When Sue tries to persuade Phillotson to release her from the marriage bond, for example, she seeks to influence him, as she has been influenced, by John Stuart Mill's ideas about liberty. Mill himself was saved by influence, as he describes in his *Autobiography* (1873): following a nervous breakdown, he found medicine in Wordsworth's poems because they expressed 'thought coloured by feeling' and helped him restore balance to his overly analytic mind, a product of his Utilitarian education.[11] Sue's breakdown represents a different kind of imbalance: thought distorted by feeling. Prior to this crisis, though, Sue is not at all the cold and unsympathetic character that some readers perceive her to be. Her ideas are imbued with emotion and therefore potently influential.

If Sue is 'a harp which the least wind of emotion from another's heart could make to vibrate as readily as a radical stir in her own' (*Jude*, p. 293), if, in other words, she is as susceptible to the emotions of others as they are to her ideas, then she is inconstant, as Kucich points out. But Hardy's novel stresses that constancy is an unrealistic ideal for sexual relationships. The empathy that moves Sue to shed tears at the sight of Father Time's tears is what makes her a sympathetic character, despite the cruelty that sometimes results from her vacillations.

Emotion in the fiction of Schreiner and Hardy is associated with women, but it is a vital component of their intellectual and ethical lives. *Jude the Obscure* develops another theme prominent in the fiction of late-century women writers: the idea that the New Woman's intellect becomes a weapon she turns against men as a means of defending herself against patriarchal injustice and freeing herself from constraints. In her relationships this exercise of power leads the New Woman to become what Hardy calls 'an epicure in emotions' (*Jude*, p. 180), usually with cruel consequences for the man or men in love with her.

Sarah Grand's *The Heavenly Twins*, like 'The Buddhist Priest's Wife' and *Jude*, poses the question of what it would be like for a woman to be in a relationship with a man without the complications of gender and sexuality. Grand's Angelica Hamilton-Wells employs her cleverness as a child to secure rights equal to those of her twin brother. She grows up well-educated but restless, without intellectual challenges. When the newly arrived choir tenor falls in love with her at first sight, she disguises herself as her brother and develops a close friendship with him. Later she is unable to account for her behaviour, though she admits to her desire for excitement and her rebellion against those who would domesticate her. Cross-dressing allows her a luxurious physical freedom; it also enables a rare sort of intellectual liberty. She says to the tenor, 'I have enjoyed the benefit of free intercourse with your masculine mind undiluted by your masculine prejudices and proclivities with regard to my sex' (*The Heavenly Twins*, p. 458). The consequences for her are therefore positive, despite the guilt she suffers after her exposure. For the tenor, however, the prank has psychologically painful repercussions, and his experience with Angelica eventually leads to his death.

Lyndall, the New Woman in *The Story of an African Farm*, shares Angelica's yearning for more possibilities than life offers a woman. Lyndall's mind and imagination help her satisfy this emotional hunger. Instead of literal role-playing, she mentally multiplies herself by participating in forms of life completely unlike her own – transcending time, gender and race, imagining herself a medieval monk, a Kaffir witch-doctor, and a variety of other selves. 'I like to see it all; I feel it run through me – that life belongs to me; it makes my little life larger; it breaks down the narrow walls that shut me in' (*Story of an African Farm*, p. 182). As both Lyn Pykett and Ann Ardis have noted, this disruption of stable feminine identity occurs in much of the New Woman writing and is often reinforced by its unconventional narrative strategies.[12] Although selflessness was expected of the traditional Victorian woman, the late-century New Woman paradoxically seeks to escape self through intellectual and emotional experiments in self-actualization, even when these experiments are hurtful to others.

Lyndall's restlessness is evident as well in her relationship with the man she loves. She explains her feelings for him by stressing his strength and power, even as she exerts her own power by refusing to marry him, though she is pregnant with his child, and by confessing that she became involved with him because 'I like to experience, I like to try' (*Story of an African Farm*, p. 206). This adventurousness, which is at once calculating and emotionally self-indulgent, is what leads her to describe herself as having no conscience (p. 176), certainly an unfair self-assessment, though it is true that she hurts those close to her through her unconventional choices. She has enough of a conscience to wish she were a better person, to prefer being good to being loved (p. 201). Schreiner encourages us to recognize Lyndall's burden of guilt but also to question where the New Woman's responsibility begins and ends in a patriarchal society that so circumscribes women's freedom.

In her relationship with Jude, Sue is very much like Angelica and Lyndall because she too feels emotional restlessness followed by compunction. Like these other New Women, Sue is 'venturesome with men' (*Jude*, p. 182). She enjoys tormenting Jude by having him walk down the aisle with her as practice for her marriage to Phillotson. She explains that she likes to do interesting things that 'have probably never been done before' (p. 180). But her pleasure evaporates when she realizes that her 'curiosity to hunt up a new sensation' causes Jude pain (p. 180). Living with an openness to possibility, Sue also strives to be responsible and compassionate. The novel shows us how difficult it is for her to balance concern for her own needs with her desire to avoid hurting others.

All three of the women in these novels evade commitment and seek to gain emotional satisfaction from their relationships with men in daring, unpredictable, intellectually self-conscious ways. Their behaviour is understandable but also sadistically flirtatious.[13] The novels waver between evoking admiration for these New Women and the new ethics of possibility that they bring to their relationships, and judging them for turning their backs on a traditionally feminine ethics of care. Writing about flirtation, Adam Phillips asks,

> what does commitment leave out of the picture that we might want? If our descriptions of sexuality are tyrannized by various stories of committed purpose – sex as reproduction, sex as heterosexual intercourse, sex as intimacy – flirtation puts in disarray our sense of an ending. In flirtation you never know whether the beginning of a story – the story of the relationship – will be the end; flirtation, that is to say, exploits the idea of surprise.[14]

Surprise is sprung on the man by the woman in each of these novels: Angelica surprises the tenor when he realizes that she is a woman, not an enchanting boy. By refusing to marry or to make a commitment, Lyndall surprises the father of her baby, who, she realizes, will continue to love her as long as she resists his mastery. And Sue surprises the men in her life at every turn: by marrying Phillotson as a way of getting back at Jude for concealing his own marriage, by refusing to sleep with Jude even after leaving her husband for him, by returning to Phillotson as a penance after the death of her children. In each novel, the story of the relationship is shaped not by the man's choice, but by the woman's restless discontent and unwillingness to be the traditional heroine of such a story.

Although the men are hurt by this new kind of flirtation that takes away their power, the novels also encourage us to recognize the positive ethical consequences of a 'flirtation that puts in disarray our sense of an ending'. Temporarily, all three heroines win for themselves a better kind of love and relationship by avoiding commitment. The sexual equality, friendship and freedom that they achieve in their relationships with the men they love is short-lived and contingent on circumstances beyond their control. But this new kind of romantic relationship imagines potential, even if it is potential that never fully blooms. Thus in New Woman fiction, flirtation, a stage of courtship that the respectable, modest Victorian woman was advised to disdain, plays an important role in the development of a more radical sexual ethics.

If these experimentally flirtatious women characters 'put in disarray our sense of an ending', their stories and the norms of late-Victorian culture eventually manage to contain them. The emotion that has energized the thinking of these women does indeed become debilitating in the end, though it is important to see that, depressing as it is, the punishing plot reveals not the author's beliefs about what the New Woman's fate should be, but his or her recognition of what it most often was.

Both *The Story of an African Farm* and *Jude the Obscure* counterpoint the New Woman character with a traditional woman, Em and Arabella respectively, and in both novels the conventional, respectable woman thrives while Lyndall and Sue suffer, one literally dying and the other metaphorically dying through self-sacrifice. *The Heavenly Twins* also focuses primarily on two women, though as Kucich points out, the counternarratives of Angelica and Evadne are self-cancelling (*Power of Lies*, p. 252). They reveal Grand to be more conservative than Schreiner or Hardy because not only are both of her heroines punished and subdued by social strictures, both are redeemed by the superior wisdom of men. The resolutions of their stories underscore the novel's emphasis on the interdependence of women's and men's ethics. As Evadne points out in her criticism of gendered moral education, 'So long as men believe that women will forgive anything they will do anything' (*The Heavenly Twins*, p. 92). Once women's morality changes, men's will too. This point is not cancelled when it is reversed: with their greater power and education, men can do much to help women socially, intellectually and ethically. But what is disturbing about Grand's conclusion is that both Angelica and Evadne cling pathetically to their male rescuers – in contrast to Sue and Lyndall, who make choices that defy the men they love.

The Heavenly Twins begins with a portrait of Evadne as a reader and thinker but also a loving, warm-hearted person, who fears that her unusualness as an intellectual woman will have painful emotional consequences: 'I don't want to despise my fellow-creatures. I would rather share their ignorance and conceit and be sociable than find myself isolated even by a very real superiority' (*The Heavenly Twins*, p. 37). Like the heroine of 'The Buddhist Priest's Wife', however, Evadne finds that for much of her life her fate is to be alone, stranded because of her difference and her principled stands, including her refusal to consummate her marriage to her syphilitic husband, with whom she nevertheless lives because of her father's skill at exploiting her emotionally.[15] Once she promises her husband not to involve herself publicly in intellectual or political work, Evadne is left with no outlet for the tremendous energies apparent from the novel's opening study of her character. By the end of *The Heavenly Twins*, the early focus on Evadne's reading has given way to Dr Galbraith's narration – his reading of her life as a broken spirit, a woman who has collapsed into hysteria. Her state is very much like that of Sue Bridehead at the end of *Jude the Obscure*. Sue becomes 'creed drunk', as Jude describes her, clinging not to a man but to the religious and moral orthodoxies she had rejected all her life (*Jude*, p. 411). Schreiner's heroine similarly turns against herself. After having lost her baby as Sue loses hers, Lyndall struggles with a wasting illness and judges herself 'weak' and 'selfish'; the 'old clear intellect' (*Story of an African Farm*, pp. 247, 252) resurfaces moments before her death, but her final psychological state, like that of the other New Women in this fiction, is marked by yearning. Countering the stereotype of the New Woman as merely an 'intellectualized, emancipated bundle of nerves',[16] Grand, Hardy and Schreiner all depict the late-Victorian feminist as someone who feels as deeply as she thinks and, in fact, suffers because her emotions and ideas are so difficult to disentangle.[17]

The cultural containment of these women that occurs at the end of each novel re-establishes separate-spheres ideology by associating women with emotion that overwhelms reason. As we have seen, however, the novels attempt to counter this stereotype while also acknowledging its destructive power. Schreiner, Grand and Hardy delineate a subtle, complex and ethically promising relationship between emotion and reason in the lives of these early feminists, only to expose all that militates against this new sense of self: social ostracism with its attendant guilt and isolation, the risk of causing pain to loved ones and, perhaps above all, the internalized social norm of the woman as emotional and therefore not capable of reason – or if intellectual then not truly feminine.

Hardy deplored what he described as the cosmic joke that emotions were allowed to develop in a such a defective world, and yet he recognized the ethical force of emotion. Too often, critics who stress Hardy's difference from the New Women writers slip into a twentieth-century version of separate-spheres thinking, characterizing Hardy as on the side of reason, wary of the feminine and the emotional, even though there is little in his novels to support such an interpretation. Like Olive Schreiner and Sarah Grand, Hardy encouraged his readers to rethink conventional ideas about women and feeling, as difficult as that was during an age just beginning to understand women's aspirations without fathoming how they could be realized.

Notes

1. Olive Schreiner, *The Story of an African Farm* (Oxford: Oxford University Press, 1992), p. 135. Further references are indicated by page number in the text.
2. Sarah Grand, *The Heavenly Twins* (Ann Arbor: University of Michigan Press, 1992), p. 340. Further references will be indicated by page number in the text.
3. Patricia Stubbs, *Women and Fiction: Feminism and the Novel, 1880–1920* (Brighton: Harvester Press, 1979), p. 25.
4. Lyn Pykett, *The 'Improper' Feminine: The Women's Sensation Novel and the New Woman Writing* (London: Routledge, 1992), p. 169.
5. Pykett, *The 'Improper' Feminine*, p. 174.
6. Gail Cunningham's discussion of Hardy in the context of New Woman writing is representative of the many critics who describe Hardy's approach as something other than feminist: 'The areas of interest which led his novels to converge on the New Woman fiction were sexual morality in general, and a pervading cynicism about marriage. Neither of these need necessarily imply a specifically feminist approach: indeed in many of his novels Hardy's view of women, and his ideas about sex and marriage, seem to pull him uncomfortably in different directions.' Gail Cunningham, *The New Woman and the Victorian Novel* (New York: Harper and Row, 1978), p. 81.

7. Olive Schreiner, 'The Buddhist Priest's Wife', in *Daughters of Decadence: Women Writers of the Fin de Siècle*, ed. Elaine Showalter (New Brunswick: Rutgers University Press, 1993), p. 92. Further references are indicated by page number in the text.

8. Laura Green, ' "Strange [In]difference of Sex": Thomas Hardy, the Victorian Man of Letters, and the Temptations of Androgyny', *Victorian Studies*, 38 (1995), 523–49 (p. 544); Thomas Hardy, *Jude the Obscure* (Oxford: Oxford University Press, 1987), p. 159. Further references to this edition are indicated by page number in the text.

9. John Kucich, *The Power of Lies: Transgression in Victorian Fiction* (Ithaca, NY: Cornell University Press, 1994), pp. 210–11. Further references will be indicated by page number in the text.

10. Penny Boumelha observes that the similarity of Jude and Sue marks a change in Hardy's fiction: 'There is no sense that Jude and Sue inhabit different ideological structures as there is in the cases of Clym and Eustacia, or even Angel and Tess': *Thomas Hardy and Women: Sexual Ideology and Narrative Form* (Brighton: Harvester Press, 1982), p. 141. Laura Green also identifies this similarity between its male and female protagonists as one of the features of *Jude* that make it the most radical of Hardy's novels (' "Strange [In]difference of Sex" ', p. 527).

11. John Stuart Mill, *Autobiography of John Stuart Mill* (New York: Columbia University Press, 1960), p. 104.

12. Lyn Pykett makes this point in her discussion of George Egerton's fiction (*The 'Improper' Feminine*, p. 173). Ardis observes, more generally, that in New Woman writing heterogeneity has replaced 'the humanistic model of integrated selfhood or "character". A monolithic model of New Womanliness [is] not [...] substituted for the old model of the "pure woman"': Ann L. Ardis, *New Women, New Novels: Feminism and Early Modernism* (New Brunswick: Rutgers University Press, 1990), pp. 113–14.

13. Laura Green makes the intriguing point that 'linguistic pedantry occurs with remarkable frequency in moments of flirtation or jockeying for position between male and female characters' (' "Strange [In]difference of Sex" ', p. 536). In Schreiner's novel, too, flirtation is as intellectual as it is emotional. Lyndall's lover says to her, 'I like you when you grow metaphysical and analytical', and she thinks, 'he was trying to turn her own weapons against her' (*Story of an African Farm*, p. 204).

14. Adam Phillips, *On Flirtation* (Cambridge, MA: Harvard University Press, 1994), pp. xviii–xix.

15. A. R. Cunningham ('The "New Woman Fiction" of the 1890s', *Victorian Studies*, 17 (1973), 176–86) identifies two main types of New Women heroines: the 'bachelor girl', a designation appropriate for Sue, Lyndall and Angelica, since this type was thoroughly unconventional in her thinking; and the New Woman of the 'purity school', a designation that fits Evadne since she is unusually intelligent but not willing to abandon traditional Victorian moral values and ideals.

16. Hardy, Preface to the 1st edn of *Jude the Obscure* (Oxford: Oxford University Press, 1987), p. xxxviii.

17. It would be instructive to compare the dramatic psychological breakdowns of these New Women to the emotional collapse suffered by heroines of

earlier Victorian novels, such as Gwendolen Harleth in George Eliot's *Daniel Deronda* (1876). Unlike Evadne, Gwendolen glories in the superiority that isolates her from others until that isolation breaks her spirit. Then, like Evadne, she is overcome by hysteria. Reaching out to Deronda for moral guidance and advice about how to establish loving connections with others, Gwendolen, unlike Sue and Lyndall, moves hopefully into the future. Eliot's heroine suffers for her difference, but she is not so different that she cannot reintegrate herself into society. These New Women are unable to do so because their efforts to conform lack conviction and authenticity. They reject gender expectations more rebelliously than even the most rebellious of earlier Victorian heroines.

12
Don Pickwick: Dickens and the Transformations of Cervantes

Angus Easson

The origins of *The Pickwick Papers* (1837) and of Mr Pickwick are well enough known, not least from Dickens's own, understandably proud, flourish in the 1867 Charles Dickens Edition Preface. The idea being propounded of the sporting misadventures of a cockney Nimrod Club, to be published in monthly parts, Dickens pressed for 'a freer range of English scenes and people'. The publisher, Edward Chapman, gave way and 'My views being deferred to, I thought of Mr Pickwick, and wrote the first number'.[1] While not denying the originality of *The Pickwick Papers*, there is no need to swallow whole the parthenogenical spontaneity of Pickwick springing fully clothed, in tights and gaiters, from his father's head. Dickens had a large inheritance, and the kinship of Pickwick and of *The Pickwick Papers* to Cervantes's *Don Quixote* and to a Quixotic tradition was early acknowledged by others, if never explicitly by Dickens. In May 1841 Washington Irving wrote to Dickens in a long and admiring letter that 'Old Pickwick is the Quixote of commonplace life, and as with the Don, we begin by laughing at him and end by loving him'.[2] And while Dickens was keen in 1867 to quash claims made for the illustrator Robert Seymour as the true if not the 'onlie' begetter of Pickwick, we may note Edward Chapman's evidence that Seymour's first sketch 'was of a long, thin man', Chapman claiming credit for describing to the artist 'a friend of mine', 'a fat old beau who would wear [...] drab tights and black gaiters'.[3] While Seymour drew 'long, thin men' readily enough – Nathaniel Winkle is one such – Don Quixote's attenuated form might seem to lie behind Seymour's sketch and Pickwick's short fat form to be a deliberate reversal of Cervantes's scheme, corporeally shadowing Quixote's squire Sancho Panza, just as Dickens develops Cervantes's contrasting but complementary pairing in Pickwick and Sam Weller.

The first is not Don Quixote nor the second Sancho Panza, and yet knight and squire are recognizable forebears of master and servant. The Don and Sancho first possessed Dickens's imagination through that 'little room upstairs' in the house at Chatham where the family's books were kept, from which, in Dickens's childhood days, '*Roderick Random, Peregrine Pickle, Humphrey Clinker, Tom Jones,* the *Vicar of Wakefield, Don Quixote, Gil Blas,* and *Robinson Crusoe* came out, a glorious host, to keep me company'.[4] Those childhood books were sold off during his father's financial struggles in London, and the copy of *Don Quixote* we know Dickens to have possessed, he bought in March 1841: an 1820 edition in four volumes, with notes by Lockhart and illustrations by Richard Westall.[5] There are few comments in Dickens's letters on *Don Quixote*, but since they include references to the preface, the galley slaves, the spurious continuation, pilloried by Cervantes in his own Second Part, and the observation that some of the best things are in that Second Part,[6] they suggest Dickens had read the novel through and through.

In what follows I want to trace three separate yet intertwined threads. The first depends on the obvious, that Dickens read *Don Quixote*, yet read the novel also through a tradition of transformation and rewriting, particularly within the English picaresque tradition of Fielding and Smollett. This tradition of course did not merely transplant the knight's exploits into an English setting. Through creative reading, the second strand, it metamorphosed Don Quixote from an insane figure of fun (if he had ever truly existed in so primitive a form) to an idealist whose passionate imagination justified his endeavours, however futile the gross world of self-interested sanity might declare his antics. The third thread lies within *Pickwick Papers* itself. As well as being part of this dual tradition of reading and rereading, Dickens himself shifted his perception of Pickwick, effectively reread and rewrote Pickwick during the novel's serialization, as Don Quixote has been reread and rewritten over the centuries. The grotesque Pickwick of the novel's opening (retrospectively read as a benevolent idealist at his very starting out from Goswell Street on his travels) changes to a Quixotic figure, no longer the absurd butt of antiquarian and pseudo-scientific satire but a Fool of God who seeks to act for good and whose benevolence preserves him even amidst embarrassment and ridicule. Dickens drew in technique and in passional development upon Cervantes and his progeny – exemplified here by Smollett, as well as by reference to the Romantics – even while his own creative nature was stimulated by this inheritance.

How did Dickens read *Don Quixote*? A tradition of its understanding, deeply seated in the practice of the English novel tradition, had been developed critically by eighteenth-century sensibility and by Romanticism. Romanticism, in Germany and in England, valuing the subjective self and emphasizing the self-created world of mental reality, peculiarly privileged the imaginative and hence ideal world, a world mentally created and aspirational: that very world, the Romantics proclaimed, which was projected and inhabited by Don Quixote himself. This reading developed in opposition to the claim that Quixote's insanity is constantly challenged within the novel and made self-evidently absurd by the substantiality of what is and must be the real world. Not that *Don Quixote* has ever really been read exclusively from either such naïvely reductive positions. Much in Cervantes's novel enforces Quixote's insanity and inability to cope with the reasonable world, just as much makes a more varied or open or ironic case: whether the Duke and the Duchess in their tricks upon Don Quixote were not as mad as he, for example, or the mystery of what occurred in the cave of Montesinos. Romantic readings of *Don Quixote*, admitting the grotesque and the ideal as intertwined, fusing them through the esemplastic agency of dream activity, are exemplified in Wordsworth's Quixotic vision in Book V of *The Prelude*. Wordsworth's friend, while reading Cervantes's novel, muses on 'Poetry and geometric Truth' and in a dream finds himself amongst desert sands:

> To his great joy a Man was at his side,
> Upon a dromedary, mounted high.
> [...]
> A Lance he bore, and underneath one arm
> A Stone; and, in the opposite hand, a Shell. [7]

This visionary Quixote, a mix of Cervantes's hero and the knight's supposed historian, Cide Hamete Benegeli ('I fancied that he was the very Knight / Whose Tale Cervantes tells, yet not the Knight, / But was an Arab of the Desart, too' (*Prelude*, V.123)), is striving to save the stone and the shell, geometry and poetry, from 'the fleet waters of the drowning world' (*Prelude*, V.136). Though Wordsworth's poem was not published until 1850, its response is typically Romantic in its combination of grotesque and visionary, using the shifting phantasmagoria of a dream to suggest wider truths, obscure and yet obscurely revealed in the liberating under-world of sleep. The outsider (the Bedouin or mad errant) who is yet saviour is both Romantic and Christian, and ties in with European (particularly German) Romantic interpretations of Cervantes.[8]

But if Dickens was no great reader of the Romantics and certainly could not have anticipated *The Prelude*'s 1850 publication, he would be familiar enough with the larmoyante sensibilities of Henry Brooke's novel, *The Fool of Quality* (1766–72). Here, the figure of the 'Author', in dialogue with his 'Friend', urges that Don Quixote is a true hero in contradistinction to those who, in 'spreading desolation and calamity', have been acclaimed such:

> How greatly, how gloriously, how divinely superior was our hero of the Mancha, who went about righting of wrongs, and redressing of injuries, lifting up the fallen, and pulling down those whom iniquity had exalted! [...] If events did not answer to the enterprises of his heart, it is not to be imputed to the man but to his malady; for, had his power and success been as extensive as his benevolence, all things awry upon earth would instantly have been set as straight as a cedar.[9]

This passage, Janus-like, glances back to Cervantes and forward to Dickens in its identification of 'benevolence' as key to our reading of Quixote. Yet it highlights also a modern opposition. The tradition that reads Quixote through tears and through idealistic aspiration, that finds in the madman a hero who would seek to preserve mental powers constantly threatened, in Wordsworth's words, by 'the waters of the deep / Gathering upon us' (*Prelude*, V.130), has been challenged by Anthony Close in *The Romantic Approach to Don Quixote*, his 1978 study of this critical metamorphosis of Cervantes. Such a tradition (or traditions), Close claims, 'perversely ignores the obvious' about Cervantes's novel. For Close, the obvious is that Cervantes is a comic artist – satirist, ironist, parodist, or whatever. The Romantic tradition has idealized the hero and denied the novel's satiric purpose, further compounding the error by insisting that the novel is symbolic. Close naturally does not deny the existence of this line of interpretation nor its influence – the purpose of his book is to trace its historical development, to explain it, and to show why he must regret it.[10] Certainly, at starting out and for some way on, Dickens embraces the satiric purpose of *Don Quixote* in his own satire upon the Pickwick Club's scientific and antiquarian obsessions. Mr Pickwick is a butt, not an idealist, when discoursing on the source of the Hampstead ponds or engaged in the paper war over Bill Stumps His

Mark, so that 'to this day the stone remains an illegible monument of Mr Pickwick's greatness, and a lasting trophy of the littleness of his enemies' (*Pickwick Papers*, pp. 136–7).

Yet Dickens comes out of a Romantic and eighteenth-century tradition of reading and rewriting *Don Quixote* which placed it at the head of that English picaresque tradition which rewrote 'rogue' as 'road'. The development of the picaresque tradition through *Joseph Andrews*, Fielding's comic epic in prose, with Parson Adams as a Christian Quixote, is familar enough, and the landscape of the eighteenth-century novel is littered with self-proclaimed Quixotic progeny: Charlotte Lennox's *The Female Quixote* (1752), for example, and Richard Graves's *The Spiritual Quixote* (1773).[11] Amongst the novels that came out of that 'little room upstairs' in Chatham, Dickens names three of Smollett's and then or later he would have read Smollett's Quixotic *Sir Lancelot Greaves* (1760–61). Smollett's errant knight highlights the shifts of sensibility and throws up consequent technical solutions to the challenge of a mad hero. Though not so openly labelled as the Quixotes of Lennox and Graves, Smollett's hero quickly reveals his parentage when, amidst a storm from which travellers on the Great North Road have taken refuge, the door of the Black Lion bursts open and 'in stalked an apparition, that smote the hearts of our travellers with fear and trepidation. It was the figure of a man armed cap-a-pie'.[12] This knight in armour proves to be Sir Lancelot Greaves, as absurdly accoutred as Quixote a century before, though his armour is of better quality than the Knight of the Sad Countenance's, a 'sartorial' detail that, along with money and social standing, serves to hitch Sir Lancelot a rung or two up the hierarchy of sensibility. Smollett, at this introduction of his hero, in the first of several conscious references to literary predecessors, links him to yet another figure armed cap-a-pie and hence to another mad idealist whom the eighteenth century read as Quixotic, at odds with the sanity of the external world. The political hack Ferret exclaims 'Hey day! what precious mummery is this? What, are we to have the farce of Hamlet's ghost?' (*Sir Lancelot Greaves*, p. 9). Hamlet, whose belief in a mental world sets him in opposition to Claudius's real one, a Quixote proved right by a ghost and yet his mental faith condemned as madness, was early valued for his sensibility. Fielding's critique of Garrick's Hamlet proclaimed the insane hero as norm, both in acting style and in audience sympathy.[13] Smollett allows an intertextual play between his narrative and Cervantes's, so explaining Sir Lancelot's conduct and excusing it by playing to a model.[14] Hamlet comes in aid

of Greaves's youthful idealism, an enforcement of the heroic nature of
Quixote. The two apprentices disguised as soldiers have read their *Don
Quixote* (pp. 107–8), and the surgeon at the Black Lion, playing up to
Captain Crowe's desire to emulate Sir Lancelot and be a knight errant
too, points out that 'Don Quixote was dubbed [knight] by his land-
lord' (*Sir Lancelot Greaves*, p. 52). This consciousness of literary predecessors internal to the narrative is not something Dickens admits to,
nor does he, as Smollett does, directly model episodes on Cervantes –
the disastrous vigil Captain Crowe keeps (*Sir Lancelot Greaves*,
Chapters 6–7), reworks the Don's vigil on his first expedition, as well
as drawing upon later mishaps when Quixote is tied up by Maritornes
(*Don Quixote*, Part 1, Chapters 43–4).

More clearly linking Smollett back to Cervantes and forward to
Dickens is the treatment of Sir Lancelot and of narrative problems
that arise from such a hero. Smollett has determined on a hero distinctly different from Don Quixote. Instead of a man old like
Quixada (or Quesada) – 'verging on fifty' (*Don Quixote,* Part 1, p. 31) –
we have a young man, handsome, in love not with some imaginary
Dulcinea but with a girl of flesh and blood, whose supposed rejection
of him has turned his wits. He is wealthy (indeed, he solves many
problems by his money and his social standing) and his madness is
justified by his sensibility and by the way he has been treated, the
victim of a plot by his beloved Aurelia's uncle Darnel. Sir Lancelot
displays sensibility and idealism: even when he is mad, his actions
are justified (by the narrative: the reader may think his behaviour
dubious or downright wrong). He argues anyway that madness and
honesty are not incompatible (*Sir Lancelot Greaves*, p. 60), itself a
staging post in a general argument (overlapping with the Romantic
view of Hamlet), first that idealism and madness are indeed compat-
ible and next that madness is idealism in the face of the dishonesty
of the world. In representing this admirable hero, Smollett solves the
'problem' technically by displacement. The burlesque element that
lies in Cervantes and Don Quixote is thrust upon Captain Crowe – a
good-hearted sea captain and one of Smollett's linguistic obsessives.
Crowe, determined to be a disciple in chivalry, provides the parodic
material that Lancelot does not, whether by his vigil (treated at
length and farcically where Sir Lancelot's is related briefly by Tom
Clarke) or by his knockabout encounters on the highway. Crowe is a
comic character and his being an absurd errant does not call errantry
into question, nor does he have to be mad to sally forth. This process
of displacement is part of a strategy that is supported by two other

effects. First, Sir Lancelot, mad in disappointed love, proves not all that mad, but rather eccentric, his derangement proof of the depth of his sensibility: his feelings, still equally intense, are socially accept-able when Aurelia is again an accessible object of love. He soon relin-quishes his errantry in armour for the determined pursuit of his Aurelia: the knowledge that she is in danger and the *éclaircissement* he has with her clear his mind. At not much over half way through the novel (*Sir Lancelot Greaves*, p. 135), Greaves resolves to abandon his armour. His character is motivated by admirable sensibility, not exclusively possessed by an *idée fixe*. Second, Smollett structures his narrative so as to enforce the essential sanity and heroic suitability of Sir Lancelot. This relates to a strategy observable in Cervantes, but here handled to a different purpose. How does an author sustain an extended narrative based upon seemingly a single idea (chivalry in the modern world) without mere repetition? Cervantes offers various solutions and different procedures in each part of his novel – or rather in each of the knight's three expeditions. The first is brief (*Don Quixote*, Part 1, Chapters 2–5); the second is extended by the intro-duction of Sancho and by the variety (in genre and material) of the inserted narratives; the third expedition (the novel's second part) as well as some inserted material (Camacho's wedding, for example), extends through the Duke and Duchess's knowledge from reading Part 1 of knight and squire, from which springs the comic interplay of the distressed gentlewoman and the government of the island. Smollett, to prevent Sir Lancelot being too absurd and so alienating his claims to sensibility, not only displaces grotesqueness into Crowe and (as in the great original) into Lancelot's squire Timothy Crabshaw. He also has the career of Lancelot, up to his appearance in the Black Lion, narrated by Tom Clarke, the telling of which (with interruptions) occupies more than a quarter of the book and so qualifies the immediacy of folly. With Crowe's buffoonery and Crabshaw's misfortunes and Lancelot's abandonment of madness and armour, the reader has little direct experience of an insane Lancelot. All this helps keep him clear of parody or irony, and allows him a properly heroic and modern role in the plots to kidnap both Aurelia and himself that are necessary before his reunion with Aurelia. Even when 'mad', Lancelot is not the object of satire but, as in the election and the confrontation with Justice Gabble, its channel. Dickens was in turn to cast over Pickwick's nakedness the 'drab tights' of sensibil-ity and modern heroism. While Dickens did not directly adopt Smollett's narrative strategies, such features prove important because they indicate narrative problems of the kind Dickens had himself to address, in adapting Quixote and the norms of sensibility.

The fact is that Dickens himself made remarkable progress artistically during the course of writing *Pickwick Papers*. He may claim in the 1867 Preface that Pickwick is revealed gradually in an unforced or natural way, as the oddities of a man in real life impress us first, the better part of him only known as we are better acquainted (*Pickwick Papers*, p. 724). But the readers are right. If Pickwick changes and 'becomes more good and more sensible' (p. 724), the change is not wrought by the author's initial conception being worked logically out. Rather, Dickens's own developing powers and concerns led him to rewrite Pickwick during the novel's publication. He could not go back and revise what had been published serially, even if in 1867 he could offer a restrospective apologia for the transformation. There was no need for Dickens to be ashamed of this technical process (obviously, he was not ashamed of its consequences, since he claims Pickwick's goodness and sense as part of his intended execution) nor for him to deny that the conception did change, though the result is not a grossly improbable effect. This change was, though, part of a developing sense of his own powers and of the story's potential, marked, as the original Preface acknowledges (*Pickwick Papers*, p. xxiv), by the virtual abandonment of the 'machinery' of the Club once Pickwick and the story began to develop. The 'editor', so largely the narrative's voice of irony in the treatment of Pickwick, effectively vanishes as do the minutes of meetings and the reports from notebooks, and with that editor goes, if not all at once, the ridicule of Pickwick.

Early on, Dickens's satire is at the expense of Pickwick's myopic fatuousness. The disparity between Pickwick's perception and the reader's, a chasm of sympathy, is clear as Pickwick at Rochester cheerfully notes his impressions of the licentious soldiery:

It is truly delightful to a philanthropic mind, to see these gallant men, staggering along under the influence of an overflow, both of animal, and ardent spirits; more especially when we remember that the following them about, and jesting with them, affords a cheap and innocent amusement for the boy population. (p. 14)

The disparity of vision remains, but Pickwick's role is recast by Dickens from implacable imperception to a horrified incomprehension of man's inhumanity to man. The 'philanthropic' Pickwick of Rochester is a man without understanding or sensibility: the comedy, of course,

lies in that very blockishness. In the Fleet, Pickwick may not comprehend, may not be able to encompass the horrors that have opened to
him, but his very realization of failure to understand stresses his new
and active sensibility. To be aware of injustice is not therefore to find
or know of a solution, but awareness marks the first hesitant steps to
unite feeling and action. Pickwick's emotions in the Fleet make him for
the reader a channel of shared feelings that in their humanity far tran-
scend the pleasing tears of sensibility. Pickwick sets out as an observer
of ponds and cabmen's horses and inscribed stones. While he never
loses this curiosity in the world about him, he duly comes to distin-
guish between accidence and essence.

Even at his most absurd, Pickwick is not, as is Don Quixote, mad in
his perception of the world, however incongruous the gap between
observation and understanding at Highgate Ponds or Rochester and
Chatham. Cervantes juxtaposed a lunatic's misperception against the
truth of an objective reality – and the Romantic interpretation, to go
no further back, questions how illusory Quixote's vision must be or
how real that external world.[15] Dickens, like Cervantes, exploits temporal and spatial order, destabilizing the apparently certain, but
doing it through a Romantic subjectivity, centred by means of the
narrative voice in the character – very unlike Cervantes in this
respect, who represents Quixote, but does not directly enter his mind
or perceptions, who holds off from rather than embracing his hero.
The rest of this essay seeks to enforce how Dickens, through a different (and indeed shifting) conception of the Quixotic personality,
technically, makes Pickwick, while a descendant of the Don, his man
rather than Cervantes's. Spatial representation is stressed, since
Pickwick's experience of *terra incognita* in the Fleet is so crucial to the
novel's final effect. Three episodes are considered which offer
(though not in chronological order) staging posts in Dickens's shifting perception of Pickwick, before the Fleet, a familiar topos of the
novel, is again revisited.

Spatial confusion, whether over his vanished library or the caves of
Montesinos or the inns he comes to, is a characteristic of Quixote.
Pickwick is well aware of what an inn is, whether the Blue Lion or the
White Hart or the George and Vulture: you take rooms and you pay –
or you stop on a coaching stage and payment is demanded for a meal
you have no time to eat. For Dickens, though, increasing emphasis on
the character's subjectivity means that such places, however inherently
stable, can seem to expand and distort; even their reassuring familiarity
can be a deception. When Pickwick descends from his bedroom in the

Great White Horse at Ipswich to retrieve his watch, the stairs expand in flights below him like some Piranesi fantasy; the stairs once descended, passage after passage opens out, and room after room: 'again and again, when Mr. Pickwick got into some narrow passage, and began to congratulate himself on having gained the ground-floor, did another flight of stairs appear before his astonished eyes' (p. 275). His return is yet more fraught with difficulty. Eventually Pickwick finds the sanctuary of his own room again, only for it to prove not his but Miss Witherfield's. As if by magic, a stable building expands and extends, and the reassuringly identical room proves to be a (comic) trap. The narrative voice provides the stairs ('did another flight [...] appear') and the hazards of the bedroom are only too embarrassingly real.

True, delusions and destabilization of the ordered world also occur in Cervantes. Indeed, while Cervantes juxtaposes Don Quixote against a stable realistic world, he often introduces things which, however rationally explained, have disconcerting effects upon not only characters but also readers. Don Quixote's household bewilder their master after the inquisition of the library by walling up the room and pretending a magician has removed it, books and all. Their invention is taken up by Quixote as a convenient subsequent explanation of his discomfiture – the work of the magician Freston, who later 'changes' the giants to windmills so Quixote shall not have the glory of the exploit. Elsewhere, Cervantes defamiliarizes things, whether the ladies travelling by coach, accompanied by monks and wearing masks amidst the dust of their progress, or the pageant of death. But Dickens enforces the idea of Pickwick as in thrall to supernatural powers. An example early in the novel, at Eatanswill, where Pickwick is still conceived by Dickens as butt, nonetheless shows a transitional stage in the character's evolution. The easy scorn evoked by Pickwick's observations at Rochester is qualified by the narrator's allowance that Pickwick was baffled as well as buffetted. When Dickens plants Pickwick amidst the excitement of an election, he may be concerned, like Smollett, to show the chicanery and worthlessness of both sides (*Sir Lancelot Greaves*, pp. 74–8). But, unlike Greaves, Pickwick does not intervene; rather he is the subjective centre of buffetting as by some magical power. And while Pickwick's bewilderment is rationally explained by his hat being thrust over his eyes, the work of Quixote's enemy Freston is now the hero's experience, not his folly:

He describes himself as being surrounded on every side [...] by angry and ferocious countenances, by a vast cloud of dust, and by a dense crowd of combatants. He represents himself as being forced from the carriage by some unseen power, and being personally engaged in a pugilistic encounter; but with whom, or how, or why, he is wholly unable to state.

Pickwick Papers, p. 155

This is a transitional episode; we laugh still against Pickwick, even amidst the nightmare phantasmagoria. Yet Dickens seats the centre of consciousness, however ironically qualified, within Pickwick himself and so increasingly challenges whether the external objective world is the true reality.

The sense that Dickens rewrites Pickwick between Rochester and Ipswich is further enforced by another embarrassment before that intrusion into Miss Witherfield's bedroom: the vigil in the garden of Westgate House at Bury St Edmunds. As Ipswich had involved spatial illusion, so Bury St Edmunds draws on walled gardens and locked doors and draws as well on dramatic illusion, a crucial source of comedy in Cervantes and Dickens. Cervantes, in designing such tricks, relishes the opportunities to confound the stage-managers themselves. The sealing up of Quixote's library and the tale elaborated by his household of its transportation only further entangles Quixote in delusion. Chief of all, perhaps, in its disconcerting outcome, is Sampson Carrasco's expedition as Knight of the Mirrors, hoping to defeat Quixote and so send him home, with its humiliating and painful consequences for Sampson.

Dickens exploits dramatic illusion, and there are early confusions of disguise and mistaken identity – most obviously centring around Jingle and Job Trotter, who combine the professions of actor and picaro. At first Pickwick is little more than Jingle's farcical victim, but the elaborate humiliation of Westgate House confounds Jingle (though Jingle is unaware of this), because Dickens provides Pickwick with a motive that aligns him with Quixote for justice and for action. Pickwick may be fooled; no elopement is foiled; yet success is not of itself the touchstone of Romantic endeavour. We never see Jingle professionally engaged, upon the stage, nor indeed discover by allusion or quotation any of his roles. But he is always the actor and the apparent master-manager of illusion – always, that is, until the Fleet, where putting on a brave show he breaks down and sheds tears as true as those that run down Pickwick's waistcoat at the end of the interview, evidence of his repentance and in marked contrast to Job's waterworks, tears of sensibility as false as those of an allegory on the banks of the Nile. Jingle is confounded in the Fleet, where acting ceases. And yet all his acting proves to be misdirected: his tricks, ironically, lead Pickwick to make friends, to engage Sam, so that the alleged failures of Quixote's enterprises become Pickwick's achievements through the unconscious agency of the picaro Jingle. Jingle had been the unwitting cause of Pickwick meeting Sam – and the cause therefore also of Bardell v. Pickwick and in turn of Pickwick being in the Fleet to be the salvation of Jingle. He is confounded indeed, yet himself redeemed, in the process.

After his flight from Mrs Leo Hunter's fancy-dress breakfast, Jingle promotes dramatic illusion and the scenario of the supposed elopement from the girls' school is put into action by Job. The eloping pupil is non-existent, just as Jingle is a non-existent suitor – though we might pause to ask whether this was something Jingle intended but aborted, perhaps another layer in multiple illusions of the kind Cervantes is so disconcertingly good at. Westgate House is not imagined by Pickwick to be a castle; but it is imagined by him to be the site of an elopement. Job and Jingle have conjured up that illusion, concocted a scenario into which Pickwick enters pat, as on to a stage (emphasized by the enclosure of wall and house where Pickwick is trapped), and in which Pickwick believes, as surely as Quixote does in armies (of sheep) or in the afflicted waiting woman. Yet Pickwick, if ridiculous in his concealment behind the door, has acted from the desire for good and he is akin in this to the crazed Quixote.

The writing and ciphering governess at Westgate House declares Pickwick must be mad – and Sam his keeper (p. 204). And Pickwick is thought mad by Perker and by his friends, at least in a colloquial sense, in his determination to pay neither damages nor costs. I said earlier that Pickwick is not mad: yet both these occasions, when he is seen as irrational by others, are occasions when he has determined to act, whether from good nature to prevent Jingle's wrong-doing or from principle to protest against an unjust legal system. Both occasions mark shifts in the conception of Pickwick, both mark ways in which Dickens is perceiving Pickwick as Don Quixote in a Romantic light and rewriting the character of Pickwick even as he rewrites *Don Quixote*. Unlike Jingle, Mr Pickwick is not a contriver or actor (hence his real embarrassment at Westgate House); unlike Don Quixote, he is not created as an active interventionist. He is set up (established) by Dickens as an observer, a role rooted in the very conception of the Pickwick Club and the Pickwickians' mission as the Corresponding Society. Don Quixote, it has been claimed, never produces any good by his interventions (Andrew, the farmer's boy, is beaten more than he would have been if Quixote had never interfered (*Don Quixote*, Part 1, Chapters 4, 31)), though even on a non-Romantic interpretation there is his good influence during the complications unravelled at the inn (end of Part 1) and in the conversations at the house of the Duke and Duchess. Pickwick was created not to intervene; yet he does, through good nature, and intervenes to good effect – upon the reader. This is a shift in his role within the novel and, more crucially, in Dickens's conception of the character, a shift underlined furthermore by authorial comment: 'Thus, for a second time, did Mr. Pickwick's innate good-feeling involve him in an enterprise, from which he would most willingly have stood aloof.'[16] What Cervantes's novel does assert (it may be a Romantic reading, but one surely allowed by the novel) is that there is injustice in Spain. If Pickwick at Westgate House is prompted by his good nature (a highly developed Quixotic characteristic), then his protest against Dodson and Fogg is his idealistic quest for justice when confronted by the legal system of England. The legal satire of *The Pickwick Papers* is familiar enough, as is its observation of the legal system (the professional bails, for example) and the anger in its writing. Even Perker, for all his astuteness and basic honesty, is a lawyer, subdued to the thing he works in: for him, the bails are not perjury, but a legal fiction, while Mr Watty, the Chancery client, is turned away by his clerk.

Pickwick in the Fleet is an observer: but not as in Cervantes's world, an observer of a known reality, nor any longer as a Corresponding member of the Pickwick Club. Rather, Pickwick is now the Romantically subjective observer, whose consciousness, trying to unify or create a mental world of images and understanding, is the point of connection or focus for the reader too. Sam Weller knows more about the Fleet than Pickwick and it may be that Dickens's readers also knew more – especially if they had read their Smollett (both Roderick Random and Sir Lancelot Greaves find themselves in the King's Bench) or even *Sketches by Boz* (1836–7). But the strategy is to place Pickwick and reader together as the portrait is taken in the prison lodge (*Pickwick Papers*, p. 512) and Pickwick is conducted through the galleries and rooms of this inferno. Don Quixote constantly represents a disparity between what is 'out there' and what he perceives. So with Pickwick, there is a disparity, even while Pickwick's responsive imagination seeks to grasp the meaning of his experience. His comment on the little cells in the Fair, which he identifies as coal cellars – 'unpleasant places to have to go down to; but very convenient, I dare say' (p. 513) – is an attempt ('but very convenient') to adapt to circumstances, rudely dashed though it is by Roker's insistence that people live there, and die there too. But instead of laughing at Pickwick's failure, we find it part of our own exploration in uncharted territories: Pickwick and reader are travellers both. Dickens adventures into the Fleet, as later he was to map Jacob's Island or have Bucket take Mr Snagsby into the infernal circles of Tom-All-Alone's. Pickwick may in the end retreat into his room: but he has aided Jingle and Job, and will aid Mrs Bardell. He has no perpetual supply of money or patronage, like Sir Lancelot Greaves, to solve everyone's problems (though even Sir Lancelot does not attempt to empty the King's Bench). Still, he and the reader have perceived how the law, claiming to be justice, works and how the individual seems helpless to overturn the system, however good nature may help Jingle or Job or Mrs Bardell. The satire here runs against the author/editor, though, not against Pickwick. The narrative voice, not Pickwick, is, deliberately, ironized. When Pickwick says 'Take that, Sir' to Job (p. 537), the author, seemingly reluctant, demands, 'Must we tell the truth?' 'That' then proves not to be a blow, but something which chinked, 'and the giving which, somehow or other imparted a sparkle to the eye, and a swelling to the heart of our excellent old friend, as he hurried away'. True feeling is not solipsistic, the delightful but merely egotistical sensation of sensibility. Charity (combining a Romantic and a Christian virtue) is active and unself-regarding, as Pickwick's 'hurrying away' here testifies. It is not the retreat of the indifferent observer but the proper modesty of a Quixotic hero.

Dickens knew his *Don Quixote* – and knew the later Quixotic tradition. He uses satire and burlesque, often enough against Pickwick early on, but he also and increasingly turns to the idealizing of Quixote generated by the reading and rewriting of Cervantes. Pickwick in the Fleet is a different conception from Pickwick at the Highgate Ponds and in that difference lies the greatness of character and of novel. *The Pickwick Papers* enters, as the passage from Brooks's *The Fool of Quality* suggested, into the eighteenth-century debate, in which Cervantes has his part, about greatness and the nature of the hero. Not Achilles or Julius Caesar are great, but Don Quixote and Mr Pickwick. Mr Pickwick, a fat man, is embodied from the shadow of a thin man. Don Quixote, the Knight of the Sad Countenance, stands in the creative light that floods upon Dickens, not to obscure but to promote Pickwick's creation two centuries later.[17]

Notes

1. Charles Dickens, *The Pickwick Papers*, ed. James Kinsley (Oxford: Oxford University Press, 1988), p. 723. Further references are given in the text by page number in this edition. For Miguel Cervantes's *Don Quixote*, references are to J. M. Cohen's translation (Harmondsworth: Penguin, 1950). Part 1 was published in 1604, Part 2 in 1614; Alonso Fernández de Avellaneda's spurious continuation, which prompted Cervantes to hasten the writing and publication of Part 2, was published in 1614: Cervantes makes reference to Avellaneda in the later chapters and in the Preface of his own Part 2.
2. *The Letters of Charles Dickens*, eds M. House, G. Storey, K. Tillotson (Oxford: Clarendon Press, 1965–), II, 269n. (26 May 1841).
3. John Forster, *The Life of Charles Dickens*, ed. J. W. T. Ley (London: Cecil Palmer, 1928), pp. 75–6.
4. Forster, *The Life of Charles Dickens*, p. 5; Forster quotes Dickens's own words, from the Autobiographical Fragment and *David Copperfield* (1849–50).
5. See *Letters*, II, 229 and note for the purchase; IV, 718 for the library inventory of 1844; and the *Catalogue of the Library of Charles Dickens from Gadshill* ed. J. H. Stonehouse (London: Piccadilly Fountain Press, 1935), p. 19 for details of the edition.
6. *Letters*, V, 50, 654, 465 (and VII, Supplement, 894); VIII, 153.
7. William Wordsworth, *The Prelude*, 1805 version, ed. Ernest de Selincourt (London: Oxford University Press, 1933, rev. 1960), V, 64; ll. 76–7, 79–80. In the 1850 version, the poet himself has the dream.
8. For Romantic approaches to Cervantes, see Anthony Close, *The Romantic Approach to Don Quixote* (Cambridge: Cambridge University Press, 1978), Chapter 2 (pp. 29–41 on the German Romantics). Also on the Germans, see Alexander Welsh on Schiller in *Reflections on the Hero as Quixote* (Princeton: Princeton University Press, 1981), pp. 71–5.
9. Henry Brooke, *The Fool of Quality*, introduced by Francis Coutts (London: John Lane, The Bodley Head, n.d. [*c.* 1920]), I , 88–9. I owe this passage originally to Close, *The Romantic Approach to Don Quixote*, pp. 42–3.
10. Close, *The Romantic Approach to Don Quixote*, pp. 1–2; the quotation is on p. 2. One extreme of the counterview, discussed by Close in Chapter 5, is that of Miguel de Unamuno: 'I consider myself more Quixotist than Cervantist, and that I attempt to free Don Quixote from Cervantes himself, permitting myself on occasion to go so far as to disagree with the manner in which Cervantes understood and dealt with his two heroes' (*Selected Works of Unamuno*, trans. Anthony Kerrigan (Princeton: Princeton University Press, 1967, repr. 1976), III: *Our Lord Don Quixote*, p. 4; from the foreword to the 2nd edn, 1914). Close notes (*The Romantic Approach to Don Quixote*, p. 157) that Unamuno's view of Quixote as 'a symbolic myth-figure' has been 'deeply influential' and its effects 'unfortunate'.
11. On the Quixotic tradition in England see Robert Alter, *Partial Magic: The Novel as Self-Conscious Genre* (Berkeley: University of California Press, 1975), and Walter L. Reed, *An Exemplary History of the Novel: The Quixotic versus the Picaresque* (Chicago: University of Chicago Press, 1981); see also Welsh, *Reflections on the Hero as Quixote*. Welsh notes that quixotic heroes need not be nominally linked to Quixote, citing for example *The Vicar of Wakefield*

(1766) and *Tristram Shandy* (1760–7). On Quixote's influence elsewhere, see Harry Levin, *The Gates of Horn: A Study of Five French Realists* (New York: Oxford University Press, 1963); and for A. A. Parker's reservations about the looseness of the term 'picaresque', in general and in Alter's *Rogue's Progress: Studies in the Picaresque Novel* (Cambridge, MA.: Harvard University Press, 1964), see A. A. Parker, *Literature and the Delinquent: The Picaresque Novel in Spain and Europe 1599–1753* (Edinburgh: Edinburgh University Press, 1967), Chapter 1.

12. Tobias Smollett, *Sir Lancelot Greaves*, ed. David Evans (London: Oxford University Press, 1973), p. 7; further references will be given in the text by page number in this edition.

13. For Fielding's critique, see *Tom Jones*, ed. R. P. C. Mutter (Harmondsworth: Penguin, 1966), Book 16, Chapter 5, pp. 757–60.

14. Cervantes himself plays intertextually between his own narrative and, variously, the chivalric romances, the 'history' of Cide Hamete Benegeli, the first part of *Don Quixote*, and Avellaneda's spurious continuation.

15. 'There cannot be a greater mistake than to consider "Don Quixote" as a merely satirical work [...] through the crazed and battered figure of the knight, the spirit of chivalry shines out with undiminished lustre' (William Hazlitt, 'On the English Novelists', in *Lectures on the English Comic Writers* (London: Oxford University Press, 1907), p. 141). See Walter Scott's comparison of Quixote with Parson Adams ('Fielding', in *Lives of the Novelists* (London: Oxford University Press, 1906), pp. 11–12) and Carlyle's characterization of Cervantes as 'so gentle and genial, so full, yet so ethereal in his humour' ('Jean Paul Friedrich Richter', in *Critical and Miscellaneous Essays*, 4 vols (London: Chapman & Hall, [n.d.]), I, 13).

16. Dickens, *The Pickwick Papers*, p. 197. The first time had been when he withdrew over Tupman's costume for Mrs Leo Hunter's (p. 180). The reference back does not significantly ironize this second occasion; rather, for the reader, it emphasizes the change in Pickwick from buffoonery to benevolence.

17. Unamuno made the general point in 1905: 'Each generation has added something to this Don Quixote, and he has been transformed and has grown greater all the time [...]. Don Quixote could not be the same man [...] in nineteenth-century England as in seventeenth-century Spain, he has been transformed and modified in England, giving proof thereby of his powerful vitality and of the intense realism of his ideal reality' (*Our Lord Don Quixote*, pp. 451–2). On transformations, see also Jorge Luis Borges, 'Partial Magic in the *Quixote*' and 'Kafka and His Precursors' in *Labyrinths*, eds Donald A. Yates and James E. Irby (Harmondsworth: Penguin, 1970), pp. 228–31, and pp. 234–6.

13
Using the Victorians: the Victorian Age in Contemporary Fiction

Robin Gilmour

One of the striking aspects of fiction in the last third of the twentieth century is the use which novelists have made of the Victorian period and its products in their fiction. By use I mean something more self-conscious than the straightforward historical novel with a period setting; rather, the kind of work which is inward with the period and the conventions of its literature, and draws on the meanings which these have come to have for us today. Michael Sadler's *Fanny by Gaslight* (1940) and Marghanita Laski's *The Victorian Chaise-longue* (1953) are early examples, but the phenomenon really gathers ground in the 1960s with such widely read and influential works as Jean Rhys's *Wide Sargasso Sea* (1966) and John Fowles's *The French Lieutenant's Woman* (1969). Since then there have been two Booker-Prize-winning novels with a Victorian setting, J. G. Farrell's *The Siege of Krishnapur* (1973) and Peter Carey's *Oscar and Lucinda* (1988); and a third, A. S. Byatt's *Possession* (1990), which concerns the researches of modern scholars into the work of a Victorian poet, Christabel LaMotte, and contains pastiches of her poetry and other contemporary writings in the shape of diaries and letters. Charles Palliser's *The Quincunx* (1989), published the year before *Possession*, is entirely a pastiche (or as Palliser prefers to call it, an 'ironic reconstruction') of the Victorian novel and the Victorian world, especially as portrayed in the works of Dickens, Wilkie Collins and Henry Mayhew. There has been a significant creative engagement with Victorian culture in recent years. Partly this is to be understood in relation to the resurgence of interest in the historical novel which is such a marked feature of contemporary literature, as in the writings of Peter Ackroyd, for example. But there is more to it than that. The Victorian period and Victorian literature offer special opportunities to the novelist today.

There are at least six uses to which Victorian history and Victorian fiction have been put in this period:

1. The historical novel written from a modern perspective and in a modern idiom, without much narratorial interference but implying a modern interpretation of the past. In a sense all historical novels are like this. The difference is one of degree and, crucially, of self-consciousness. Among many examples one might choose Farrell's *The Siege of Krishnapur* or Byatt's *Angels and Insects*.

2. Pastiche and parody, whether in the thoroughgoing form of Palliser's *Quincunx*, or in part: the poems, diaries and letters in *Possession*, the Notebooks in Graham Swift's *Ever After* (1992). This is a kind of ventriloquism from within the narrative. It is worth noting in passing that pastiche is a stylistic compliment which the Victorians themselves were capable of paying to their predecessors: Thackeray's *Henry Esmond* (1852) is partly a pastiche eighteenth-century novel and when first published appeared with an eighteenth-century typeface.

3. The inversion of Victorian ideology, as in the Flashman novels of George MacDonald Fraser, which, by installing a cad as hero, effectively stand Arnoldian values on their head.

4. The subversion of Victorian fictional norms. The classic case here would be *The French Lieutenant's Woman*, which parodies the form of the Victorian novel as it was used by Thackeray and George Eliot, with the chapter epigraphs and garrulous narrator, but uses the narratorial possibilities of the form to introduce a degree of explicit philosophizing which was then (1969) felt to be no longer available to a modern novelist. Things are different now, of course.

5. The modern reworking or completing of a classic Victorian novel, as Jean Rhys does *Jane Eyre* (1847) in *Wide Sargasso Sea* or Emma Tennant *Tess of the d'Urbervilles* (1891) in *Tess* (1993); or its incorporation in a digested form, as is *Great Expectations* (1860–1) in Graham Swift's *Waterland* (1983).

6. The research novel. This is a work which, recognizing the prominence which the study of Victorian literature and culture plays in contemporary academic life, builds that into the structure of the novel, making it the subject or focus of the book: *Possession* (again), David Lodge's *Nice Work* (1988), to some extent Graham Swift's *Ever After*.

Behind these different invocations and evocations of the Victorian world and Victorian literature there is, however, something of a paradox. The period is an inviting one for parody and experimentation just because it is so seeming-solid and so unselfconscious in the expression of its official attitudes; and because these attitudes are held so often in an unreconstructed way and so garrulously and directly expressed in its fiction. But it is an inviting one for the reader also and for much the same reasons, because it offers a solidity of characterization and a lack of formal self-consciousness not available in modern writing and for which there seems to be a real appetite. Only in this way, it seems, can one explain the co-existence of an experimental use of the Victorian novel with the expanding market for a more traditional one, of which the current availability of all forty-seven of Trollope's novels (and in paperback) is only the most striking example. Tradition has created the conditions by which experiment can work, but experiment will sometimes unwittingly repay tradition in the old coinage. The modern version may set out to expose the inadequacies and silences of the Victorian novel, but its effect is often to give the unsophisticated reader a density and a satisfying solidity which contemporary fiction may seem to lack. (And sometimes the purpose of sophisticated experiment is to deliver unsophisticated narrative pleasures, as I shall suggest later.)

This is well illustrated in the case of perhaps the most famous of all pastiches of Victorian fiction, *The French Lieutenant's Woman*. The narrator's commentary, once considered the most daring 'experimental' feature of the novel, now seems rather dated. It is, for example, difficult to take a passage like the following altogether seriously:

> He seemed as he stood there to see all his age, its tumultuous life, its iron certainties and rigid conventions, its repressed emotion and facetious humour, its cautious science and incautious religion, its corrupt politics and immutable castes, as the great hidden enemy of all his deepest yearnings.[1]

That one could generalize about the age so glibly and without qualification now seems terribly old-fashioned. But I suspect that is not why many people continue to read and enjoy *The French Lieutenant's Woman*. It is because beneath the often jejune commentary there is a powerful quasi-realistic novel, which plays with certain stereotypes of Victorian literature – the monster matron, the dainty drawing-room belle, the cockney manservant – in order to establish by contrast the seriousness of the central protagonist and his predicament, and to evoke the erotic power in his quest for the mysterious, elusive Sarah Woodruff. It is as if we had been given a modern version of a Hardy novel.

The French Lieutenant's Woman belongs in the same category of pastiche as, a generation later, does Charles Palliser's *The Quincunx*; although Palliser has refused the label, choosing instead that of 'ironic reconstruction': 'I intended that the novel should be neither a historical novel nor a passive pastiche', he wrote in the Afterword to the paperback edition, 'but rather that it should be an ironic reconstruction of the Victorian novel'.[2] It is massive (1202 pages in the Penguin edition), with a bafflingly intricate legal plot turning on wills, codicils and inheritances. In true Dickensian fashion the hero (whose ancestor, Huffam, has one of Dickens's middle names) shuttles between high life and low, gentility and poverty; and sometimes worse than poverty. It is a highly intertextual novel. There are dusty, devious, elderly lawyers; a Chancery suit; a pestiferous city burial ground in which the hero's mother is buried; a swell-mob and a Yorkshire school; a penniless governess; a jolly (but deceptive) Dickensian Christmas. Detecting these echoes is part of the pleasure of the novel, but there are darker period elements, derived partly from the novelists but more from Mayhew, which Palliser picked up at the age of eleven and found offered

> a different perspective on the same world as the one described by Dickens [...]. I was fascinated by the harsh and brutal lives of these street people, who come briefly into hearing, tell their extraordinary stories of suffering and injustice (often in language of striking beauty and directness) and then disappear, without leaving even their names.
>
> *Quincunx*, p. 1209

The novel gives a voice and a setting to the lives of these people, and is often at its most impressive when dealing with cold and poverty, the sheer struggle to keep warm and find the pennies with which to buy food. Nothing is more powerful in the book than its portrayal of the narrator's mother's decline from genteel rural comfort to death in a city slum, stripped bare of everything but a brass-substitute wedding-ring; and there are remarkable descriptions, more explicit than anything in Dickens or Collins, of scavenging in the sewers or the pain and humiliation of life below stairs in a fashionable family. These scenes are truly unforgettable in their detail and period feel, and yet their realism consorts oddly with the fantastic elaboration of the structure and plot, and the unconvincing (to this reader at any rate) names given to the characters: Mompesson, Palphramond, Fortisquince. Palliser is a highly sophisticated writer, deeply versed in the Victorian period, and no doubt he intends the juxtaposition of the two. Indeed he has said as much in the Afterword to the novel, where he declares that he

> wanted to write a novel that would contain this 'monstrous' sense of the sprawling, haphazard and 'given' nature of reality, and yet would at the same time gradually reveal itself to be carefully designed and patterned so that the effect would be a kind of dialectic between chance and purpose, between accident and design, and between Victorian and Modernist fiction.
>
> *Quincunx*, p. 1213

This is almost too knowing. It is not the pastiche that lets Palliser down, but the plotting and patterning he needs to create and sustain a fictional universe that will have the density of *Bleak House* (1852–3) and the internal ordering of *Ulysses* (1922). One admires him for this heroic ambition while realizing that it would take a Dickens or a Joyce to bring it off.

Pastiche is also at the centre of Byatt's *Possession* – pastiche of Victorian poetry, letters and diaries – but the narrative is located in the present and moves backward, the research of the two young scholars having important influences on their lives in the present. Similarly Graham Swift's *Waterland* and *Ever After* are novels set in the present but deeply informed by a sense of the Victorian past, whose contemporary significance they interrogate. *Waterland* is narrated by a history teacher, Tom Crick, coming to terms with the fact that he is being forced to take early retirement. His headmaster no longer believes in the usefulness of history as a subject and intends to close the Department down. Crick is under challenge from another quarter, too, from one of his pupils who believes that the past does not matter, that the only history worth studying is the history of the present day. His narrative, ostensibly a history lesson about the French Revolution, is really an exploration of the nature of history and its relation to storytelling, as one of the book's epigraphs indicates: '*Historia* – a) a narrative of past events, history. b) any kind of narrative: account, tale, story'. The other epigraph, 'Ours was the marsh country', comes of course from *Great Expectations*, and links Swift's evocation of the Fens with the most famous marshes in English literature. Tom Crick is under challenge to justify history and he does so by telling the story of his family, which reaches from the mid-eighteenth century to the present day. It is a family saga, a Faulknerian tale of dynastic grandeur ending in incest, imbecility and murder. It is also an autobiography in which history and the private life intersect and counterpoint one another, as when we are told that while Hitler was making his invasion plans in Paris, Tom Crick the future teacher was reading *Hereward the Wake* in a first edition of 1866 (Swift is obsessed by dates).

Waterland is a playful and self-reflexive novel. It is not just about history but about one man's problematic contemporary relation to history, and this awareness is built into the novel's structure. Published in 1983, its background is the Afghan crisis and the missile build-up of the Thatcher–Reagan years. The fear of the End of the World runs through the novel; the spokesman for this fear, Price, is Tom Crick's most astute classroom critic, for whom it invalidates the study of history. Tom argues passionately that the past is not meaningless, that there is a necessary relationship between history and the real:

> Yes, yes, the past gets in the way; it trips us up, bogs us down; it complicates, makes difficult. But to ignore this is folly, because, above all, what history teaches us is to avoid illusion and make-believe, to lay aside dreams, moonshine, cure-alls, wonder-workings, pie-in-the-sky – to be realistic.[3]

The past bogs us down literally, for although *Waterland* is not a realistic novel, its darting speculativeness is earthed in the remarkably evocative landscape of the Fens, with its rivers and locks and barges and dredgers, which human beings struggle to drain and put to productive use. The flatness of the Fens represents the uneventfulness of reality, which Crick the history teacher contrasts with the violent eventfulness of war and revolution: 'Reality is uneventfulness, vacancy, flatness. Reality is that nothing happens' (p. 34). Drainage is the never-completed human struggle to impart some meaning to the process.

Swift is interested in dates, history, and the genealogy of his characters. Also in the genealogy of the landscape, the way locks, canals, bridges, railway lines form what the narrator in *Ever After* – looking from a hill over road, railway-line, barge to the hay-rick in the distance – calls 'the living palimpsest' of history.[4] Both kinds of genealogy are at work in *Waterland*. Present is linked to past in the rise and fall of the brewing Atkinson family, a typically Victorian story of accumulating success through several generations until it falls apart on the eve of the Great War; and their story is linked to the genealogy of the narrator through the incestuous union of the last Atkinson and his daughter, out of which comes Tom Crick's idiot brother. There is a genealogy of landscape, too, where the building of locks and canals are dated to the individuals who created them and the needs they are designed to serve. They are also a symbol in the novel of a different, more dogged kind of progress than the Victorian Empire-builders understood. As Tom Crick says in his retirement speech: ' "it's progress if you can stop the world slipping away. My humble model for progress is the reclamation of land. Which is repeatedly, never-endingly retrieving what is lost" ' (p. 291).

Retrieving what is lost could also be described as the activity at the heart of Swift's research novel, *Ever After* – the loss of the narrator's actress-wife through cancer, and the lost family-life of his Victorian ancestor, Matthew Pearce, whose notebooks he inherits. Pearce is a Victorian engineer whose apparently happy marriage is brought to an abrupt end for reasons that the novel does not make entirely clear. His notebooks begin on the second anniversary of the death of his son Felix and end with his departure from the family home, having quarrelled irrevocably with his clergyman father-in-law on the subject of evolution; personal loss leading in typical Victorian fashion to loss of faith. The narrator's own guilty stepfather has left him a fortune in his will and a closed fellowship in a Cambridge college. But he finds an academic purpose to justify his privileged existence only when the Pearce Notebooks come to him.

It is possible that Swift may have been influenced by Byatt's *Possession* (*Ever After* was published two years after Byatt's novel) since both are novels in which the central figure attempts to uncover the secret life of a Victorian ancestor or artist; and both provide pastiches of the Victorian artefacts into which their protagonists research. Byatt is immensely more ambitious in this task than Swift. She is aware of – although her novel does not ultimately endorse – the contemporary challenge to the concept of the unitary self. And she obviously enjoys, and registers very well, the ups and downs of literary research. Swift is different. *Ever After* is less respectful of the academic life than *Possession*. He does not suffer from fashionable doubts about the existence of a unitary self. *Ever After*, as the title indicates, is about the loss of individuals only too powerfully registered as individual: chiefly the narrator's actress-wife Ruth, whose death by suicide in the face of incurable illness is the central event of his life; and the lost family, lost faith, and ultimately death of Matthew Pearce.

The relationship of past to present is more enigmatic in *Ever After*. *Possession* is something of a literary detective story leading to the discovery of documents which explain all, or nearly all. The Notebooks in

Ever After reveal a classic (perhaps too neatly classic) Victorian loss of faith, brought on by the discovery of a fossil and the death of a child. But they do not reveal the why or the how of the break-up of Matthew Pearce's marriage, except in showing his banishment by his clergyman father-in-law and suggesting that his wife might have been guilty of adultery, nor quite why it should matter so much to the narrator. A shared experience of loss? Certainly it is not as a document of cultural history that he is interested in the Pearce Notebooks. It is 'the personal thing' that matters to him: 'It is knowing who Matthew Pearce *was*. And why he should matter so much to me' (p. 49).

Perhaps *Ever After* never quite answers that question satisfactorily. The idea that a happily married man, even in the Victorian period, would let intellectual disagreements drive him from his home, strains credulity a little. Perhaps Swift intends a teasing incompleteness, to suggest the final unknowability of the past. But there is something very satisfying about the way, as in *Waterland*, he establishes links and continuities between the Victorian past and the present. Matthew Pearce passes into oblivion but his favourite daughter Lucy lives on until only a dozen years before the narrator is born, and his notebooks survive to be fought over by modern scholars. *The Origin of Species*, the source of contention between Pearce and his father-in-law, was published in the same year, 1859, as Isambard Brunel died – the great Victorian engineer who designed the Great Western Railway on which, the narrator discovers in the course of the novel, his own father had worked. Finally, and threading the novel like an example of the Darwinian co-existence of accident and design, there is the rosewood mantelpiece clock which Matthew's father gives them as a wedding present and which descends through the family to end up in the narrator's college rooms. Ruth makes it her business always to keep it wound and it stands as a witness to the inescapability of time and the survival of love.

Graham Swift is unusual in that he seems to use the past as the Victorian novelists did, to embed his narrative in time and history and to give it a greater resonance by doing so (one could argue for this historical presence even in a novel so different from *Ever After* as his recent, Booker-Prize-winning *Last Orders* (1996)). The case of David Lodge is rather different. Lodge is a paradoxical, not to say schizophrenic literary figure, an academic who has championed the cause of theory and experiment but whose own fiction usually stays within the tradition of comic realism. *Nice Work* is something of an exception to this rule, an intertextual novel which uses a Victorian classic to ask some hard questions about contemporary Britain. It is a modern

version of Elizabeth Gaskell's *North and South* (1855), in which a contemporary Margaret Hale, Robyn Penrose – expert in the industrial
novel, feminist, theoretician, and temporary lecturer in English at
Rummidge University – is sent out by an Industry Year scheme to
'shadow' a local industrialist, Vic Wilcox (the name Wilcox carrying
associations of Forster's *Howards End* (1910) where the Wilcoxes are the
'business' people). The parallels with Gaskell's novel are fairly obvious,
and the chapter epigraphs – from *Sybil* (1845), *Shirley* (1849), *Hard
Times* (1854), and *North and South* itself – link *Nice Work* to the classic
Victorian 'industrial' or 'Condition-of-England' novels. This allows
Lodge, as Steven Connor says, 'to borrow in [his] own characterisation
of the condition of England something of the integrating reach and
perspectival authority it ascribes to its predecessors in social-realist
fiction of the nineteenth century and afterwards'.[5] At this level Vic and
Rummidge stand for the traditional industrial culture of making and
selling things which is being devastated in the Thatcherite 1980s; at
the theoretical level he represents realism and a belief in the unitary
self. In the course of the novel Robyn learns to register the reality of
industrial Rummidge, and like Margaret Hale in Gaskell's novel she
rejects her parents' comfortable world on the South Coast (' "You don't
know what the real world is like down here," ' she tells them[6]) and
ends up lending Vic money to set up his own business after the factory
in which he has been employed is closed down by its parent company.
At the theoretical level she represents, and speaks for, Derridean deconstruction and against what she has been taught to see as bourgeois
notions like character and romantic love. The narrator introduces her
as '[a] character who, rather awkwardly for me, doesn't believe in the
concept of character' (Lodge, *Nice Work*, p. 39). This is awkward for
Lodge indeed, since what the novel demonstrates is how much more
powerfully registered is the realistic impulse than the theoretical voice
which calls it into question. Lodge the novelist operates rather differently from Lodge the literary theorist. The landscape of Midlands
England in the grip of recession, the dirt and noise of the factory, the
harshness of industrial relations, the hard questions which Vic Wilcox
is allowed to ask about the privileges of academic life, and the continual awareness of a world beyond academia – all these give a power to
the novel's realism which threatens to overwhelm Robyn's other world
of self-conscious theorizing. Vic loses her and in one sense he loses the
argument (it is a nice touch to find him reading Arnold's *Culture and
Anarchy* (1869) before one of their last meetings, the most *passé* of
humanist texts to a contemporary theorist); in another the solidity of

his world, a very Victorian solidity, wins her respect and makes the reader aware of the unsubstantiality of her colleagues, lovers, parents. We may even be left at the end feeling that Robyn herself is something of a 'shadow'.

Having looked at some of the different uses to which novelists have put Victorian literature and the Victorian past in recent years, I want finally to venture some possible explanations for the phenomenon. Clearly it is very various, so no single set of explanations will do; and equally clearly fashion has something to do with it, although novelists would not evoke the Victorian past if they did not feel that this enabled them to see things in a new or different way. One theme that I have touched on but not developed is the feminist re-writing of classic texts: a woman novelist who had read *Wide Sargasso Sea* and Gilbert and Gubar's *The Madwoman in the Attic* (1979) would never read *Jane Eyre* in the same way again, and might feel inspired to give other Victorian classics a similar treatment. Then the contrast between the harsh public ideology of the period and the poverty it sanctioned, and the fugitive domesticity of the middle classes, is both interesting in itself and a forerunner of recent historical experience. One hesitates to make too easy a link with the Thatcherite 1980s, but in a period when 'Victorian values' were being publicly celebrated it would be strange if writers did not explore them and the society which produced them. Intellectually, there is the modernity of the period's mental life, about which we now know so much more, and what might be called a Darwinian consciousness can be sensed in several of these novels. But it has been less important, paradoxically, than its opposite. Using the Victorians has offered a sophisticated way to get back to the unsophisticated, or at least to certain powerful narrrative simplicities that the contemporary novel has been wary of: the pleasures of plot (as in *The Quincunx*), Romance (the subtitle of *Possession*), romantic love (as in *Ever After*); as well as the tantalizing sublimations of desire and death about which the modern novel post-Lawrence and Joyce has been so impatient. A. S. Byatt's 'Morpho Eugenia' (in *Angels and Insects*) is a good example of a novelist evoking the sensuality which the restraints of convention both controlled and aroused, and then springing the corrupt truth (incest as anagram of insect) on the reader at the end.

The larger context for all this is the expansion of British higher education in recent years and the concomitant growth in the paperback publishing of Victorian fiction. The study of Victorian literature and history has developed immensely as a result of the expansion of tertiary education, the growth of social and cultural history as intellectual disciplines, and the seemingly inevitable drift of English Studies towards the twentieth century, which has left Victorian literature central to an English degree to an extent it was not in the past. Here I do not entirely agree with John Sutherland when he says in his excellent *Longman Companion to Victorian Fiction* that 'our map of nineteenth-century fiction has shrunk to Lilliputian dimensions. The tiny working areas of the "canon", the "syllabus" and the paperbacked "classics" are poor reflections of what the Victorian novel actually meant to Victorians'.[7] Perhaps so, but the *range* of Victorian fiction available in paperback is surely greater, and better edited, than it has ever been. Looking through the latest World's Classics catalogue one notes M. E. Braddon's *Lady Audley's Secret* (1862) and *Aurora Floyd* (1863), ten works by Wilkie Collins, eleven by Elizabeth Gaskell, Geraldine Jewsbury's *The Half Sisters* (1848), Le Fanu's *In a Glass Darkly* (1872) and *Uncle Silas* (1864), the major Thackeray, and all forty-seven of Trollope's novels (plus two volumes of his stories) – something that would have been inconceivable twenty years ago, when even a complete Trollope in hardback was being talked about as a Utopian project. We are living through a Golden Age in the popular publishing of eighteenth- and nineteenth-century fiction. An editor at Oxford University Press has told me that the student market is their first consideration in commissioning a new title but that they are anxious to expand their list by including titles they know will never be big sellers, subsidizing them if need be from sales of popular classics. (Trollope apparently is something of an exception to this rule: his readership is a more general one.) What this means is that since *Tess of the d'Urbervilles* is studied in many schools and colleges, and just about every English Department in the land, she will keep Collins's *Poor Miss Finch* (1872) (for example) in print. I doubt if many undergraduates read *Poor Miss Finch*, or even know who wrote it, but somebody must, and the very availability of such minor Victorian fiction is an invitation to explore beyond the canon.

These contextual developments have helped to create a readership for the novels I have been discussing which is much more sympathetic, better informed, and less condescending than was the case in the 1960s. As for the novelists themselves, one cannot stress enough the variety of the forms taken by their preoccupation with the Victorians, and that, in a sense, is just the point: it has become established as a truly experimental aspect of their fiction. There is, however, one feature common to most of these novels. The past is another country, as the narrator of Hartley's *The Go-Between* (1953) famously has it. But the Victorian past is not another country here: it exists in dynamic relation to the present, which it both interprets and is interpreted by. Evoking the Victorians and their world has not been an antiquarian activity but a means of getting a fresh perspective on the present.

Notes

1. John Fowles, *The French Lieutenant's Woman* (London: Panther, 1971), p. 315.
2. Charles Palliser, *The Quincunx* (Harmondsworth: Penguin, 1990), p. 1212. Further references are given in the text by page number in this edition.
3. Graham Swift, *Waterland* (London: Picador, 1984), p. 94. Further references are given in the text by page number in this edition.
4. Graham Swift, *Ever After* (London: Picador, 1992), p. 199. Further references are given in the text by page number in this edition.
5. Steven Connor, *The English Novel in History 1950–1995* (London: Routledge, 1996), p. 77.
6. David Lodge, *Nice Work* (Harmondsworth: Penguin, 1989), p. 306. Further references are given in the text by page number in this edition.
7. John Sutherland, *The Longman Companion to Victorian Fiction* (London: Longman, 1988), p. 1.

14
Women, Spiritualism and Depth Psychology in Michèle Roberts's Victorian Novel

Susan Rowland

In the Red Kitchen by Michèle Roberts is a contemporary feminist novel partly set in the Victorian London of female Spiritualist mediums.[1] Its two other temporal sites are Ancient Egypt and London in the grim 1980s where 'Victorian values' have restored homelessness and poverty. The novel hinges upon imagining together two related nineteenth-century issues: Spiritualism with its preponderance of female mediums, and its implications in the succeeding discourse of depth psychology. By depth psychology I refer to the theories of Sigmund Freud and C. G. Jung who were both concerned to theorize upon the unruly bodies of women a medical discourse of hysteria, defining as 'the unconscious' what had earlier been attributed to the occult. Only the Victorian portion of *In the Red Kitchen* is assigned historical sources in the 'Author's Note', which cites Alex Owen's essay in *Language, Gender and Childhood* and Elaine Showalter's *The Female Malady*.[2] Specifically feminist histories, these sources mark a new development in the historical novel as the products of *feminist* academic research of the 1970s and 1980s becomes absorbed into fictional writing. In its examination of the genesis of depth psychology with its gender politics, erotic drives and occluded relationship to Spiritualism, *In the Red Kitchen* is a continuation of feminist research challenging, but not pretending to replace, traditional history. The novel corresponds to Robin Gilmour's arguments about contemporary fictions with a Victorian setting.[3] It is a research novel employing historical material in its portrayal of Flora Milk, fictional descendent of historical Florence Cook, a medium of ambiguous career in the London of the 1870s.[4] *In the Red Kitchen* gives fictional voices to the women marginalized in official records of Spiritualism and male-generated theories of depth psychology. By so doing, the novel inverts Victorian norms to suggest fictional, cultural and erotic drives implicated in the theoretical discourses of hysteria, Freud's female Oedipus complex, and Jung's notions of the unconscious. I will be examining a further, uncited source for the novel, Jung's doctoral thesis, to demonstrate how Roberts's fiction both utilizes and critiques Jungian theory from a feminist perspective by situating it historically in its nineteenth-century Spiritualist antecedents.[5]

Before giving some account of nineteenth-century female Spiritualism and its links to hysteria, it is worth outlining the main events of the novel.[6] *In the Red Kitchen* has five female narrator–writers who do not read each other's texts but whose stories comment on each other as characters and give sometimes violently conflicting versions. Three of the five narrators are linked through Spiritualism with Flora Milk, the Victorian working-class medium based on Florence Cook, the pivotal figure. The Hattie she conjures up as her spirit-guide could be the contemporary Hattie who seems to be living in Flora's house in 1980s London and/or she could be Hat, daughter of Pharaoh and later Pharaoh herself in Ancient Egypt. King Hat is devoted to erasing signs of her female gender so that she can rule and be immortal. When her plan for eternal life through the assumption of masculine power fails, she decides to project herself forward as a ghost to find future women to write her spirit, 'one whose hand will dance to my spelling' (p. 133), she writes with obvious ambiguity. Similarly, contemporary Hattie sees a child ghost, probably Flora, and King Hat may well be her childhood fantasies of Egypt generated by the abuse she suffered from an uncle. She says: 'At night, in my narrow white bed encircled by white curtains, I escaped into another country called Egypt where I was King' (p. 35).

The Victorian site is 'home' to the other two narrators: the angry Rosina Milk, Flora's sister and assistant, if and when she resorts to 'tricks' in her Spiritualist practice, and Minnie Preston, the relentlessly patriarchal wife of Sir William, the investigator. Flora and Rosina go to stay with the Prestons. While William's cruel probings of Flora and spirit-guide Hattie amount to sexual exploitation upstairs, downstairs, Flora's private seances with Minnie suggest that she, Minnie, may well have smothered her dead daughter Rosalie. The reader has to choose between Flora's and Minnie's version of events since they conflict so violently. Finally, William takes Flora to Paris where she is exhibited as an hysteric at Dr Charcot's Salpetrière hospital. Returning from Paris pregnant, Flora marries Rosina's young man which cements the rift between the sisters. The gravestones which contemporary Hattie finds in a London cemetery suggest that Rosina marries the object of her epistolary narrative, a Spiritualist benefactor named Mr Redburn whom she initially contacted to allege Flora's deceit as a medium. Minnie is not the only patriarchal-identified woman who may well have killed. Hat in Egypt marries her father and decides that she needs to dispose of his favourite concubine. By contrast, the romance of contemporary Hattie with the object of her writing, her male lover only known as 'you', is comparatively benign, but she does suffer a miscarriage. The presence of 'you', an obvious site for the reader's engagement with the text (in a romantic and erotic sense) serves to underline the novel's status as a feminist text interrogating gender and patriarchal power, not blaming men. 'Romance' in the more overtly patriarchal periods, Ancient Egypt and Victorian London, is structured through and against patriarchy, as romance with the father that does not protect the daughter from oppression on gender grounds.

Some details of Spiritualism will be useful to illuminate the novel's critique of Victorian culture. Communication with spirits, supposedly of dead people, has been known throughout history, but the modern phenomenon of Spiritualism began in America in March 1848 with poltergeist activity in the home of adolescents Kate and Maggie Fox. The two young women soon discovered that the knocking they heard showed signs of an intelligent grasp of the alphabet, and a newspaper campaign in the *New York Tribune* helped to launch their careers as spirit mediums. Spiritualism, noted for its female mediums, spread rapidly to Europe where its appeal was disseminated through populist channels of newspaper journalism. Female mediumship became a lucrative career for middle-class and some working-class women. Spirit communication developed from table-rapping, through automatic writing where the medium held the pen and the spirit supposedly guided it, to the spirit speaking through the body of the medium. Many mediums also managed a 'materialization' of a spirit where the medium would probably be tied up and locked in a cabinet, the room darkened and a fully physical bodied 'spirit' would emerge who could be touched and held.[7]

Florence Cook in the 1870s materialized a spirit called Katy King, while her fictional counterpart, Flora Milk, produces Hattie King or King Hat. Clearly, the potential for fraud was immense and some unscrupulous mediums were exposed by Spiritualist investigators.[8] *In the Red Kitchen*'s Rosina charges Flora with using all the tricks of her historical predecessors: 'collapsible rods to make spirit arms, trick slates with messages already written on them, rubber gloves to feel like spirit hands [...] gauze coated with luminous paint [...] tossed out to make a ghostly cloud' (p. 1).

To turn to specific source material, *In the Red Kitchen*'s use of Showalter and Owen demonstrates fiction's interventions in historical discourse by re-staging historical rumour as a narrative possibility but not unambiguous fact in the novel. Owen gives a succinct account of the known events surrounding the unproven rumours of an affair between the Spiritualist investigator, Sir William Crookes, and Florence Cook, upon which Roberts bases Flora's contested allegations of sexual interference from William Preston:

> Florence Cook was born in 1856 to respectable working parents, and as a young medium lived with her family in Hackney. She was the eldest of three daughters, all of whom claimed to be mediums, and began giving séances at the age of 15. At first she was only able to produce vague spirit faces which appeared in the gloom of gas or candlelight, but after 'Katie King' became her regular spirit control the manifestations swiftly increased and improved. By 1873, Florence, in complete trance but hidden from view behind a heavy curtain, was able to produce the full-form materialisation of 'Katie'; that is, a young female figure would emerge from behind the curtain, completely covered from head to foot in white robes, and would pass among the sitters [...]. Charles Blackburn, a wealthy and devoted spiritualist, undertook to make a regular annual payment to Florence so that she could remain 'private'.
>
> During the early part of 1874 Blackburn passed the management of Florence's séances to the scientist William Crookes who was engaged in a laboratory investigation of the young girl's powers. Crookes was clearly enamoured of 'Katie', if not Florence, and his ardent espousal of the spirit's authenticity, together with his interest in other young mediums like Miss [Mary Rosina] Showers, began to earn for him the dangerous reputation of a philanderer.[9]

Here, *In the Red Kitchen* simplifies its sources. Florence Cook's cross-class friendship with the middle-class medium, Mary Rosina Showers is collapsed so that 'Rosina' can be the name of a younger sister with whom the historical Florence did have a rivalry. The early benefactor of Florence Cook, Mr Blackburn, becomes Mr Redburn: first the instrument of Rosina's revenge for the loss of her lover and then her means to a middle-class life as his wife. Florence Cook's spirit guide 'Katie King' becomes Hattie King, almost certainly to exploit the greater linguistic possibilities of Hat, Hate, Hattie, but Roberts's Rosina manages 'the materialisation of Katy King' (p. 147) in a return of the repressed historical record. William is closely modelled on Sir William Crookes, and Roberts exploits the ambiguities of his relationship with the young working-class medium, Florence Cook.

Owen also connects mediumship to hysteria. As she describes, William Crookes certainly wrote of his faith in the genuine nature of the materialized spirit, Katie King, and while he did not cite any connections to hysteria, there were those at the end of the century who did.

> [T]o imagine, I say, the Katie King of the last three years to be the result of imposture does more violence to one's reason and common sense than to believe her to be what she herself affirms.[10]

> The acts of the hysteric, again, are like those of the medium and the poltergeist child... the study of hysteria paints for us in rather coarser colours just such a weakening of the moral sense, such an inextricable mingling of imposture and reality and such examples of unnatural cunning posing under the mask of innocence, as we find in mediumship.[11]

After Flora is investigated by William (and perhaps sexually abused by him), he takes her to Dr Charcot's Salpetrière hospital in Paris where she is exhibited as an hysteric in his famous public spectacles of female hysteria patients. None of this applies to the historical Crookes and Showalter's analysis of Charcot becomes the source. Showalter quotes a witness to one of Charcot's theatrical exhibitions of his hypnotized female hysteria patients at Salpetrière:

> Some of them smelt with delight a bottle of ammonia when told it was rosewater, others would eat a piece of charcoal when presented to them as chocolate. Another would crawl on all fours on the floor, barking furiously when told she was a dog, flap her arms as if trying to fly when turned into a pigeon [...]. Another would walk with a top hat in her arms rocking it to and fro and kissing it tenderly when she was told it was her baby.[12]

This very passage is re-imagined in the novel from a female soon-to-be participant's point of view, not that of the relatively detached male audience. Flora sees the events as an enactment of naked patriarchal power:

Dr Charcot is a ringmaster: the first woman drops on all fours, sniffs the legs of her chair, waggles her rump, barks.

Dr Charcot is a magician: the second woman takes the top hat he offers her, cradles it in her arms, rocks it to and fro as she walks up and down the dais and croons to it.

Dr Charcot is God: the third woman hops on one leg, arms outstretched, squawks, tries to fly.

Dr Charcot is a great artist: the fourth woman accepts the piece of charcoal he gives her and begins to eat it, drooling with pleasure.

(pp. 124–5)

In the Red Kitchen does not claim to be history but it does claim to be adding to history a perspective: women's perspective, however fictional in this text, which the empirical written record may have suppressed. Roberts here adopts the metaphor of the circus to display patriarchal power made visible. Interestingly, Showalter points out that Charcot did not believe that hysteria was exclusively a female disease, and that Salpetrière contained male patients although they were not exhibited.[13] Roberts omits the implication of masculinity in hysteria, a point not missed by Pat Barker in *Regeneration*, the first volume of her War Trilogy which draws on Showalter's following chapter on male hysteria as shell shock.[14]

Before considering the third textual source, that is, C. G. Jung's thesis, I want to elucidate the novel's treatment of women and Spiritualism in its distinctive narrative structure. Flora conjures up contemporary Hattie and/or King Hat. Contemporary Hattie sees a child ghost who may be Flora, while King Hat could be Hattie's fantasies of omnipotence spun in response to sexual abuse. The novel is structured upon the ontological ambiguity of its narrators: mediums or ghosts? Fantasies or tricks? Indeed, the connections between the three main narrators in the novel – King Hat, Flora, Hattie King – could be defined in any one of three ways but not confined to one definition. Firstly, they are mediums connected by Spiritualist practice; secondly, they stand for each Other's autonomous and creative unconscious, and thirdly they are fictions or tricks to each other. In effect, the three main narrators could be mediums, women in touch with a creative unconscious, or fiction writers: they operate in an ontological field which includes all three possibilities in a continuum, not one to the exclusion of the others. In terms of the female figures standing for the unconscious Other, I would argue that Roberts is using Jungian psychology here, as in earlier novels, because this unconscious is proactive, autonomous and compensatory.[15] For example, whatever 'Hattie' is to Flora, she is capable of guiding Flora out of the prison that Salpetrière becomes for her. Flora says of Hattie: 'She is my white rope [...]. She leads me out. She delivers me, into the sunshine' (p. 130).

In this narrative form, where the main narrators are mediums and/or Jungians and/or creative writers, it is impossible to find any secure subject position from which to re-construct the story. Hysteria becomes embedded in narrative art. History and fiction are depicted as contingent forms. As mediums, the narrators make the claim that they are recording an historical 'truth', but their Spiritualist practice cannot be isolated from the possibilities of unconscious powers and fiction making. Of course, all these ontological possibilities take place within a text defined as a 'novel', not the history of Florence Cook and William Crookes. Nevertheless, the text poses questions about the status of the imagined Other and artistic inspiration. Just what powers does an artist tap into when 'creating' fictional voices? Do mediumship or the creative unconscious provide appropriate models for narrative art? *In the Red Kitchen* is not history, but its fictional nature claims to be Other to history, in a way that is differentiated but not wholly different from historical discourse. It is a fiction, moreover, which imagines the voices of women like Florence Cook, which are subordinated in official 'history'. It offers an hysterical history, employing fiction both to interrogate the apparently disinterested status of traditional accounts and to recover marginalized women in a fictional form that problematizes the concept of fiction in connection with occult and unconscious drives. It is important to stress that not one of these conflicting narratives is presented as the 'historical truth', the master narrative which operates to subordinate all the Others. Indeed, the novel deliberately exposes the power structures involved in defining one narrative as 'history' and the rest as fiction within the novel's own boundaries. The greatest clash is between the accounts of Minnie Preston and Flora Milk (pp. 90–8). Where Minnie cites her beneficence to the poor young medium, vilely repaid by scandalous allegations against her god-like husband, Flora depicts adulterous deceit and child-murder in Minnie, sexual abuse from William. The sympathetic reader is much more inclined to Flora's side but to over-rule Minnie is to dismiss her own patriarchal suffering and very real fears of death through excessive child-bearing (p. 11).

The novel makes the power operations inherent in such a form of reading visible in the scene where Flora is exhibited in Salpetrière. She hears the doctors talking in French and thinks she hears the subject as 'women' and 'history': 'Isterry, History? And then famm. History and women?' (p. 124). However, an educated reader, knowing the 'history'

of Charcot and Salpetrière, may conclude that Flora has heard but mis-
interpreted the word for *hysteria*; the doctors are talking about hysteria
and women. Surely this, historically speaking, is the case? Yet, because
this is a novel, not history, and we *like* the victimized and courageous
Flora, I would argue that the reader is given a choice about whether to
completely discount working-class Flora and stick to official history. To
do this, the novel makes it clear, is to side with the male doctors
against Flora, and hence adopt the masculine gaze of theory (here of
hysteria) that objectifies women as Other to its dominant modes. *In the
Red Kitchen* makes the reader examine the tracks of desire in interpret-
ing a text as well as offering a feminist critique of history's tendency to
encode patriarchal literary forms which marginalize or exclude the
feminine voice. Clearly, in the reading of the Salpetrière scene, the
reader is not going to ignore the masculine designation of hysteria, but
credence may also be given to Flora's definition of the scene as being
about history and women: hysteria in this novel is also about the
history of women's lives. The novel teaches the reader not to choose
exclusive versions of events, not to designate some of the female narrators as wholly Other to the reader's credence or sympathies. Since no
hierarchy of narratives is possible in the text without defining one or
more women as liar, fantasist or pathological (which is exposed as
patriarchy's method), the novel encourages hysterical reading, the
failure to find a secure subject position as a way to incorporate an
acknowledged fiction like *In the Red Kitchen* into our reading of traditional history. Such novels claim to be history's Other, both as fiction
and as a text aiming to recuperate what has been marginalized in
history as feminine, untruthful, occult or fantasy.

　To turn to depth psychology is to approach a discourse which also has
founding narratives composed by scientific males practising upon female
hysteria patients whose voices do not represent themselves in the writings.[16] The recent collection of essays *In Dora's Case* offers a thorough critique of Freud's practice with his female patients.[17] Freud's view of the
predominantly female disease of hysteria famously changed in the late
nineteenth century. Whereas Freud once believed that hysteria resulted
from repressed memories of sexual abuse, he later decided that such abuse
had no reality outside the mind of the patient, that it was in fact fantasy.
Such a theoretical turn fuelled his concept of the Oedipus complex with
its female equivalent, the daughter's incestuous desire for the father.[18]
When *In the Red Kitchen* takes the reader to Charcot and Salpetrière, it
visits the place where Freud learned his technique of hypnosis (later aban-
doned) and observed hysteria patients.[19] In depicting occult disturbances

summarily redefined as hysteria, *In the Red Kitchen* sites itself at the genesis of depth psychology.

However, the novel makes two precise moves in relation to Freudian theory. Firstly it reinstates 'real' sexual abuse as a possible cause of psychic symptoms, particularly with contemporary Hattie's traumatic memories of her 'uncle'. Then the novel suggests that the daughter's romance with the father can be understood as an erotic expression of patriarchal subjection: the daughter's fear of and desire for 'male' powers. In other words, a cultural and feminist theory of sexual desire is offered rather than Freud's biological formulation. As Flora alleges about the photographs of an hysteria patient in Salpetrière (documented by Showalter): 'the mad girl in white. But she's not mad, she's angry' (p. 130). Just as this fiction offers a different history of hysteria, so it could be said to provide an hysterical version of official psychoanalytic history. An hysterical version may be one that makes use of fictions, performances, art, and which fails to provide a fixed subject position, as in this novel where Flora's account and Hattie's tale of abuse are only single-voiced strands in a plural text with no absolute hierarchy of truth and lies.

Charcot has a distinct historical role and so bears the weight of psychoanalytic history in the text with being a proto-Freudian character. Jung's presence in *In the Red Kitchen* is more complex. On one level, Minnie Preston recalls meeting a 'Mr Charles Young, whom I understand to be writing a doctoral thesis on the psychology of the phenomena we were about to witness' (p. 48). Is this the fictional shade of Carl Gustav Jung, who in reality did not haunt seances in London in the 1870s (the period of Florence Cook and Flora Milk), but whose attendance at the seances of a female medium cousin in Switzerland in the 1890s forms the basis of his doctoral thesis? Jung's document performs the translation of a female medium into an hysteria patient, becoming the opening text of his *Collected Works* and the inauguration of his later psychology. If William Crookes is the model for William Preston's treatment of Flora Milk only until the fictional characters meet at Salpetrière (for Crookes always believed in Cook as a medium, not as an hysteric), then it is C. G. Jung who anticipates the later William, as an enthusiastic attender of seances but one who is willing to collapse the medium into the hysteric. Moreover, Jung argues that his cousin's hysteria coincides with Freud's revised conclusions about the disease as symptoms of repressed sexual desire. He calls all the stories that the medium provides through spirit voices, 'romances', even 'family romances'. Jung's medium's spirit guide was called Ivenes. He wrote:

These family romances [...] had a pretty gruesome character: murder by poison and dagger, seduction and banishment.[20]

Our patient's 'romances' throw a most significant light on the subjective root of her dreams. They swarm with open and secret love affairs [...]. It is the woman's premonition of sexual feeling, the dream of fertility, that has created these monstrous ideas in the patient. We shall not be wrong if we seek the main cause of this curious clinical picture in her budding sexuality. From the point of view the whole essence of Ivenes and her enormous family is nothing but a dream of sexual wish-fulfilment.[21]

This early work shows Jungian ideas at their most Freudian because Jung assimilates his current theory of spirits, that they are repressed desires acting as separate personalities, to Freud's dream theories. 'As repressed thoughts [...] they begin to lead an independent existence as autonomous personalities. This behaviour calls to mind Freud's dream investigations which disclose the independent growth of repressed thoughts.'[22]

However, if depth psychology had not yet split into two hostile schools, this thesis still anticipates key aspects of a distinctively Jungian theory. One node of future theory is the phrase 'autonomous personalities', which alerts the reader to Jung's fundamental notion of the autonomy and creativity of the unconscious. Additionally, the depiction of Ivenes's, the spirit-guide's, role in relation to the female medium anticipates Jung's theories of the 'self', a superior governing unconscious personality to which the ego becomes a subject in psychic interactions with the unconscious.[23]

As well as the Freudian and proto-Jungian elements, there is a third subtext to this seminal document for Jungian psychology which also reappears in *In the Red Kitchen*, and that is eroticism. Jung's thesis conceals vital evidence about his own relationship to the medium–patient. We do not learn that she is his cousin, that he promoted the seances for years longer than indicated and that the medium's family finally had to remove her from Jung's influence.[24] The term 'romances' (which is used throughout the English edition read by Roberts) to designate the fictional status of the medium's productions seems to both reveal and suppress an erotic drive within the seances. Jung was also greatly interested in the Spiritualist writings of the historical William Crookes prior to his own attendance at seances. Therefore, when the barely educated medium Hélène Preiswerk produces a spirit-voice claiming kinship with Florence Cook, the reader may wonder at the extent of Jung's own influence on his medium. Is he as 'objective' as the erotically invasive fictional William Preston? Jung wrote: 'Ivenes had to embody herself at least once in every two hundred years; apart from her, only two human being shared this fate, namely Swedenborg and Miss Florence Cook (Crookes' famous medium). [The medium] called these personages her brother and sister.'[25]

Certainly, if Jung describes Florence Cook as 'Crookes's famous medium', he is equally constructing Preiswerk in his doctorate as *his* famous medium who can be medicalized though his writing for his own professional gain. Effectively, William Preston in *In the Red Kitchen* is a William Crookes who becomes C. G. Jung. Crookes may have had an affair with Florence Cook but did not assimilate mediumship into hysteria as Jung's doctorate does, writing of Preiswerk's 'hysterical attacks [...] when she enacts dramatic scenes, has visionary experiences etc'.[26] William Preston is a fictional re-staging of Crookes and Jung as male scientists theorizing the bodies and psyches of women as Other, occult, or pathological, or fraudulent. By modelling William Preston on Crookes and Jung, *In the Red Kitchen* posits a web of intersecting erotic, occult and medical narratives at the genesis of psychoanalysis and Jungian psychology, where gender is the silent term in these male-generated theories of the end of the nineteenth century.

In terms of the gender politics of his writings, Jung's theory does not remain interested in female mediums. Instead the feminine becomes relegated to the spirit position, known as the 'anima' in Jungian psychology, forming the Other or the unconscious to male subjectivity. When Jung later writes of female psychology, he bases much of it on his notions of his anima, his feminine side: unconscious, erotic, non-rational.[27] For both Freudian and Jungian theory, *In the Red Kitchen* offers a cultural critique of the scientific claims of their discourse by imagining the genesis of theory as historically constituted through culture, not scientifically transcendent of it. If depth psychology claims an interest in returning to 'the mothers', then *In the Red Kitchen* seeks the mothers of depth psychology itself in the nineteenth-century women engaged in Spiritualism. In doing so the novel makes the theories 'hysterical' in disrupting their secure foundations and exposing what is Other, fictional, feminine and repressed in Freud's female Oedipus complex, his notions of hysteria, and in Jung's model of subjectivity that treats the feminine primarily as an unconscious ingredient of male subjectivity.

Michèle Roberts's *In the Red Kitchen* is not a feminist polemic about Victorian patriarchy but a textual space for imagining what is absent from historical record and some of the theoretical writings of the late nineteenth century. It is a novel which represents the history of depth psychology hysterically by suggesting fiction haunting the theories and by using fiction to suggest new aspects to theory in the imagined recovery of female voices. Such a novel, I would argue, is not Victorian literature in the traditional sense of the term, but neither is it wholly separate from our cultural methods of conceiving the past.

Notes

1. Michèle Roberts, *In the Red Kitchen* (London: Methuen, 1990). Further references are given in the text by page number in this edition.
2. Alex Owen, 'The Other Voice: Women, Children and Nineteenth-Century Spiritualism', in *Language, Gender and Childhood*, eds Carolyn Steedman, Cathy Urwin and Valerie Walkerdine (London: Routledge & Kegan Paul, 1985), pp. 34–73. Owen's article is reprinted in her book *The Darkened Room: Women, Power and Spiritualism in Late Nineteenth-Century England* (London: Virago Press, 1989); Elaine Showalter, *The Female Malady: Women, Madness, and English Culture, 1830–1980* (London: Virago Press, 1987), pp. 147–55.
3. See Robin Gilmour's essay in this volume.
4. For a comprehensive account of the career of Florence Cook see Owen, 'The Other Voice: Women, Children and Nineteenth-Century Spiritualism', pp. 42–6.
5. C. G. Jung, *On the Psychology and Pathology of So-Called Occult Phenomena*, in *Collected Works*, trans. R. F. C. Hull, 18 vols (London: Routledge and Kegan Paul, 1957–77), I, 3–88. Michèle Roberts confirmed in a private conversation with the present author that she had used Jung's doctoral thesis on a series of seances as a source for *In the Red Kitchen*. For further information on Jungian concepts, Jung's own account is helpful: *Analytical Psychology: Its Theory and Practice*, eds Mary Barker and Margaret Game (London: Routledge, 1968; repr. Ark paperback 1986). See also Andrew Samuels, Bani Shorter and Fred Plaut, *A Critical Dictionary of Jungian Analysis* (London: Routledge, 1986). The essential differences between Jungian notions of the unconscious and the more familiar Freudian version are, firstly, that the Jungian unconscious is creative, self-healing and not dominated by repression; and secondly that religious experience for Jung is an authentic form of psychic activity, not necessarily to be reduced to sexual or traumatic explanations.
6. For a powerful study of women, the occult and the feminine in Victorian culture see Diana Basham, *The Trial of Woman: Feminism and the Occult Sciences in Victorian Literature and Society* (London: Macmillan, 1992). For a

comprehensive history and discussion of the varying definitions of hysteria see essays by Sander L. Gilman, Helen King, Roy Porter, G. S. Rousseau and Elaine Showalter in Gilman *et al.* (eds), *Hysteria Beyond Freud* (Berkeley, CA: University of California Press, 1993).

7. For a comprehensive history of Spiritualism and psychical research in the period see Janet Oppenheim, *The Other World: Spiritualism and Psychical Research in England, 1850–1914* (Cambridge: Cambridge University Press, 1985).

8. For example Owen describes lawyer Edward Cox's challenges to Florence Cook and Mary Rosina Showers in 'The Other Voice', pp. 44–5.

9. Owen, 'The Other Voice: Women, Children and Nineteenth-Century Spiritualism', pp. 42–3.

10. *Ibid.*, p. 65, quoting William Crookes, 'The Last of Katie King', *Spiritualist*, 5 June 1874. Repr. in full in *Crookes and the Spirit World*, ed. M. R. Barrington (London: Souvenir Press, 1972), pp. 137–41.

11. Owen, 'The Other Voice: Women, Children and Nineteenth-Century Spiritualism', p. 67, quoting Frank Podmore, *Modern Spiritualism: A History and a Criticism*, 2 vols (London: Methuen, 1902), II, 323–4.

12. Showalter, *The Female Malady*, p. 148, quoting Axel Munthe, *The Story of San Michèle* (London: Murray, 1930), p. 296, pp. 302–3.

13. See Showalter, *The Female Malady*, p. 148.

14. Pat Barker, *Regeneration* (London: Viking, 1991). Barker cites Showalter in the acknowledgements.

15. Roberts acknowledged the use of Jungian psychology in her earlier fiction in a private conversation with the present author. For more information on Jungian theory see Samuels, Shorter and Plaut, *A Critical Dictionary of Jungian Analysis*.

16. For Freud's changing views on hysteria see *The Standard Edition of the Complete Psychological Works of Sigmund Freud*, trans. under the General Editorship of James Strachey, in collaboration with Anna Freud, assisted by Alix Strachey and Alan Tyson, 24 vols (London: Hogarth Press and the Institute of Psycho-Analysis, 1955–74), especially 'Katharina', II, 125–35; 'The Aetiology of Hysteria', III, 191–221; and 'Dora – Fragment of an Analysis of a Case of Hysteria', VII, 1–122.

17. See *In Dora's Case: Freud, Hysteria, Feminism*, eds Charles Bernheimer and Claire Kahane (New York: Columbia University Press, 1985).

18. For the Oedipus complex and especially Freud's developing views of female Oedipality see *The Standard Edition of the Complete Psychological Works of Sigmund Freud*, XVI, 333–7 and 'Femininity', XXII, 112–35.

19. Showalter, *The Female Malady*, pp. 147–8, on Freud studying with Charcot and later praising his work.

20. Jung, *On the Psychology and Pathology of So-Called Occult Phenomena*, p. 39.

21. *Ibid.*, pp. 69–70.

22. *Ibid.*, pp. 77–8.

23. The best description of the evolution of Jungian ideas of the 'self' can be found in Samuels, Shorter and Plaut, *A Critical Dictionary of Jungian Analysis*. See also Jung's own elaborations in *Analytical Psychology: Its Theory and Practice*, pp. 137–8.

24. See F. X. Charet, *Spiritualism and the Foundations of C. G. Jung's Psychology* (New York: State University of New York Press, 1993), p. 157.
25. Jung, *On the Psychology and Pathology of So-Called Occult Phenomena*, p. 36.
26. *Ibid.*, p. 65.
27. See Jung's descriptions of female psychology in C. G. Jung, *Aspects of the Feminine* (London: Ark Paperbacks, 1982).

Index

Schreiner, Olive   (*Cont.*)
  Dreams, 145–58
  From Man to Man, 148
  The Story of an African Farm, 10,
    145, 146, 147, 148, 159, 166,
    168, 169
  Woman and Labour, 153
sensation, 60, 65, 80 n. 34
sentimentalism, 8, 15
sentimentality, 13, 14, 16, 23, 27
separate spheres, 160–1, 164
Shakespeare, William, *Hamlet*, 127,
    177
  King Lear, 127
Shalkhauser, Marian, 101
Shelley, Percy Bysshe, 148, 155
Showalter, Elaine, 201, 205
Shurbutt, Sylvia Bailey, 111–12
Sidney, Philip, *Astrophel and Stella*, 47
sincerity, 49
Smith, Adam, 85
Smollett, Tobias, 174
  Roderick Random, 185
  Sir Lancelot Greaves, 177–9, 182, 185
social Darwinism, 145, 146, 147, 150,
    151
Spark, Muriel, 117, 128 n. 2
Spinoza, Benedict de, 22–3
Spiritualism, 201–14
Stevenson, R. L., *Dr Jekyll and Mr
    Hyde*, 84
Stoker, Bram, *Dracula*, 9, 81–95, 154

Stubbs, Patricia, 159
Sue, Eugène, *Les Mystères de Paris*, 60,
    77 n. 3
Sutherland, John, *Is Heathcliff a
    Murderer?*, 1
  *Longman Companion to Victorian
    Fiction*, 199
Swift, Graham, 11
  Ever After, 190, 194–6, 198
  Last Orders, 196
  Waterland, 190, 194, 196

Taylor, Alexander L., 127
Tennant, Emma, *Tess*, 190
Thackeray, William Makepeace, *Henry
    Esmond*, 190
Tit-Bits, 93
Trollope, Anthony, 191

Unamuno, Miguel de, 187 n. 10, 188
    n. 17

Walsh, Susan A., 99
Wells, H. G., *The Time Machine*, 86
Wilde, Oscar, 82
Willard, Nancy, 108
Woolf, Virginia, 'Modern fiction', 2
Wordsworth, William, 165
  'Preface' to *Lyrical Ballads*, 27
  'Resolution and Independence',
    121, 127
  The Prelude, 175, 176